CRACK CLIMBING
The Definitive Guide

MOUNTAINEERS
OUTDOOR EXPERT
series

CRACK CLIMBING
The Definitive Guide

Pete Whittaker
Illustrations by Alex Poyzer

MOUNTAINEERS
BOOKS

I started this project with one goal in mind—to provide a resource of crack climbing knowledge: the go-to place to learn about this craft. I hope that everyone who picks up the book—even the very best climbers in the world—can learn something (I certainly have from writing it), or at the very least think about a crack climbing concept in a different way.

So, to the readers: this book is written for you.

 MOUNTAINEERS BOOKS is dedicated to the exploration, preservation, and enjoyment of outdoor and wilderness areas.

1001 SW Klickitat Way, Suite 201, Seattle, WA 98134
800-553-4453, www.mountaineersbooks.org

First published simultaneously in Great Britain and North America in 2020 by Vertebrate Publishing, Sheffield, and Mountaineers Books, Seattle.

VERTEBRATE PUBLISHING
Omega Court, 352 Cemetery Road, Sheffield S11 8FT, United Kingdom
www.v-publishing.co.uk

First edition: first printing 2020, second printing 2020

Copyeditor: John Coefield
Design: Mountaineers Books
Layout: Peggy Egerdahl
Illustrator: Alex Poyzer
Front cover design: Jane Beagley
Frontispiece: *The author finger jamming on* Mustang *(F8a) at Caderese, Italy* (© Paolo Sartori)
Back cover photograph: *Brittany Griffith on* Boothill *(5.12b), Maverick Buttress, Long Canyon, Utah* (© Andrew Burr)

Library of Congress Cataloging-in-Publication data is on file for this title at https://lccn.loc.gov/2019010571

Printed on FSC®-certified materials

ISBN (paperback): 978-1-68051-215-1
ISBN (ebook): 978-1-68051-216-8

An independent nonprofit publisher since 1960

Contents

Preface

One of my earliest crack climbing memories is of a notorious route on Peak District grit-stone called *The Vice*—a short, steep hand-and-fist crack that requires a bit of brute force and tenacity, but with the correct techniques is not overly difficult. A confident twelve-year-old me spotted the HVS (5.10) grade in the Stanage guidebook, thought "that's within my ability," and then spent the next 20 minutes dangling on the end of a tight rope with my feet paddling the air and brushing the ground.

I managed only a single move.

It's not uncommon to have a heartbreaking experience when you start crack climbing as the techniques required are so far removed from anything you might have previously learnt in climbing. But stick with it. Since my own demoralising efforts on *The Vice*, I have gone on to repeat or establish many of the world's hardest crack climbs. Miles of outdoor crack experience and indoor wooden crack training, along with many hours of crack climbing coaching, have given me the experience and the confidence to write this book.

My goal from the start was to provide a single point of reference for crack climbing technique. The aim is to show you the different techniques and give you an understanding of why and how you use them. Then you can put them into practice with confidence and your climbing will improve.

You'll also have the privilege of learning from some of the world's best crack climbers. Every climber can learn something from the likes of Lynn Hill, Alex Honnold, and Peter Croft.

If you think that this book isn't for you and that you will never go crack climbing, think again. Remember the pocket on that boulder problem you were trying? Or those tufas on that sport climb? There are jams in and between those. Many sport climbers and boulderers miss opportunities to jam, instead pinching, crimping, and squeezing around obvious jamming spots. Pick up this book, learn the craft, and make climbing easier for yourself.

If everybody who reads this book learns just one thing that benefits their climbing, I'll be a happy author.

Get jamming!

Opposite: *Aubrey Hodges gets fingers in* Crime of the Century *(5.11c) in Squamish, Canada.* (© Irene Yee)

Mike Hutton making an early morning ascent of Don Whillans's classic gritstone hand crack The File *(VS 4c) at Higgar Tor in the Peak District, UK.* (© Mike Hutton)

A Note

This book has a mountain of information buried inside of it. A lot of it is illustrated, which will help you to visualise what I'm explaining. However, there is a lot of information which is only described in words.

After a while a book of words describing actions can become heavy and overwhelming. Even when you are focused it can be difficult to visualise the actions described in those words.

To overcome this, I propose two solutions:

- *Use this book like you would a guidebook.* Find the information you are looking for, focus on that information, and don't become distracted by information in the rest of the book (because, at that time, the rest of the book is not needed). If you lose focus, put it down and pick it up another day. Total focus with a particular section is the key to success.
- *Mimic in real life the words that are printed on the page.* Use your fingers, hands, arms, legs, and feet to literally go through the actions in the air as you are reading about them. You might look like a total wally on the bus, at the train station, or on the climbing wall, waving and flapping your arms and legs around, but I guarantee it will help you learn.

A NOTE ABOUT SAFETY

Safety is an important concern in all outdoor activities. No book can alert you to every hazard or anticipate the limitations of every reader. The descriptions of techniques and procedures in this book are intended to provide general information. This is not a complete text on crack climbing technique. Nothing substitutes for formal instruction, routine practice, and plenty of experience. When you follow any of the procedures described here, you assume responsibility for your own safety. Use this book as a general guide to further information. Under normal conditions, excursions into the backcountry require attention to traffic, road and trail conditions, weather, terrain, the capabilities of your party, and other factors. Keeping informed on current conditions and exercising common sense are the keys to a safe, enjoyable outing.

—Mountaineers Books

Before we begin, it's worth summarising some of the key terms that you'll come across while using this book. It should also be noted that for simplicity's sake, and unless otherwise stated, the techniques described in this book assume that a crack takes a vertical line up a vertical rock face.

CRACK FEATURES

Boxed crack—a crack with a back. Essentially the back of the crack prevents you from delving deeper: maybe because of a wall, a narrowing or a chockstone preventing you from doing so.

Corner wall—the crack wall becomes the corner wall when the crack wall extends past the crack edge, outside of the crack feature entirely, and forms a corner (a large offset).

Crack edge/arête—where the crack wall meets the rock face. Easily identified if it's sharp and square cut.

Crack entrance—the point where the space inside of the crack meets the space outside of the crack.

Crack wall—the inside walls of a crack.

Flare—a rounded and more sloping feature. When a crack is described as "flaring" you can likely presume the crack edge/arête is a difficult feature to distinguish (i.e., the crack wall blends into the rock face).

Offset/corner—where one crack edge is set forwards of another, either a little (an offset) or a lot (a corner).

Pod—a slightly larger opening (in comparison to the general width) within a crack feature.

Rock face—the walls outside of the crack.

Splitter—a uniform crack separating two rock faces.

TECHNIQUE TERMINOLOGY

Bomber—a jam that is incredibly positive. You could probably hang a car off yourself from something this good.

Gaston—taking a hold with your palm facing away from you, with your thumb pointing towards the floor and elbow out to the side, is known as a gaston. Imagine trying to prise open elevator doors.

Guppy/cup—the act of wrapping the palm of your hand around a rock feature, then using your fingers and thumb to clamp either side of it. Imagine wrapping your hand over the top of a large eggplant . . .

Jam—a body part placed actively or passively in a crack feature.

Movement—the way the body moves to make upwards progress.

Positioning—the way the body is positioned on the rock to achieve movement.

Stack—two body parts used in combination in the crack as a single unit.

Technique—the way in which you place a body part into the crack.

JAM STABILITY

At the beginning of each technique, the jam is listed as either being a powerful, marginal, balance or resting jam.

Balance jam—a jam that is poor; you shouldn't expect to be able to pull or push on this kind of jam. You might use this jam to help gain purchase so that you can move other body parts, and you will need to be able to put weight through other body parts when using this jam. This jam alone will not keep you in the crack and on the rock.

Marginal jam—a jam that can be pulled or pushed on; this should be done with care and precision to ensure the jam sticks. A subtle movement within this jam can make it suddenly feel very poor and possibly lead to a failure of the jam.

Powerful jam—a jam that can be used forcefully (powerfully) for pulling or pushing. It will feel positive and you should seek out this kind of jam. If it is done correctly you could hang from this jam and nothing else.

Resting jam—a jam which is very solid and can be used powerfully, but which can often restrict body movement. This kind of jam is very useful for resting or placing gear from.

BODY PARTS

The book assumes you know the names of the main body parts (i.e., that you know your knee from your elbow), but the different parts of the hand are a little more complicated. Here's a breakdown of how I've referred to the components of the hand throughout this book.

KEY TO ILLUSTRATIONS

 Contact area between rock and body part.

 Red arrows show different amounts of pressure and direction of pressure when skin touches rock. The dotted red arrow indicates an area that cannot be seen and that may be hidden by another body part.

 Black arrow shows different amounts of pressure and direction of pressure when skin touches skin.

 Pressure on the wall behind a body part we can't necessarily see.

 Movement of a body part: twisting, rotating, flexing, etc. The letters indicate the order in which these movements should be performed.

 Direction of push or pull to enable the climber to move off a jam. If the arrow points towards the body part which is jamming, this indicates a pushing action. If the arrow points away from the body part which is jamming, this indicates a pulling action.

 Twisting point around which the body part should move/pivot.

 Front-on view

 Side-on view

 Bird's-eye view

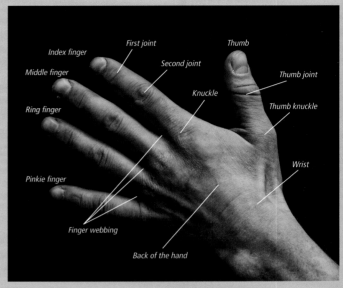

Index finger · First joint · Thumb · Second joint · Thumb joint · Middle finger · Knuckle · Thumb knuckle · Ring finger · Wrist · Pinkie finger · Finger webbing · Back of the hand

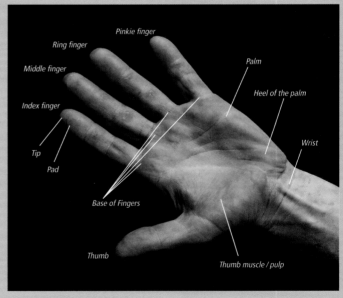

Ring finger · Pinkie finger · Palm · Middle finger · Heel of the palm · Index finger · Tip · Pad · Wrist · Base of Fingers · Thumb · Thumb muscle / pulp

Opposite: *Roger Brown soaking up the atmosphere on the granite hand crack of* Living in Paradise *(VS 4c) at Paradiset, one of the many crack venues on Norway's magical Lofoten Islands* (© Mike Hutton)

CHAPTER 1

The Five Rules of Crack Climbing

There are five basic rules to abide by when it comes to climbing cracks. If you follow these rules and apply them to all aspects of your jamming techniques then you will experience less pain and a higher level of enjoyment and success. The different techniques and jams covered throughout this book will refer back to these principles; but while you might return to this chapter later, it's important to make sense of these five rules at the outset.

RULE 1: FILL THE SPACE EFFICIENTLY

Crack climbing is climbing the spaces between and inside the rock. So, with all jams, you should try to fill those spaces as efficiently as possible. You therefore want to insert as much of the body part you are jamming with inside the crack before you even start doing any of the techniques needed to execute the jam itself.

Many people start performing the dynamics of the jam before the body part is fully in the crack. This means they get less

surface area of jam touching the rock—and therefore a poorer jam. Why use only two fingers on a large crimp when you could use all four? It's the same with jamming: why insert only half of your hand when the crack can gobble your hand to wrist depth? Get that body part right in there.

There are three points to remember when filling the space efficiently:

1. **Put the body part** going into the crack **into its thinnest dimension/ orientation**: a thin cross section means more of the body part can be inserted into the crack.
2. **Relax the body part** going into the crack: a relaxed body part will be easier to wiggle and ease in and will better mould to the crack's shape. A tensed-up body part will form a rigid block which will stop you getting it further inside. Let's try to understand this concept better:

    Imagine you have a large, rectangular stone brick and you want to fit it through a smaller round hole (square peg/round hole concept). The logistics of this are impossible: first, the brick is larger than the hole you are trying to fit it through; second, its shape is different. However, imagine this brick was made of plasticine: you would be able to press, mould, and squeeze the plasticine brick through the hole to the other side. The stone brick is rigid and keeps its shape: it definitely can't fit through the hole; whereas the plasticine brick is soft, malleable, and can change its shape to fit through the hole. So, make those body parts soft and malleable like plasticine when you insert them into the crack.

3. **Expand the body part** and make it rigid (using one of the jamming techniques covered in this book) **only when it is inside the crack**: an expanded body part will fill the space more efficiently and will have more surface area in contact with the walls of the crack. And a rigid body part with a solid shape will struggle to come out of the crack. So, take that plasticine body part that you have just inserted into the crack and make it rigid—and it won't come back out! Winner winner jamming dinner.

These three points sound very simple, but people often neglect one of them—usually the first or second—which consequently makes it difficult to achieve a solid jam.

RULE 2: USE YOUR BODY AS A JAMMING DEVICE

When the part of your body that you want to jam with is inside the crack, you have to expand it to fill the space and make it stick. There are lots of different ways that this jamming and expansion can be achieved.

Let's imagine your body is a rack of gear, with lots of different shaped and sized pieces. What you do with your body when you are crack climbing is the same as what you do with your climbing gear: insert it into cracks.

A rack of gear has lots of pieces of different sizes, from the smallest micronuts through to the biggest cams and Big Bros. Likewise, your body has lots of **different size options** available to insert into the crack, from the diameter of your little finger right through to the length of your whole body.

Your gear has lots of options for ways it can expand and twist to make sure it sticks in the rock. Your body also has lots of **twisting and expanding mechanisms** thanks to the movement in your joints.

Your gear generally needs two or more points of opposing pressure to stay in place. Your jam also needs **two or more points of opposing pressure** on the crack walls to make it stick. (It's important to remember that a jam will only work when body parts are touching both sides of a crack feature.)

There are two ways that your body can jam: **passive** and **active**.

Passive (like placing a nut): the jam is created by constrictions in the rock which allow a body part to be slotted in and wedged, enabling your jam to stick. The jam works because the constriction becomes too small for the body part to pass through. This type of jam requires minimal strength so you should try to use this type of jam as a first option.

Active (like placing a camming device): the jam is created by a range of movement from you—either by twisting, rotating, or expanding. A downwards force (your weight pulling on the jam) along with this movement of the jam creates outwards pressure and friction on the crack walls enabling your jam to stick. A downwards force (or pull) is hugely important in making the jam stick. Let's try to understand this concept better:

Imagine you placed a camming device into the rock and hung a car from it. It would be impossible to retrieve this camming device; you wouldn't even be able to move it. However, if you swapped the car for a feather, you would be able to move or rotate the cam easily inside the crack and retrieving the camming device would be simple.

The same principle applies to jams. The more weight you put through a jam, the better it will stick (provided that your force of outwards pressure against the crack walls can match up to the weight you are putting through it). So, if you lean back, put your weight through it, and trust the jam, it will feel more positive. Maybe climbing with a car attached to you would in fact make it easier!

PASSIVE (STATIONARY) JAMS
CHOCK JAMS

The crack will give you wider and narrower spots (constrictions) to jam between. If you first insert your jam into a wider part and then slide it into a narrower part, it will automatically lock—with no effort required from you—due to the constriction in the rock being smaller than the body part you have inserted. You should always look for passive jams first as they require the least amount of strength. Your body gives you lots of different sizes of chocks to place, ranging from the sizes of your fingers and toe knuckles, right up to your body as a whole, with everything in between—hands, feet, knees, and so on. No strength or twisting is required from you to secure the jam; it is naturally secure as it is not able to pass through the narrowest section of the constriction. The gear example is the placing of a nut: an equivalent jam would be sliding a hand jam into a constriction (figure 1).

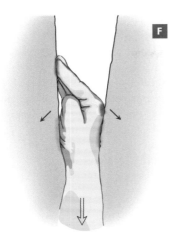

Figure 1. Hand wedged like a nut

EXPANSION JAMS (PASSIVE)

It is possible to place into a crack a body part which is larger than the crack entrance itself. The body part you are inserting just has to be able to mould to the crack's shape, so a softer exterior to the body part you are inserting works better for this—your forearm or your leg, for example. If you manage to put a body part into a crack which is bigger than the crack itself, the body part will naturally want to expand back to its original shape. This passive act of expansion is what makes this kind of jam stick.

Instead of a gear example, imagine an unpoppable balloon. If you pushed an unpoppable balloon into a crack, it would narrow to fit through the gap, but would then want to expand back to its original shape. By expanding, it would exert opposing outwards pressure on the walls and therefore would stick inside. Exactly the same principle works when you are squeezing your body part into a crack. Your forearm or your leg should be like an unpoppable balloon. Bear in mind that this will work with only a few body parts, as not every body part can squidge down easily and then expand again . . . without breaking bones!

ACTIVE (MOVEMENT) JAMS
TWISTING JAMS

If you insert a body part into the crack in its narrowest profile, when you twist it, it will give you a bigger profile, helping you fill the space and create the opposing pressures needed on the crack walls to make the jam stick. The movement of a body part outside of the crack can act as a lever to help generate a greater twist (although it should be noted that a lever doesn't necessarily have to be used to create twist). For example, the movement of the forearm, when executing a thumb-down finger jam, emphasises the twisting of the fingers inside the crack. With twisting jams, it is important to pull or push in the direction that the lever is moving. So, with our finger jam example, the lever is moving down, and this means you should keep a consistent downwards pull. If you start to pull out or up the jam won't work. The gear example is the twisting of a cam hook.

ROTATIONAL JAMS

This is where one side of a jam remains stationary and acts as a pivot point for the other side of the jam (the movement point) to move around. Where the movement point of the jam touches the crack wall, an outwards/downwards force is exerted from your body weight. This force creates an outwards pressure against the crack walls at the pivot and movement points, making the jam stick. The gear example is the rotational forces of a Big Bro; an equivalent jam would be the rotation of the forearm in a chickenwing jam.

EXPANSION JAMS (ACTIVE)

This is a jam that acts like a camming device. You insert a part of your body into the crack in one shape, then when it is inside the crack you can tense, expand, or reshape the jam to make it bigger. A downwards force (your body weight), along with the outwards force put on the crack walls via the expansion of the jam, is what makes the jam stick. It differs from a passive expansion jam because you are actively tensing, expanding, or reshaping the body part.

Expansion jams are particularly useful because you can pull in a 360-degree rotation around the jam and it should be just as solid in any direction: you can either pull down, out, up, or push away on the jam. For example:

Pulling down: the jam is used in the same way you would use any jam. You pull down on it in order to move your body up.

Pulling out: this could be used if you are at the start of a horizontal section after climbing some vertical terrain, for example at the start of a roof. You make an outwards

pull on the jam in order to reach out into the horizontal roof.

Pulling up: this could be used if you are undercutting and need to pull up on the jam in order to make a move up.

The gear example is the expansion of a camming device; an equivalent jam would be the expansion of a hand jam.

COMBINATION JAMS

You can use single or multiple body parts for combination jams.

Using single body parts: a single jam can be inserted into the crack and then two or more of the above techniques can be performed at the same time. This often creates a much more solid jam. An example

---

COMMON MISTAKES TO LOOK OUT FOR:

- Not first looking for passive jams.
- Not keeping the correct direction of pull on twisting jams.
- Trying to use twisting jams in a 360-degree rotation like can be done with expansion jams.
- Pushing or pulling your weight through the pivot point rather than the movement point on rotational jams.
- Making poor contact on one of the crack walls when using expansion jams.
- Trying to use jams individually when placing them in combination rather than letting them complement one another and work together in harmony.

of this would be using the active expansion and twisting actions in the cup and twist technique for a hand jam (see Chapter 3).

Using multiple body parts: if a single body part isn't big enough to fill the space on its own, you have to use a combination of jams. All of the above techniques, either passive or active, can be used in combination with multiple body parts. The gear example is using a slider nut; an equivalent jam would be using different combinations of hand stacks.

RULE 3: KEEP EVERYTHING IN LINE WITH THE CRACK

All body parts should be twisted and orientated in such a way that makes their final position—before you move up on them—parallel and in line with the crack. Let's try to understand this concept better:

Imagine that climbing a crack is like climbing a ladder. Easy! The legs of the ladder represent the edges of the crack and each ladder rung is a jam. Now imagine you're climbing the ladder and your limbs and body are parallel with the ladder's legs. Your elbows will be pointing downwards as this generates the best force for pulling yourself up with your arms. Your knees are pointing upwards as this generates the best force for pushing yourself up with your legs. If your elbows and knees start twisting out to the side, then this will affect their ability to pull up and push down on the ladder's rungs. It will start to feel like you are pulling and pushing outwards to the side—and climbing efficiency

COMMON MISTAKES TO LOOK OUT FOR:

- Trying to open the crack like an elevator door. This will make your elbows rise up and point out to the side—no longer in line.
- Pressing your feet onto the insides of the crack walls in a smearing action. This will make your knees point out to the side—again, no longer in line.
- Being bunched up. If your hands and feet are too close together, both your elbows and knees will have a tendency to point outwards and away from being in line with the crack.

will be lost. Exactly the same principles apply when climbing a crack: elbows should be down and knees should be up. When everything is in line with the crack, effective jamming is in action. If your body parts aren't in line, you will not be able to pull up and push down as effectively. Climbing a crack is like climbing a ladder.

RULE 4: USE STRUCTURE NOT STRENGTH

With all crack climbing, you use the frame (structure) of your body to stay in and on the rock. Joints, ligaments, and bones: you are aiming to lock these into the crack in such a way that you can hang off them using minimal or no muscle/tendon contraction.

WHAT IS THE "STICK-SLIP POINT"?

The point where the jam goes from sticking and you are able to pull on it, to slipping and failure. This failure is not to do with pump/power/fatigue or any other physical aspect; it's purely related to the jam slipping because not enough twist, expansion, or rotation has been put through the jam and therefore there is not enough friction to hold it in the crack.

Imagine a body with no soft tissue, just a skeleton with ligaments holding the bones together. If you twisted, rotated, and expanded the skeleton's bones you would be able to create shapes which could fit and lock into cracks without any "holding power" from the absent muscles and tendons. This is what you are trying to achieve when using your body in a crack.

You are **locking** your body *into* the rock. **Not holding** your body *on to* the rock.

- *Joints* twist, rotate, flex, and extend. If you perform these actions correctly for the right size crack they will automatically lock, and you will only need to use limited holding power. Use these actions to lock your body into the rock rather than holding yourself on to the rock.
- *Ligaments* hold the bones and joints together and stop them from separating. When you hang from the joints, you are also hanging from the ligaments. Hanging from joints and ligaments uses a lot less energy than hanging from muscles and tendons. Imagine dangling off a pull-up bar one-handed: you would be able to do it for a lot longer with a straight arm (hanging from bones and ligaments) than with a bent arm (hanging from muscles and tendons).

This means you can hang from the rock using your body's structure rather than its strength. This is a valuable tool: make sure you use it.

- *Bones* are different sizes and widths. If you slot your bones into the correct-sized crack they will jam without you having to use any strength. Use different sizes of bones to lock yourself into the rock, instead of holding yourself on to the rock.

COMMON MISTAKES TO LOOK OUT FOR:

- Feeling like you are holding on to the rock.
- Crimping, or any other finger grip position, inside or on the edge of the crack. If you feel as though you are using any normal climbing grip, it will mean you are trying to hold on to the rock rather than making your body parts fit into the rock.
- Climbing bunched up with arms and legs bent. If your arms and legs are continuously bent, you will be using a lot more muscular strength, rather than the structure of your body.

■ *Skin* is your contact point with the rock. This contact between the rock and your skin has friction which keeps you on the climb. Friction is an essential part of jamming as a lot of the time there is a great deal more skin contact than in any other style of climbing. Hands, arms, legs, torso, you name it—you'll probably use it against the rock while crack climbing. Jams rely on friction to stay in the crack. Use your body parts to get more friction against the rock, as larger amounts of friction will mean you won't have to hold on as hard. If you practise where the "stick-slip point" is, then you can learn to climb whole routes just above this threshold, gaining maximum efficiency from friction and using less strength. Structure not strength!

RULE 5: MORE SURFACE AREA BETWEEN SKIN AND ROCK EQUALS A BETTER JAM

The more contact that your jam has with the rock, the better it will feel. By orientating your jam correctly to the rock's profile, you will get more surface area of the jam touching the rock and therefore a more solid jam. Let's try and understand this concept better:

Your climbing partner has made you a jam sandwich. Between the two slices of bread is a layer of strawberry jam. They pass you the sandwich, but when you bite into it you find they haven't spread the jam right to the edge of the slice, so all you get is a mouthful of bread. You find they

COMMON MISTAKES TO LOOK OUT FOR:
- Using the incorrect side of your body (whether right or left) to execute the jam.
- Using only passive and active jams when combination jams could be used: i.e., just using a cupping action in a cupped hand jam, when in fact cupping and twisting can be used.

have only spread the strawberry jam in the centre of the sandwich and there is barely any surface area of strawberry jam touching the bread. Very disappointing. You ask if the jam can be spread right to the edges of the bread to cover the whole area. You try the sandwich again; this time you get a mouthful of strawberry jam and the *jam* sandwich tastes great!

Let's take this strawberry jam sandwich example and apply it to crack climbing. The slices of bread represent the crack walls and the strawberry jam represents our body jam. When you put your jam in between the crack walls, if there is minimal surface area contact between skin and rock when you engage the jam, then just like your strawberry jam sandwich, the end product will be disappointing. However, if you create lots of surface area contact with your jam and the crack walls, then just like your fully spread strawberry jam sandwich, the taste—of success—will be sweet.

More surface area between skin and rock equals a better jam.

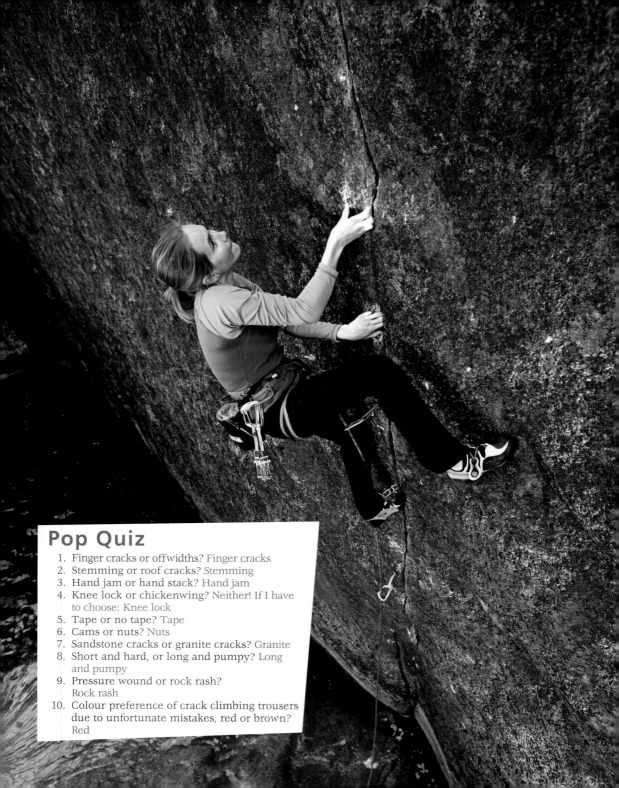

Pop Quiz

1. Finger cracks or offwidths? Finger cracks
2. Stemming or roof cracks? Stemming
3. Hand jam or hand stack? Hand jam
4. Knee lock or chickenwing? Neither! If I have to choose: Knee lock
5. Tape or no tape? Tape
6. Cams or nuts? Nuts
7. Sandstone cracks or granite cracks? Granite
8. Short and hard, or long and pumpy? Long and pumpy
9. Pressure wound or rock rash? Rock rash
10. Colour preference of crack climbing trousers due to unfortunate mistakes, red or brown? Red

BETH RODDEN

Beth cemented herself as one of the best with repeats of many of America's hardest cracks and corners. She then stepped things up in 2008 with her own route, The Meltdown (5.14c), in Yosemite, an incredibly tenuous and delicately powerful testpiece. Such is its difficulty, The Meltdown waited over ten years for a second ascent, by Carlo Traversi, who called it "a benchmark in the history of climbing."

FAVOURITE CRACK CLIMBING AREA?

Yosemite. It's hard for me to think of crack climbing without thinking of the Valley. It's where I learnt to crack climb. I spent my first few seasons living out of my two-door hatchback car in the parking lot of Yosemite Lodge. I'd wake each morning and try to convince anyone to go out climbing with a skinny little sport climber and promise not to drink too much water or complain too much. It's the most humbling climbing area I've ever been to, constantly teaching me that 5.8 can challenge or thwart you at any time in your climbing career. But aside from the history and the humbling nature of the climbing, it just has so much good, fun climbing. I find the Yosemite granite challenging and to be the best type of climbing, making you have both good technique and strength. I've been climbing there for almost 20 years and whether I get to climb on something I've done a hundred times, or something that I've never been on before, it's so fun for me to climb on the impeccable granite and have an adventure.

FAVOURITE CRACK CLIMB?

One of my all-time favorite pure crack climbs is *The Phoenix* (5.13a) in Yosemite. I flashed the route back in 2002. It has everything from pure finger locks, to thin hand jams. It's slightly overhanging, gets you pumped out of your mind, and is everything you'd want in a crack climb. It's hard to beat its location right next to Cascade Falls and with beautiful vistas of the lower Valley. I've gone back a couple times when I'm feeling the desire to get pumped and a

good workout, and I'm never disappointed in my decision to return. Definitely a great one!

MEMORABLE CRACK EXPERIENCE?

I've long been trying to redpoint *Ahab* in Yosemite. It's a route at the base of El Cap and my nemesis. I'm terrible at wide climbing, but I love a good challenge. One day I thought that I might be able to do it cleanly on top rope: I was feeling fit, I remembered what I did from the previous week, all things were going in my favour. I started up the climb and got into position. I squirmed and squeezed and grunted and groaned and thought I was making great progress. My shoulders were burning, my knees were sore, and my ankles bloody. I thought for sure I was near the top of the hard part—when I looked down I found that I was only a few feet off the starting ledge. Alas, wide climbing still eludes me. Randy [Puro] walked up and promptly flashed it after my failure, which to this day is one of the most impressive sends I've seen.

THE KNOWLEDGE

Start easy in Yosemite; build a good base. If you are climbing much harder sport or gym routes, the harder-rated climbing might feel easier to you, but inevitably on a long route, you are going to encounter some real Yosemite old-school climbing which will be like nothing you've encountered in the gym or at the crag before. So make sure you are at least somewhat comfortable on that stuff—I'm still learning this lesson!

Opposite: *Beth on* The Meltdown, *Yosemite National Park, California* (© Corey Rich/Cavan Images)

SUMMARY: THE FIVE RULES

1. *Fill the space efficiently:* insert as much of the body part as possible into the crack **before** executing the jam.

2. *Your body is a rack of jamming devices:* your body has lots of different sizes and shapes and ways of moving and expanding. Use these body "tools" to jam, twist, rotate, and expand to make the jam stick.

3. *Keep everything in line with the crack:* imagine climbing a crack like you would climb a ladder.

4. *Structure not strength:* you should be hanging from joints, ligaments, and bone. You should **lock** your body *into* the rock, **not hold** your body *on to* the rock.

5. *More contact equals a better jam:* by using the profile of the rock and your body, in unison, you will maximise contact area with the rock, and have more friction and therefore a better jam.

Jasmin Caton on Tantalus Wall *(5.11c),* Squamish, Canada *(© Andrew Burr)*

Opposite: *Mike Holland screaming on the classic* Swedin-Ringle *(5.12-), Indian Creek, Utah* (© Drew Smith)

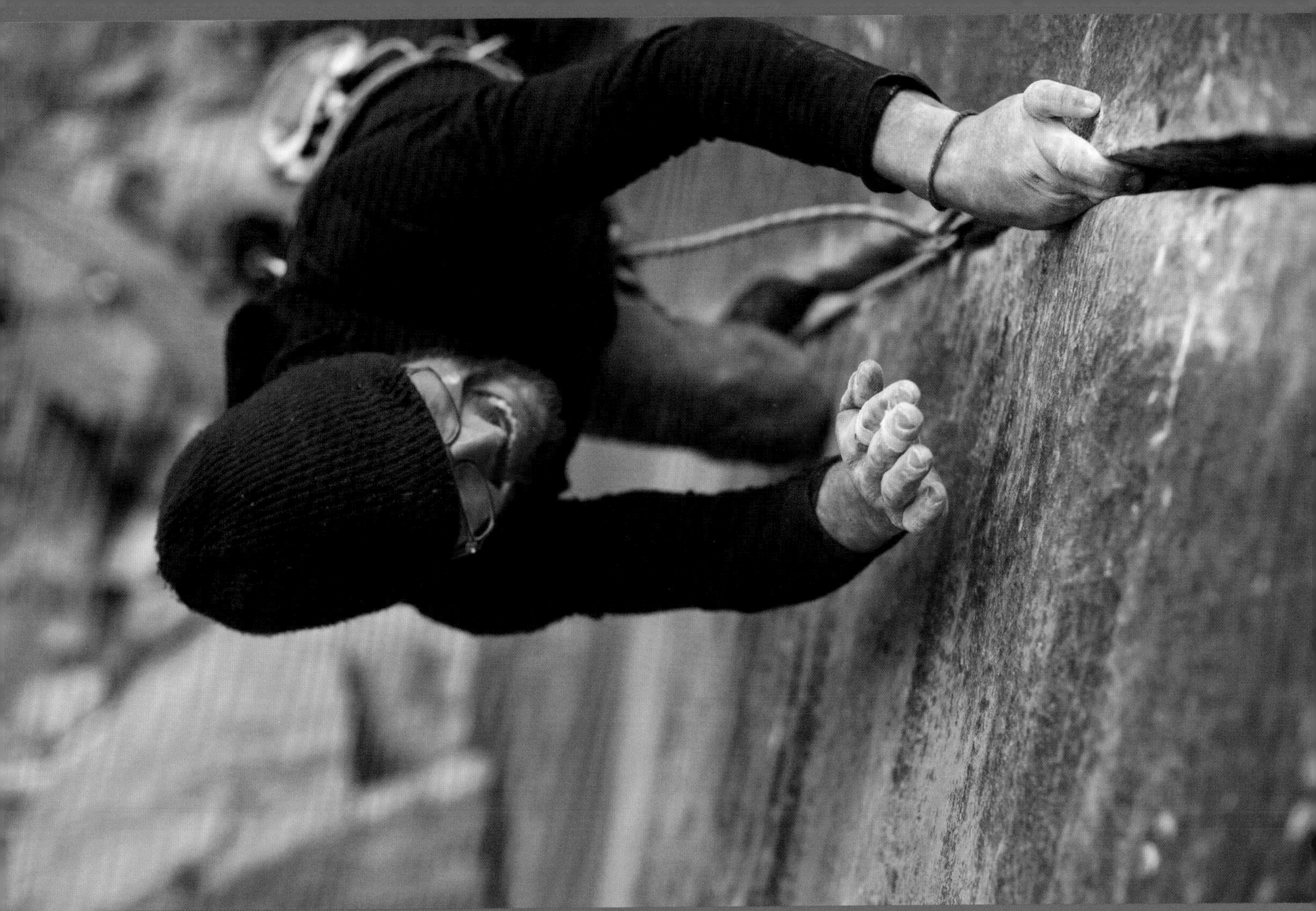

CHAPTER 2

Finger Cracks

Finger cracks are one of the most fickle sizes, as a small variation in crack or finger size can make a big difference in difficulty. Just one millimetre larger or smaller can be the difference between a move feeling easy or impossible.

Imagine a thin crack. Two people walk up to the route. One is a ballerina and one is a lumberjack. The ballerina has hands as thin as paper and fingers the width of matchsticks. The lumberjack has hands the girth of a tree trunk and sausage-like fingers. The ballerina climbs and dances up the rock, fingers locking and jamming with ease, whereas the lumberjack can't fit a single sausage inside the crack and topples like a felled tree. Now, if we were to widen the crack by a few millimetres and again take our two climbers, we would find that our ballerina's fingers would rattle inside the crack and she would have to use more difficult techniques to make them stick, whereas our lumberjack's fingers would lock and jam easily. With finger-width cracks, very small changes can make a big difference.

The thought of sticking your body's smallest digits into a crack, twisting them in ways they haven't evolved to twist, and then pulling your body weight up on them, obviously makes people queasy and dislike this type of climbing. Fair enough! However, with the correct techniques, finger cracks can be climbed with relative ease.

This chapter covers crack sizes where you can insert only the tips of your fingers inside the crack, right up to the width where you can use your thumb and fingers in combination, but can't yet fit the knuckles of your hand inside.

HAND TECHNIQUES IN FINGER CRACKS

LOCKER FINGER CRACKS

The dreamy finger jam: your fingers should sink, seat, and twist into the jam like a key in a lock. They will be buried inside the crack up to the base of your fingers and the jam will feel good.

Thumb-down jam: index finger
powerful jam, active twisting jam

As this is an active movement jam it can be used to great effect on complete splitters

28

where there are few constrictions to passively jam between. (Remember when inserting a body part into a crack to always look for constrictions to jam passively first.)

1. Orient your hand into the thumb-down position (index finger and thumb towards the ground, pinkie finger towards the sky), pointing your elbow out to the side away from the centre of your body. The back of your hand should be facing towards you, as if you were saluting someone.

2. Bend your hand, at the wrist, away from you so the tips of your fingers are now pointing towards the crack. Because you are bending from the wrist and not the knuckles your fingers should be relaxed and able to move freely. They are also in their thinnest orientation.

3. Insert your fingers into the crack up to their base, with your thumb on the outside of the crack.

4. Flatten your palm and forearm against the rock face; this creates a small amount of expansion in the finger pulp of skin at the base of your fingers.

5. Imagine there is a metal rod running up your forearm and through your wrist (so that you cannot bend or flex the wrist). Keeping this rigidity through the wrist and forearm, rotate your elbow and forearm down and in line with the crack. It is important to keep your forearm and palm close to the rock. If they move away from the rock, you will find yourself pulling out on the jam and not down. An outwards pull will negatively affect the quality of the jam, most likely forcing you

into the dreaded elevator-door-opening technique (gastoning/backhanding the edge of the crack).

6. As you rotate with your elbow, your fingers will start to twist inside the crack (clockwise, if jamming with your right hand, anticlockwise if jamming with your left):

   ■ your index finger will bite into the rock
   ■ your middle finger will also bite (but slightly less so)
   ■ your ring finger will gain some friction; however, it is common and correct for it to start rotating out of the crack and to leave it stacked on your front two fingers
   ■ your little finger will come out the crack and should be placed against the crack wall

7. Your hand and forearm will now be parallel with the crack and you are ready to use the jam to move up on the route. When you start to pull up be careful not to move your palm and forearm away from the rock. Pull down on the jam, not out (figure 2).

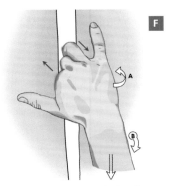

Figure 2. Thumb-down jam: index finger

Thumb-down jam: middle finger
powerful jam, active twisting jam

The same thumb-down jam can be performed but with your index finger out of the crack and your middle finger as the bottom finger in the jam. This can be useful if:

- the crack is ever so slightly too thin to fit your index finger in comfortably (it's not uncommon for the index finger to be slightly fatter than the middle finger)
- you have done multiple jams using your index finger and this is becoming increasingly painful

Pinkie-down jam: little finger
powerful jam, active twisting jam

Although this jam has active movements to it, it works much better if you look for constrictions and aim to place it passively. And while there is some twisting involved in this jam, there is not as much as in thumb-down jams, which means that if you don't find constrictions the jam can be marginal, feel like it is slipping, and be very strenuous to make work. However, if you can find the right spot, it can feel more restful than thumb-down jams—and can often be better than holding a massive jug.

1. Orient your hand into the pinkie-down position (pinkie finger towards the ground, index finger and thumb towards the sky), with the tips of your fingers pointing straight at the crack. Keep your hand relaxed. Your arm will be in line with the crack with your elbow pointing downwards—it is important to remember this and keep your arm in this position.

2. Insert your fingers into the crack, up to their base if possible. Look for constrictions that narrow down to become thinner than your pinkie finger, so that your finger can passively jam. Slide your fingers down into the constriction until your pinkie finger bites.

3. Whether you keep your index finger inside or outside of the crack will depend on how deep your fingers are inside the crack. As a basic rule, if three or more fingers have been inserted all the way to the base of the fingers, then keep the index finger inside. Also, if the jam is placed passively, this will reduce the need to rotate the wrist (see next step), meaning you can keep the index finger inside. If the jam isn't placed passively, you will need to rotate more at the wrist and so the index finger will naturally start to twist out of the crack. If only one or two fingers go all the way to the knuckles, then keep the index outside. However, this is a guide: using feel to decide is often the best way.

4. This next part involves a very subtle twisting motion to make the jam work effectively. Being delicate is the key to success with this jam. Imagine placing a key into a "tricky to open" lock: using force and twisting vigorously will not work; you should gently and lightly feel for the best spot until it clicks into place. It is the same with this jam: don't use brute force and over-twist; wait for it to click into place.
   - Flatten your palm against the rock (keeping your thumb outside the crack) and then rotate it

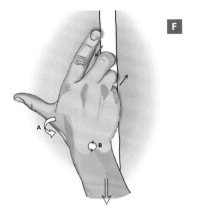

Figure 3. Pinkie-down jam: little finger

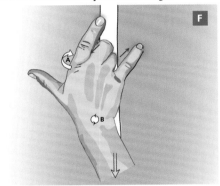

Figure 4. Pinkie-down jam: ring finger

downwards. It is important with this jam to rotate from the wrist and not the arm. Your forearm should already be in line with the crack so there is no need to move it.

■ Rotating from the wrist will twist the fingers into the crack, making them stick. If jamming with your right hand your fingers should start to twist anticlockwise, and vice versa (figure 3).

Pinkie-down jam: ring finger
powerful jam, active twisting jam

You can also execute pinkie-down jams with your ring finger as the bottom finger (figure 4). The same technique is used as with pinkie-down finger jams, the only difference is that your ring finger is the one biting into the constriction. Your little finger can either stay inside the crack (where it will be of limited use as it is too narrow to passively wedge) or move outside. Keeping it outside the crack will help to emphasise the twisting action on your ring finger. This technique is useful if:

■ the crack is too wide for your little finger to jam, meaning it keeps sliding through the crack

■ you have done multiple jams using your pinkie finger and this is becoming increasingly painful

BAGGY FINGER CRACKS

A difficult size of jam, in between the security of good finger locks and ring locks (later in this chapter). A large amount of twisting force is used with these jams to get enough rotation in the fingers to enable them to make solid contact with the crack wall. They are a bad size and, I won't lie to you, can cause some discomfort on the joints and skin from the amount of twisting.

Thumb-down jam
powerful jam, active twisting jam

The same starting techniques apply with this jam as with a normal thumb-down locker jam, however because the crack is slightly wider you will be getting less surface area of jam touching the rock. In this scenario you can do two things:

- Put greater pressure through the points touching the crack walls. To do this, you have to emphasize the forearm rotation to increase the amount of twisting from your fingers.
- Create more surface area touching the crack walls. To do this, you can insert your thumb into the crack and slot it upwards underneath your fingers. You can put opposing pressure through the pad and back of your thumb against the crack wall to create outwards pressure. You can also rest your fingers on the tip of your thumb (figures 5 and 6).

Pinkie-down jam
powerful jam, active twisting jam
This jam again requires a large amount of twisting force. Be very careful doing it pinkie down as the jam can start to over-open the knuckles on your hand which can be painful and result in hand injuries.

All the same starting principles apply as if performing a locker pinkie-down jam, however an emphasized twist of the wrist is needed at the end to make this jam work effectively. It is most likely that the pads of your index and middle fingers will be touching one side of the crack and the opposing pressure comes from the backs of your ring and pinkie fingers touching the opposite side of the crack. If there is any kind of crack offset, you can also get useful pressure from the backs of your pinkie and ring finger knuckles (figure 7.)

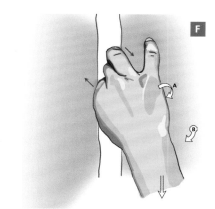

Figure 5. Baggy finger cracks: thumb-down jam

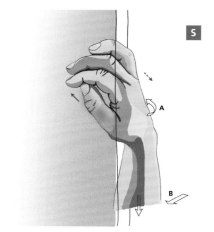

Figure 6. Baggy finger cracks: thumb-down jam

- If using your left hand, emphasize the twist in your wrist in a clockwise orientation
- If using your right hand, emphasize the twist in your wrist in an anticlockwise orientation

BAGGY FINGER CORNERS
balance jam, active expansion jam

If the crack is in a corner and you can't use standard baggy finger locking techniques, then you can use the corner wall to your advantage.

Size 1 (narrower)

1. Place your fingers into the crack as you would when executing a standard thumb-down baggy finger lock.
2. Instead of actively rotating the elbow down and twisting the fingers in, bridge your thumb across the gap of the crack below your index finger. The width will be so that you can place the tip of the thumb on the crack edge and the thumb joint on the corner wall. The thumb position is very similar to the starting position that you would use when performing a ring lock (see later this chapter).
3. Now, at the same time, push the backs of your fingers against the crack and corner walls (the pads of your fingers are unlikely to be touching the opposite crack wall due to the crack width) and push the tip of your thumb into the crack edge, to create two opposing pressures (figure 8).
4. When you push the tip of your thumb into the crack edge, push out and down. This helps to rotate the thumb joint up and into the corner wall with more force.
5. It's useful to note that the use of the thumb in this technique can also be applied if you were performing a standard baggy finger lock in a corner (i.e.,

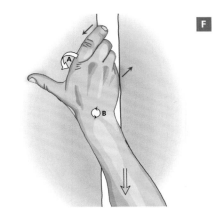

Figure 7. Baggy finger cracks: pinkie-down jam

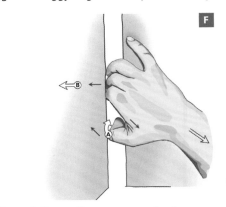

Figure 8. Baggy finger corners: size 1

if you were to rotate the elbow down and actively twist the fingers into the crack). If you're twisting and the jam still feels like it might slip, then using the thumb will give a little extra support. You could even start to rest your fingers on the tip of your thumb. In this case you'd essentially be performing a very narrow ring lock.

Size 2 (wider)

This is a variation to the above technique for slightly wider cracks.

Exactly the same principles and positioning apply, however as the crack will be too wide to bridge the thumb across, you will just be using the pad of your thumb and backs of your fingers to generate opposing pressures through the crack edge and corner wall.

A cunning little extra tip (which is useful if you have short pinkie fingers), is to use your pinkie finger (as well as your thumb) to push out against the crack edge.

The finished position will have the back of your front three fingers (index, middle, and ring) pushing against the crack and corner wall, with the pads of your thumb and pinkie finger pushing against the crack edge (figure 9).

TIPS FINGER CRACKS

This jam sits either before, on, or only just past the first finger joint. As you have minimal skin in contact with the rock, tips jams are the most marginal of the finger jam techniques. They can feel awful in the wrong circumstances, however there are subtle tricks which can make even the most impossible moves doable. File those cuticles down and get those chisel tips out as things are about to get thin and every micrometre makes a big difference.

The same basic hand positions can be used with this jam as with traditional finger jams: either thumb down or pinkie down.

Thumb-down tips jam
marginal jam, combination jam (active twisting and crimping)

The same starting principles should be applied with this jam as if you were doing a normal thumb-down finger jam. The crack will be very thin so it will be tempting to put all your fingers into the crack to try to gain more purchase. However, if you put three or more fingers in the crack, you won't achieve the

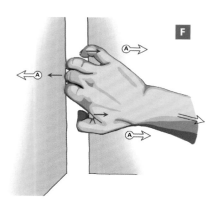

Figure 9. Baggy finger corners: size 2

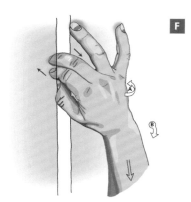

Figure 10. Tips finger cracks: thumb-down jam

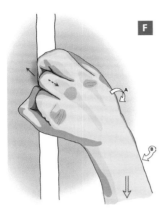

Figure 11. Tips finger cracks: crimped fingers

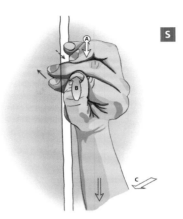

Figure 12. Tips finger cracks: crimped fingers

correct twisting action which is crucial to keeping this jam in place. You will end up crimping or pulling on the edge of the crack, which defeats the point of trying to jam. With this jam you should concentrate on using your index and middle fingers to jam and leave your other digits outside of the crack (figure 10). This doesn't mean you have to neglect these digits; you can use them and your thumb, in lots of different ways, as secret weapons to give you more purchase:

■ Wrap your thumb over the two jamming fingers in much the same way as you would use your thumb if you were crimping (figure 11).

■ If your finger jams are solid, use the jamming fingers as a platform: stack your ring and pinkie fingers on top of your jamming fingers in a half-crimped position. If the jam is good enough to take the power from your crimping fingers, overall you will achieve a stronger position and be able to put more weight

through the jam. If your finger jams feel extra solid, you can blend this technique with the previous technique and also use your thumb over the top of your jamming fingers for extra downwards pull. The overall position will create a crimped finger jam, which if performed well can be very effective (figure 12).

■ If your finger jams are less solid or feel insecure, use your thumb as a platform: place your thumb sideways on the edge of the crack beneath your jamming fingers and rest your fingers on the tip of your thumb. (See figure 10.)

Pinkie-down tips jam
marginal jam, combination jam
(active twisting and crimping)

The same starting principles apply for this jam as with a normal pinkie-down finger jam, however, concentrate on your pinkie and ring fingers inside the crack and keep your middle and index fingers and thumb outside.

As with thumb-down tips finger jams, the fingers on the outside of the crack can be used to help complement the jam. They can be used individually, as a pair, or as a whole unit.

- *Middle finger:* the middle finger can either rest on the edge of the crack, or, if there are crystals, lumps, or bumps outside of the crack to rest your finger on, you can use these.
- *Index finger:* look for pebbles, crystals, lumps, bumps, pockets, or rock indentations—anything that you can put your finger in or on in a half-crimp or drag position that will give you extra purchase.
- *Thumb:* look for exactly the same features that you looked for to use the index finger. However, aim to use your thumb in opposition to the fingers that are inside the crack, so you are in effect making a pinch position and pulling in towards the crack. If using the thumb to pinch, ensure you keep the fingers twisting inside the crack and don't turn the jam into a pure pinch grip.

TIPS IN CORNERS

Further techniques and tricks can be used when you have tips finger jams but in a corner or offset crack. Offsets occur when one side of the crack wall protrudes out from the other crack wall, essentially making a little corner. As well as the crack, with a corner or offset you have the extra bonus of a side wall, which you can use in a number of different ways.

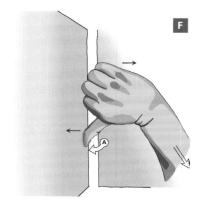

Figure 13. Tips in corners: thumb sprag

Thumb down: thumb sprag
balance jam, active expansion jam

The thumb sprag is a technique I use a lot with awful jams. Simply place the pad of the thumb on the corner/offset wall just below where the jam is and press hard into the wall.

The useful thing about this technique is that you only need an offset that is the same width as the pad of your thumb to make it effective; this can range anywhere from a small crack flare to a full-blown corner crack.

Spragging your thumb on the wall pushes the fingers that are inside the crack against the opposing crack wall with a slightly greater force, which on a marginal jam can make a big difference.

The thumb sprag can also be used in combination with a half crimp on the edge of the crack if a tips jam can't be performed (for example, if the crack is too shallow or flared). Crimp on the edge of the crack and sprag on the opposing offset (figure 13).

Pinkie down
marginal jam, active twisting jam

All the same rules and tricks apply with pinkie-down tips in corners, as with standard pinkie-down tips jams, i.e., the use of your fingers and thumb outside the crack to help complement the jam. However, the difference here is that you have a corner wall to gain friction from.

The following technique will only work if the back of your hand/fingers face the corner wall as you start the technique.

Follow the first four steps of the standard pinkie-down tips jam (earlier this chapter) all the way to the final stage: the subtle wrist rotation (step 4).

As with any pinkie-down finger jam, the final rotation of the wrist will help complete the jam and make it feel solid. However, as you complete this motion in a corner it is likely that the side of your hand, below your pinkie finger, will come in contact with the corner wall: use this to

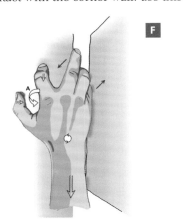

Figure 14. Tips in corners: pinkie down

your advantage. Push and nestle it into the corner wall and gain extra friction from this new skin/rock contact point (figure 14).

If you're really lucky you might even be able to get the side of your forearm involved and gain some extra friction from this as well.

It should be noted that this way of gaining extra friction from the side of the hand can also be used if you use a thumb-down position (your hand must oriented so that the back of your hand/fingers are against the corner wall). However, it will be the side of your hand below the thumb knuckle which will come into contact with the corner wall.

Tight corners: thumb down and pinkie down
marginal jam, active twisting jam

This technique can be used on any width of corner finger crack where the angle of the corner starts to become tighter, however it is especially useful on tips finger cracks, as the jams on this width often feel more marginal; this technique can offer that little bit of extra support.

As a guide, it generally starts to become useful when the corner is at less than a 90-degree angle. The tighter/smaller the angle, the more effective the technique.

Follow all the procedures of a normal thumb-down tips finger jam—or the procedures from larger finger crack widths if the crack is wider.

As you rotate your forearm down and twist your fingers into the crack, allow the sides of your hand to twist into the tighter angle of the corner.

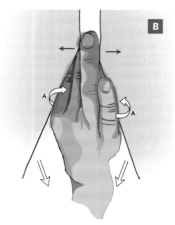

Figure 15. Tight corners: thumb down

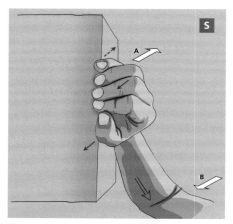

Figure 16. Tips in corners: thumb bridge (side-on, viewed through corner wall).

If you're using your right hand—and twisting in a clockwise motion—the back of your hand below the base of the thumb/index finger will gain friction from the left wall and the palm/side of the hand below the pinkie finger will gain friction from the right wall.

You can even start to get the thumb involved like you would on a normal thumb-down hand jam. Tuck it into the palm and push it towards the little finger. This will raise the index knuckle and help push it into the crack wall.

The overall position of the hand will start to represent a very flared thumb-down hand jam, with the tips of your fingers locked in the crack at the back (figure 15).

While this technique works better in a thumb-down position due to the twisting action that occurs in the hand, it can be done—albeit with a bit more difficulty—with a pinkie-down jam.

Thumb down and pinkie down: crimped thumb bridge

Use standard crimping techniques to crimp the crack edge. As you crimp gain extra friction from the thumb joint and second joint of the fingers coming into contact with the corner wall or offset. This technique can be used in both a thumb-down and pinkie-down orientation (figure 16).

RING LOCKS

The ring lock is a difficult jam and requires practice to perfect it. This is because it entails using two different jams (an expansion jam and a twisting jam) in combination to form the final solid jamming position.

The crack will be too wide to get a solid finger lock; even twisting your fingers hard won't prevent them from slipping through the crack. However, the crack is still too thin to be able to start getting parts of your hand in. You need to start thinking laterally now: fingers and thumb need to work in harmony to make the jam stick.

Ring locks work best in a thumb-down position and there are two techniques to use, depending on the width of the crack.

Size 1 (thinner)
powerful jam, combination jam (active expansion and twisting)

1. Insert your thumb into the crack in its thinnest orientation. This should be with your thumbnail facing one side of the crack, the pad of your thumb facing the other, and the tip of your thumb pointing towards the sky.
2. Bend your thumb at the joint and bridge it across the gap, so the pad of your thumb touches one crack wall and the joint plus lower part of your thumb touches the opposite crack wall. Your thumb should be placed just inside the crack, close to the crack edge. It's important not to place it too deep as this will hinder the completion of the following steps (figure 17).

3. To keep the thumb in place, focus on bending it at the joint and pressing hard with the pad of your thumb into the crack wall—by doing this you will create opposing pressure through the crack walls. Your thumb will be rigid and be jammed in the crack using expansion.
4. To complete the jam all you have to do is perform a normal thumb-down finger jam (see "Locker Finger Cracks" earlier this chapter) but on top of your thumb. Your bridged thumb should have created a little V-slot between it and the rock. Imagine this slot is actually a V-slot in the rock and place your fingers passively in it in the same way as you would place a normal finger jam. This will involve rotating the elbow up and out to the side to get the fingers into the correct position: as you rotate your elbow up and place your fingers be sure you **do not move** your thumb deeper into the crack, which is tempting to do as the positioning

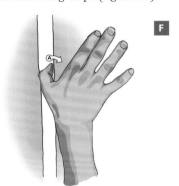

Figure 17. Ring locks: size 1 starting position

Figure 18. Ring locks: size 1 finishing position

can feel awkward. (Note that this is a difficult position to achieve correctly.) Once passively placed, perform the appropriate twisting actions of a normal finger jam (figure 18).

Either the front two or three fingers can be used, depending on size and what feels best. If using three fingers, they are likely to be crammed together. The twisting action (rotation of the elbow downwards) is very important in this jam as this is what levers the thumb into place and creates a solid chock for your fingers to jam on top of. Think: *push out* (on the crack walls) with the thumb; *pull down* (on top of the thumb) with the fingers; *rotate down* (to keep the twisting pressure on the thumb) with the forearm; *push in* with the forearm towards the rock face.

5. For this jam it is especially important to keep a downwards pull force through the jam by keeping your elbow down and forearm close to the rock. Either reach your hand a reasonable distance above you so your forearm automatically moves closer to the rock or, if the jam is close to you, forcefully push your forearm towards the rock. This jam becomes increasingly difficult if you put an outwards pull force through the jam. This outwards force occurs when the jam is too close to you and you lean back off it.

6. This style of ring lock can be altered to fit the width of the crack. Figure 17 shows a 45-degree bend in the thumb, but if the crack is slightly wider, you might be able to bend your thumb

into a 90-degree angle, so that the tip of your thumb (rather than the pad) touches the crack wall. In this case, a two-finger donut jam (later this chapter) with your index and middle finger over the top of your thumb can be very effective.

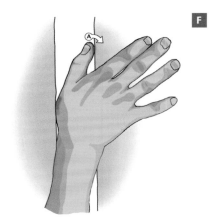

Figure 19. Ring locks: size 2 starting position

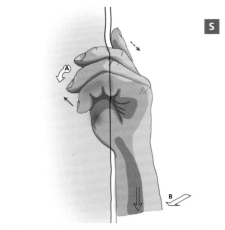

Figure 20. Ring locks: size 2 finishing position

Size 2 (wider)

When the crack becomes this wide, it is likely you will be able to start using thin-hand-jam techniques (Chapter 3). However, there are occasions when it is not possible to do that, perhaps due to the crack not being deep enough or the jam placement being shorter than the length of your hand; in those instances, this technique can be useful to have up your sleeve.

The same principles apply as with the slightly thinner size-1 variation, however the thumb positioning is different.

1. Instead of placing the joint and pad of your thumb on opposing sides of the crack, place the knuckle and pad of your thumb on opposing sides. By using the knuckle, you can bridge a bigger gap with your thumb (figure 19).
2. Now, using your front three fingers, recreate the same thumb-down finger jamming action as with the thinner size-1 ring lock jam, using the V-slot you've created with your thumb and the rock as if it were a constriction (figure 20).

Other variations

It is most common to use the front two or three fingers (in a thumb-down orientation) when ring locking. However, there are times when a different finger combination will fit the jam better and feel more solid. It is unlikely you will use one of these variations during an on-sight attempt, but while working a route when you have time to fiddle about with the jams you might just find a different combination that works perfectly. Remember that you should always

Dan Parkes enjoying the smooth slate rock on the perfectly protected finger crack of Comes the Dervish *(E3 5c) in Vivian Quarry, Snowdonia, North Wales* (© Mike Hutton)

be imaginative and creative when jamming! With the first two options below, the index finger should be left outside the crack.

- Middle-two ring lock (middle and ring fingers)
- Back-three ring lock (middle, ring, and pinkie fingers)
- Mono ring lock. Index finger works best, however middle finger can also be used. This technique would only really be used in very specific situations; if the crack is so thin that you are having to mono ring lock, then it is likely that you could be using normal finger jams and tips techniques.

FINGER BARS

The finger bar is another technique for the ring lock size of crack (bigger than baggy finger, but too small to get the back of your hand in). Although this jam can't be pulled on as powerfully as a ring lock, it is a useful tool for occasions when it is impossible to place a ring lock due to the nature of the crack: for example, if there are other rock features—a side wall or a flare—preventing you from doing so.

Finger barring can be a painful technique when you do try to pull on one powerfully as it's the type of jam that wants to bend your fingers in the wrong direction. Imagine placing your palm on the road and resting the tips of your fingers against the angle of the curb, then getting someone to cycle over the backs of your fingers. Ouch! That may be a bit extreme, but the point is they can be slightly painful even when performed correctly. However, with a small amount of pain tolerance and practice,

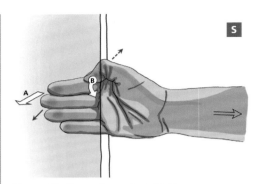

Figure 21. Finger bars: straight fingers

finger bars can come in useful when ring locks can't be placed.

Finger bars work best in a thumb-up orientation, so rotate your hand to a thumb-up position, with the tips of your fingers pointing towards the crack, and insert your fingers into the crack up to the knuckles at the base of the fingers. There are now two types of finger bar which can be performed.

Straight-finger finger-bars

marginal jam, active expansion jam

Keeping your fingers straight, place the pads of your fingers against one side of the crack and press hard into the rock with them. This will force the backs of your fingers (just above the knuckle) to put opposing pressure on the edge of the crack (figures 21 and 22).

Crimped-finger finger-bars

marginal jam, active expansion jam

Instead of keeping your fingers straight, bend your fingers at the second joint and bridge the tips of your fingers across the crack. The tips of your fingers should be

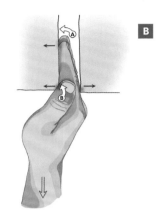

Figure 22. Finger bars: straight finger

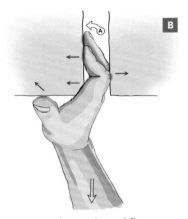

Figure 23. Finger bars: crimped fingers

producing outwards pressure through one wall and the area of finger between the second joint and big knuckle should be inserting opposing pressure through the other wall (figure 23). This technique can be good on sharp-edged cracks as it spreads the load across a larger area (rather than directing it onto one point like the straight-finger finger bar does).

Use of thumb

The thumb can either be used or not when finger barring. If it is used, tuck it into the crack (nail pointing upwards) resting above the index finger and against the same crack wall as the tips of your fingers. Push out to gain a greater outwards pressure through the crack wall (figure 22). Alternatively, if there are features on the face outside the crack, you can use your thumb as a sprag against these features. It's important not to pull on the features as you will pull the backs of your fingers away from the crack wall and will end up using the crack like a pinch. You should press with the pad of your thumb which will push the backs of your fingers even harder into the crack wall (figure 23).

DONUT JAMS
powerful jam, active expansion jam

Sometimes cracks can be shallow, so they have no depth into which you can sink your fingers. (This is sometimes referred to as a box crack). Or there can be lots of little constrictions on the edge of and inside the crack; these can lend themselves to a unique technique. This technique is the donut jam, which has nothing to do with jam donuts. It's a reference to the shape your fingers make when performing the jam—a round shape, like a donut. It was made famous by Didier Berthod in the film *First Ascent*. Didier is seen attempting the first ascent of *Cobra Crack* in Squamish with a sequence that involves him inserting his middle finger upwards into an undercut mono in the crack in the forty-five-degree wall above him.

The donut jam can actually be performed with one, two, or three fingers. (When four fingers are involved it is closer to fist jamming—see Chapter 4.) Whether you use one, two, or three fingers, the principles are the same.

One-finger donut jam

1. This is one jam which breaks the rule of "put the body part into its thinnest dimension before inserting it into the crack." Select the appropriate finger to work with the crack's width, and insert your finger into the crack with the sides of your finger against the crack walls. The pad of your finger should be facing up and your fingernail facing down, or vice versa.

2. When you insert your finger into the crack it is important to keep it as straight as possible, and not flex it at any of the joints, to make sure that it doesn't expand. If the crack is very shallow, angle your finger as you put it into the crack so that the tip of your finger doesn't hit the back of the crack.

3. Once your finger is in the correct position in the crack, use an active expansion jam to make it stick. To perform this, keep the second joint of your finger stationary and pull the tip of your finger towards the edge of the crack. The soft tissues around the second joint will expand, creating opposing outwards pressures against the crack wall, enabling the jam to stick (figure 24). As there is very little expansion happening in the finger

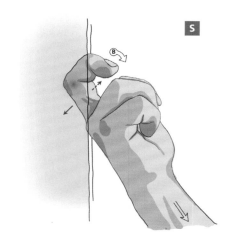

Figure 24. Donut jams: one finger

joint, this jam can have a tendency to rip out unexpectedly, which if pulling on it very hard, can result in you punching yourself in your face. A couple of little tips to help prevent this are:

- Seek out any constrictions on the edge of the crack to wrap your finger around.
- Create more expansion by pushing on your fingernail with your thumb.

4. As it is just the expansion of the finger that keeps the jam in the crack, your forearm will already be in line due to the starting position you used to insert your finger. It is important to keep this alignment with the crack when executing the jam. However, as is explained with Rule 2 of Crack Climbing (Chapter 1), the direction of

pull with an active expansion jam can be rotated 360 degrees around the jam (so you can pull down, out or up on it), meaning when finger locks or ring locks don't work due to the direction of pull, donut jams can be used as another option.

Two-finger donut jam

A two-finger donut jam is used in slightly wider cracks, usually about ring lock width. Either front-two, middle-two, or back-two fingers can be used. These combinations give you options due to subtle size differences and nuances that the crack offers. For example, one jam placement might suit the front two fingers better if there is an offset which disrupts executing the jam properly if you were to use middle or back two.

Three-finger donut jam

It would be rare to use a donut jam with three fingers as usually a thin-hands hand jam (Chapter 3) would be used. However, as with all jams, it is useful to have this option in your repertoire of jamming tricks as the rock or a single move might suit this jam better than a thin-hands hand jam. Exactly the same principles apply with three fingers as with one or two fingers, and either front three or back three combinations can be used.

Reversed donut jam

Instead of inserting your finger into the crack with the pad of your finger pointing up and your fingernail pointing down, reverse it, and insert your finger with the pad pointing down. In this reversed position either one, two, or three fingers can be used and in the same combinations as described above.

PIN SCARS

Pin scars are artificial features in the rock, a result of aid climbers hammering pegs (pins) into seams and micro-thin cracks. Over the course of years, pegs that are hammered into the rock wear the rock down, expand the seams and cracks, and enable free climbers to fit their fat, callused fingers inside the openings. Pin scars are often more rounded, shallow, and not necessarily as secure as sinker finger locks. Pin-scar-style free climbing is particularly common in Yosemite. Yosemite's granite is popular with both aid and free climbers, and lots of the free routes follow old aid lines.

As a first solution, normal finger jamming techniques should be used with pin scar features, however there are a few useful additional tips that can be of benefit.

Finger stacking
passive chock jam

One useful technique is finger stacking. With this technique a certain degree of finger strength is required, as the "jam" is more akin to holding a pocket.

1. Place your index finger into the pin scar with the pad of your finger facing down. Rest the pad of the finger in the constriction or groove at the bottom of the pin scar. Now simply use this

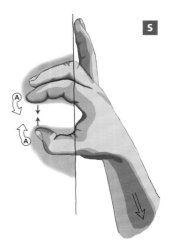

Figure 25. Pin scars: finger stacking and use of thumb

arrangement as if you were pulling on a pocket. Traditional climbing finger strength (along with a possible constriction) should be what keeps your finger in place, rather than a twisting action which occurs during normal finger jamming techniques.

2. To reinforce the "jam," stack the middle finger on top of the index finger and use the combined strength of two fingers (figure 25).

The stronger you are open-handed on pockets the easier this "jam" will be. However, you are likely to burn out your forearms more quickly as you are holding on to the rock in the same manner as holding a pocket.

Stacking can be done in a number of combinations depending on the width and depth of the pin scar and also the most

comfortable way that your fingers overlap each other. Not everyone is the same: some people can cross certain fingers over other ones with more ease or difficulty than someone else.

Here are a few suggested combinations, but see what works best for you taking into account the flexibility of your fingers, your finger strength, and the placement on offer:

- Index finger placed in the bottom of the pin scar—middle finger placed on top of index (as described above).
- Index finger placed in the bottom of the pin scar—middle finger placed on top of index—ring finger placed on top of middle
- Middle finger placed in the bottom of the pin scar—ring finger placed on top of middle
- Ring finger placed in the bottom of the pin scar—middle finger placed on top of ring
- Pinkie finger placed in the bottom of the pin scar—ring finger placed on top of pinkie

Although finger stacking doesn't feel as secure as traditional finger jamming because of the lack of twisting, it can also be used in normal finger cracks. The stack needs to be placed passively (so there must be a constriction in which your finger can sit), and it is a useful option if your fingers are sore from twisting.

Use of thumbs in pin scars

As with climbing in general, using your thumb when jamming can be the difference between something feeling impossible or easy. The use of your thumb in pin scars is no different and it can make jams or stacks feel much better.

As your fingers will already be blocking the bottom of one pin scar, your thumb will only work if there are multiple pin scars, sitting one on top of the other, no more than a thumb stretch apart. There are two techniques that you can use: they are very similar but have subtle differences.

The first technique is useful **if the upper part of the lower pin scar also constricts forming an upside-down constriction**. With your finger stack/jam in the upper pin scar place your thumb into the lower pin scar. Place it in its thinnest dimension, with the pad and thumbnail facing opposing sides of the pin scar wall. Now rotate your thumb from the knuckle towards your index finger and slot it upwards in to the constriction. Aim to jam your thumb joint passively into the constriction.

The second technique is useful **when the upper part of the lower pin scar is less constricted and more rounded**. With your finger stack/jam in the upper pin scar, place your thumb into the lower pin scar, but position it so that the pad is facing up and the thumbnail is facing down. Now pinch the upper part of the lower pin scar with your thumb, while still pulling down with your fingers. This technique is very strength dependent, and the stronger your pinch grip the easier it will be. It is unlikely you will be able to out-technique strong sport climbers and boulderers with this one!

Accomplished trad climber Debbie Birch tackles the classic gritstone finger crack of Regent Street *(E2 5c) at Millstone Edge in the Peak District, UK.* (© Mike Hutton)

Pop Quiz

1. Finger cracks or offwidths? Finger cracks
2. Stemming or roof cracks? Stemming
3. Hand jam or hand stack? Hand jam
4. Knee lock or chickenwing? Chickenwing
5. Tape or no tape? I generally tape in Indian Creek but not usually in Yosemite
6. Cams or nuts? Cams and nuts
7. Sandstone cracks or granite cracks? Granite
8. Short and hard, or long and pumpy? Long and pumpy
9. Pressure wound or rock rash? Rock rash
10. Colour preference of crack climbing trousers due to unfortunate mistakes: red or brown? Brown works best in most conditions when living the dirtbag lifestyle!

LYNN HILL

One of the most influential climbers in the history of the sport, Lynn didn't just push standards in women's climbing; she led the way and showed all climbers—both the strongest men and women of the time—what was possible. Her first free ascent of the Nose (5.14a) on El Cap in 1993 was groundbreaking. "It goes, boys!"

FAVOURITE CRACK CLIMBING AREA?

My all-time favourite crack climbing area is Yosemite, of course! I love Yosemite because of its stunning beauty, history, and vast potential for adventure. Everyone should have the experience of going to Yosemite, regardless of whether or not they are a climber, hiker, runner, or whatever activity they prefer to enjoy in this amazing natural wonderland.

BEST CRACK CLIMBING EXPERIENCE/ FAVOURITE CRACK CLIMB?

My favourite crack climb is actually a multi-pitch route called *Astroman* (5.11c) in Yosemite. It's a 10-pitch route that has a wide variety of different sized cracks, chimneys, and even some interesting face climbing near the top. The first ascent was done in 1959 by Warren Harding, Glen Denny, and Chuck Pratt. In 1975 it was climbed all free by John Bachar, Ron Kauk, and John Long.

MEMORABLE CRACK EXPERIENCE?

On one memorable day in Joshua Tree when climbing with my friend, Roy McClenahan, I learned a good lesson about making sure to place good protection. I started up what was a relatively easy crack with good hand jams and before I knew it, I was high above my last piece of protection.

I went through the motions of placing a hex (old-school protection device), but the hex didn't quite sit in the crack as nicely as I would have liked. Since I was getting tired of fiddling with this piece, I decided to just leave it as it was and move up a bit higher where I could place a better piece. The climbing eased up, so I just continued to the top, without thinking about the fact that I was essentially free soloing. As it turned out, the next piece was not any better, so I had essentially free-soloed that route. I realised that not paying close attention to each gear placement could cost the ultimate price. Now I know not to just place a piece of gear for decoration—it needs to be able to catch me should I fall!

THE KNOWLEDGE

My advice to beginners when it comes to jamming is: don't be discouraged by how it feels at first. Jamming is not very intuitive because it kind of hurts. The goal is to figure out how to best position your hand in the crack in the least painful and most efficient way possible. Once I place my hand in the crack, I don't allow my hand to move or change position. If I need to adjust the angle of my hand and wrist as my body moves upwards, I unweight it by holding on with the other hand jam and quickly adjust the position of the bottom hand.

Opposite: *Lynn on* Pudgy Gumbies *(5.11+) at Little Cottonwood Canyon in Utah's Wasatch Mountains* (© Andrew Burr)

FOOT TECHNIQUES IN FINGER CRACKS

There are some great stories of the first ascents of thin crack routes where, in order to slim their feet right down, climbers have either cut holes in the ends of their climbing shoes or have gone shoeless with only tape on their feet so they can twist just their toes into the crack. An extreme and masochistic approach, but a solution which has helped push the standard of crack climbing ever higher.

Often the most difficult thing when climbing finger cracks is the feet. With climbing shoes on, suddenly your toes and feet are a lot wider than your fingers, and what you can fit your fingers into doesn't necessarily translate all that well to your feet. Quite the opposite to normal climbing where a small handhold can often make a very positive foothold. For this reason, it is important to keep your eyes open for other options.

What follows are all the foot techniques that can be used with finger cracks. One technique isn't necessarily superior to another, however it is important to be able to select the correct technique to suit specific parts of different routes.

FEET IN SPLITTER CRACKS

Using your feet in splitter cracks can be incredibly difficult as there is minimal boot rubber going into the crack. However, there are lots of different features and techniques to be aware of. Below is an explanation of the standard toe jam, followed by other techniques and tricks to take into consideration when toe jamming.

Figure 26. Toe jam

Toe jams
powerful jam, active twisting jam

Exactly the same crack climbing principles apply to feet as to hands, so it's important to keep following the five rules of crack climbing (Chapter 1).

1. First, you need to orient your foot so that it is in its thinnest dimension. The depth of your foot is thinner than the width of your foot, so it is the depth that you need to use. You should aim to get the sole of your foot and the top of your foot parallel with the crack walls.

   ■ To position your foot correctly, first rotate inwards at the ankle so that the sole and top of your foot start to move parallel to the crack walls (big toe up, little toe down). This movement with the ankle will create half the foot positioning you need to achieve: your ankle won't be flexible enough in this direction of movement to achieve the finished position.

- Next, lift your foot up in its current position: this will move your knee away from the crack so that it is pointing out to the side. The process of lifting your foot and moving your knee away from the crack will complete the positioning and make the sole and top of the foot parallel with the crack walls and put your foot into its thinnest position to help execute the jam.

2. As with other jams, it is important to relax the body part that is going into the crack. So, make sure your toes are flat, straight, and relaxed in your climbing shoe. Curled, tensed, and bunched toes increase the profile of your foot and make it harder to insert into the crack. Lose those aggressive down-turned shoes and put some flat-soled shoes on. It is also important to relax the calf and shin muscles as tensing these will result in rigid toes.

3. Now that your foot is in the correct position and relaxed you can insert it into the crack. When inserting it, give it a little wiggle up and down and side to side: this will help to get more of your shoe and toes inside. Remember you are wearing a climbing shoe, made of rubber, which is malleable and can deform into different shapes. Make use of this so that your shoe rubber moulds and conforms to the crack's shape.

4. Your big toe, which has a slightly larger profile than the rest of your toes, will have entered the crack first. As this is the case, drop your heel slightly so the outside edge of your shoe rolls down and comes into contact with the crack. The outside edge of your shoe will be slightly lower in profile than your front point (big toe), so more of the boot will go in to the crack. This is only a very subtle movement but it can make all the difference as finger cracks are so thin for the feet (A in figure 26).

5. Now that your toes are in the crack you need to use them like a jamming device. The jam you must use is an *active twisting jam*: you will be using the lower part of your leg as a lever to twist your toes into the crack. To achieve this jam, rotate your knee (which should now be pointing out to the side, away from the crack) upwards, so that your shin bone moves in line with the crack (B in figure 26). If jamming with your right foot, your toes will start to twist anticlockwise; the twist will be clockwise if jamming with the left foot.

6. To improve this twisting action you can also rotate from your ankle so that the ball of your heel points down towards the ground. As you are only inserting your toes into the crack, it is normal for this jam to be slightly painful across the joints and knuckles of your toes. The important thing with this jam is not to "over turn" or "aggressively turn" as this can rotate the boot rubber out of the crack.

LOOK FOR FACE HOLDS

Look out for edges and footholds on the face outside of the crack when climbing finger cracks. As toe jams can be marginal, small edges, bumps, and normal climbing face holds can make for much better footholds than the crack feature itself.

LOOK FOR FOOT PODS

Another feature to look out for is toe pods (or wider spots in the crack). Even on completely splitter cracks you can usually find places which are slightly wider. You have to really look at the crack closely as wider spots might not be obvious and may be only a millimetre different in size. The pod or wider spot may have formed due to a small edge of the crack breaking, a softer area of rock crumbling, or because of a flaky section of rock fracturing. If you look closely, wider spots will appear.

When on-sighting it will be difficult to locate the perfect placements, so familiarity with the rock type and overall experience plays a big part. However, when redpointing you will be able to seek out these small pods and use them effectively.

LOOK FOR FLARED OR ROUNDED EDGES

Flares or rounded edges on the edge of cracks can often result in the outside of the crack being wider than the inside where you are jamming with your fingers. As a result, the crack can "climb wider" for the feet than it does for the fingers.

Flares and rounded edges can also be more comfortable for the feet, meaning less pain and better climbing. Remember the crack might not be flared or rounded the whole way; it could just be one section or foot placement.

LOOK FOR OFFSETS

Offsets can be useful for the feet as you are able to get more rubber against more rock creating greater friction. Most climbers will look for square-cut offsets as they are more obvious, but offsets can also be hidden in flares or rounded edges. A large rounded edge can often disguise how much one side of the crack protrudes from the other, so pay attention to the small details.

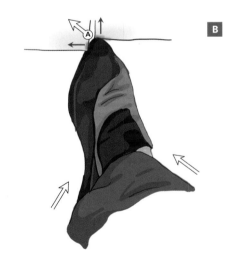

Figure 27. Foot on offset/pod

Using an offset

It is important to use the correct foot against the offset or the toe jam can actually start to feel worse. Use the sole of your foot against the offset:

- If the left wall of the crack is offset and protrudes outwards you should aim to use your right foot in the placement (figure 27).
- If the right wall of the crack is offset and protrudes outwards you should aim to use your left foot in the placement.

FEET IN CORNER CRACKS

When climbing a crack in a corner (or a large offset) there are lots of ways that you can use your feet effectively. These can be grouped into either straight-in or layback techniques.

STRAIGHT-IN TECHNIQUES

Bridging/stemming

Bridge across the corner either using edges or smears on both corner walls (figure 28). This technique works well on all corners, but is very useful on more open corners when other techniques fail to work.

Platform purchase

powerful jam, passive expansion jam

Place your foot flat (sole towards the floor) and directly into the corner, with your big toe on the edge of the crack. You will get pressure points from the corner walls on the inside and outside edges of your climbing shoe (figure 29). This technique works well if the corner is tight (less than a 90-degree angle).

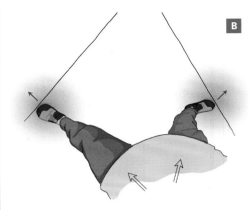

Figure 28. Bridging technique in corner cracks

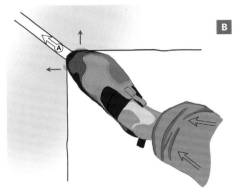

Figure 29. Platform purchase technique in corner cracks

Offwidth foot

powerful jam, passive expansion jam

Bridge your foot across the corner like you would on the edge of an offwidth. Place the back of your heel on one face of the corner and your toe on the other face (figure 30).

Figure 30. Offwidth foot technique in corner cracks

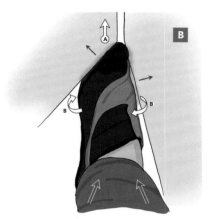

Figure 31. Corner foot jam technique in corner cracks

Corner foot jam
powerful jam, active twisting jam
This technique uses the corner (not the crack) as a baggy foot jam. Place your foot into the corner like you would place a foot jam (Chapter 3). The top of your foot will be on one corner wall and the sole of your foot will be against the other corner wall (figure 31). The tighter the corner, the better this technique will work.
   Right foot: twist anticlockwise
   Left foot: twist clockwise

LAYBACKING TECHNIQUES
These techniques work well on their own or in combination. If using them individually, always be sure to look for edges and smears for the other foot.

Pinkie toe jam
When laybacking the crack, place the out-side edge of your shoe into the crack while smearing on the crack wall with the sole of your shoe (figure 32).

Big toe jam
When laybacking the crack, place the inside edge of your shoe into the crack while smearing on the crack wall with the sole of your shoe.

CLIMBING POSITIONING

Now you have an idea of how to execute specific finger jamming techniques, it's important to know when to use them while climbing. Every finger crack has minor and subtle differences, so it is impossible to say, "use this technique for this crack" or "use that technique for that crack." What follows are positioning techniques which, while not set in stone, will provide guidance and tips for you to take away, adapt, develop, and apply to the routes that you would like to climb.

Figure 32. Pinkie toe jam technique in corner

FACE CRACKS
Positioning on vertical cracks

A vertical crack is one which follows a straight line up the rock face. Vertical in this context does not refer to the angle of the rock: vertical cracks can be overhanging, slabby or, in fact, vertical.

Hands: if the crack is completely splitter it is likely you will want to purely use thumb-down technique. It would be unusual for a crack to be so splitter from bottom to top that you would use this one technique the whole way up, however there certainly could be very long stretches of totally uniform parallel-sided cracks on certain routes. The reason for going thumb down on parallel-sided cracks is to take advantage of the extra twisting motion that the jam offers. More than likely you will struggle to get pinkie-down jams to stick as convincingly. If the crack features pods or constrictions, a mixture of thumb-up and thumb-down finger jams which complement each other will be the best approach.

Feet: there are a couple of positioning options to consider for vertical finger cracks if using feet purely inside the crack.

- Execute standard toe jamming technique (See figure 26). Don't become too bunched up; make sure you stay as in line as possible. Also, to prevent your feet from slipping, don't get too stretched out: toe jams are usually poor, and they will slip if you leave your feet too far behind.
- Use the **froggy leg position.** This breaks the rule of keeping everything in line, but it is really useful when the twisting action of toe jams doesn't work—usually because the crack is too thin or square cut. Bring both feet up to around knee level (or even slightly higher) and point your knees out to the side. Place the bottom of your right toes on the left crack wall/edge, and vice versa with the left foot. Keep both feet reasonably close together and press them outwards with opposing force; keeping the feet high and pressing them in opposition at the same time is what makes them stick and prevents them from slipping. In the finished position your knees will be pointing out to the side, with your hips close to the wall and feet high. You will be using opposing pressures rather than any twisting action, expansion, or rotation to keep the feet in place—although a small amount of subtle twisting of the feet could complement this technique, depending on the crack.

Pop Quiz

1. Finger cracks or offwidths? Finger
2. Stemming or roof cracks? Stemming
3. Hand jam or hand stack? Hand jam
4. Knee lock or chickenwing? Knee lock
5. Tape or no tape? Tape
6. Cams or nuts? Cams
7. Sandstone cracks or granite cracks? Granite
8. Short and hard, or long and pumpy? Pumpy
9. Pressure wound or rock rash? Rock rash
10. Colour preference of crack climbing trousers due to unfortunate mistakes, red or brown? Sorry, it has to be white karate pants!

JERRY MOFFATT

The strongest climber across all rock disciplines for his time, Jerry excelled at trad, sport, boulder, and comps. His first ascents from the 1980s and 1990s are still considered fierce testpieces and see few repeats today. In 1983, aged only 20, he flashed the Tony Yaniro crack Equinox *(5.12c) in Joshua Tree, and returned to the UK having repeated four of the hardest routes in the US. The following year he returned to the States and made the first onsight of the stunning crack of* The Phoenix *(5.13a) in Yosemite—the world's first onsight of this grade.*

FAVOURITE CRACK CLIMBING AREA?

Yosemite Valley is a mecca for crack climbing as far as I'm concerned. The history for me is so important and Yosemite has this in abundance. The rock is immaculate glacier-polished granite which is pretty much featureless. Having an impressive over-hanging wall split by one crack gives a route real presence. I like the fact that so many great names in the past travelled to Yosemite to push grades and standards in the world of climbing.

FAVOURITE CRACK CLIMB?

London Wall (E5/5.12b) at Millstone Edge in the Peak District is an outstanding route. It was done in 1975 by John Allen when he was just 16 years old. He had just one fall at the start which is an amazing feat in itself as it was probably the hardest route in Britain at the time. The crack splits a headwall with no routes to the right or left; it just stands out as the line on the crag. It's all finger jamming in old pin scars with the crux at the very top with your last nut well below your feet. When I started there was a programme on TV which filmed Steve Bancroft trying it—I watched it so many times. I dreamt of trying it one day, never imagining that I would do it. I got the first onsight in 1982.

MEMORABLE CRACK EXPERIENCE?

Onsighting *Super Crack* (5.12c) in the Shawan-gunks on the east coast of the States in 1982 was pretty special. I trained so hard for it and had it as an onsight goal for about a year beforehand. It's a great line with the finger crack splitting a but-tress with a small overhang at about six metres. I felt so good there was no way I was going to let go although the pressure built as I got near the top. I was 19 years old, on my first trip to America, and everything was new and exciting. *Super Crack* had only been done a couple of times and was the hardest route on the East Coast—onsighting it really put my name on the map.

THE KNOWLEDGE

Find someone who is good at cracks and copy their tape job. Also, experiment with tape.

Make sure you really set a jam before you move off it; if it's not set well, it will normally get worse as you move up. Do this no matter how pumped you are.

If you have a crack climb goal in mind, find a crack size which is similar. Set a top rope up and practise the hell out of it.

Opposite: Jerry after flashing Equinox *(5.12c) at Joshua Tree National Park, California*
(© John Bachar)

Positioning on diagonal cracks

A diagonal crack is one that doesn't follow a straight line up the rock face, but which trends across the face at an angle. For the following description, imagine the crack is trending diagonally from left to right.

Hands: the same rules apply here as with vertical cracks. If it's totally splitter, thumb-down jams will work better the majority of the time. If there are constrictions or pods, a combination of both thumb up and thumb down will work in your favour. The very important thing to remember when climbing diagonal cracks is that the elbow rotation and finishing position of the forearm must still end in alignment with the crack. If they are not in line, it is likely that not enough twisting action is occurring and you will be holding the crack edges instead of jamming between them.

Feet: if the crack is an extreme diagonal, you will be unable to keep both feet in the crack. There are two options:

If there are good face holds on the wall below the crack, using them will be the easiest option.

If there aren't any good face holds:

- Put one foot in the crack and perform a standard toe jam. Putting your foot in the crack will help relieve some pressure from the arms (remember to move your shin in line with the crack).
- Brace your other foot on the wall below you, either smearing or edging (figure 33). Putting your lower leg on the wall will stop your body rotating (flopping) away from the crack and will help keep

Figure 33. Positioning on diagonal cracks

everything rigid. Imagine your lower leg as a post, propping the rest of your body up, enabling it to climb. A great trick on easier-angled terrain with minimal footholds is to plant the whole sole of your foot on the wall sideways (heel to toe, pointing left to right, or vice versa—not up and down) rather than just smearing with the toe box of your shoe; planting the whole sole will give you the greatest amount of rubber in contact with the rock.

Positioning on offsets

An offset crack can be both a blessing and a curse. If the sequence and jams work, things will feel much easier because a greater surface area of jam will be touching the rock. However, if the sequence and jams don't fit together well, you could find yourself in a whole world of painful, rattly locks, wondering why nothing will stick.

Hands: When using a jam with an offset it's important to try to get the correct orientation of hand to coincide with the offset on offer. You should aim to get the back of the fingers and hand against the offset. If you do this, you will have more success with the twisting action of the jam and with moving your palm to be flat against the rock. The positioning you should aim for is:

- When the right-hand side of the crack protrudes forwards and produces an offset, use right hand pinkie down or left hand thumb down.
- When the left-hand side of the crack protrudes forwards and produces an offset, use right hand thumb down (figure 34) or left hand pinkie down.

Sometimes the jam won't suit the common orientation (back of the hand against the offset)—maybe your pinkie finger keeps slipping through the bottom of the jam or you have to use a specific sequence which sets you up to jam "wrong-handed"—so you will have to put your palm against the offset. There are some tricks which can help the jam work better for the "wrong" hand (palm against the offset):

- *Thumb down, palm against the offset:* Push your thumb against the offset: this will help push the backs of your fingers into the crack edge. Or, put your thumb

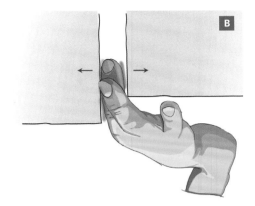

Figure 34. Offsets, thumb-down finger jam: back of the fingers against the offset

into the crack: this will give you more friction and purchase in the jam when you are unable to twist as vigorously.

- *Pinkie down, palm against the offset:* This will feel more like finger barring than finger jamming—yuck! If the offset is big enough (like a small corner), I find that executing a standard hand jam (even though it's just your fingers in the crack), actually helps push the backs of the fingers into the opposing crack edge giving greater holding power. It's a floating hand jam!

Feet: Feet in offsets work similarly to hands. There is a common foot to use depending on which crack wall is offset. You should aim for the sole of your shoe to be placed against the offset edge of the crack as this way you get greater surface area contact between rubber and rock. Execute the standard toe jam procedure; as there is something to push the sole of your foot into (an offset), you will be able to twist your foot more vigorously without fear of it rotating out of the crack. Since this is the case, twist your foot and aim to get the ball of your heel pointing towards the ground.

Sometimes an offset will run for a long section of a route; there won't be just one placement. A great trick here is to select the foot which is best suited to the offset and use only this foot in the offset crack. To do this, smear or edge with the other foot on the outside of the crack and bump your "crack foot" up to the next placement. Repeat for as long as necessary.

When an offset is bigger than the sole of your shoe, it could be considered a small corner. In this situation it can be difficult to get enough of a twisting action through your foot as the offset obstructs this movement. When this is the case, you can change from the common approach as described above and use the opposite foot (the sole of your shoe will be away from the offset) to proceed with a standard toe jam technique (just don't twist it out of the crack). It is easier to face the sole of the shoe away from the offset in this circumstance because you can angle the sole of your foot towards the ground more easily. A similar bumping sequence for the feet can be used.

CORNER CRACKS

Corner cracks add a whole new dimension to crack climbing. There are three main ways to climb corner cracks:

In layback style with jams: This is what we're going to look at. Remember, just because you're laybacking, it doesn't mean that you can't jam at the same time!

Straight in: The same positioning should be used as on face cracks.

In pure layback style: Use standard layback techniques.

Hand Techniques

Note: All hand techniques are described with the back of the hand against the corner wall and the palm wrapping around the edge of the crack.

Tips cracks: These will feel demanding to climb, so the key is to keep moving through the hard parts and rest and place gear at the better handholds. In general, your top hand should be thumb down. You will find the thumb sprag and crimped thumb bridge techniques (earlier in this chapter) come in very useful on this terrain. The bottom hand should be pinkie down. I tend to cross my hands on these types of cracks only if the sequence forces me to, which admittedly can be fairly often. If the handholds are particularly small, it will be very specific as to which hand will feel best in a placement.

Locker cracks: The positioning and way of moving with locker cracks is very similar to tips cracks, except you have better jams. Keep the top hand thumb down and bottom pinkie down and only cross hands if the sequence forces you to. On completely splitter corner cracks you might find it difficult to make the pinkie finger of your bottom hand stick in the bottom of the jam, so a pinkie-down ring finger jam could work better. One technique that does work well on locker cracks is assisted jams.

Assisted jams: These are jams where you use one good jam to assist another poor jam.

Place one good jam with either your top or bottom hand (it has to be good). If you placed your top hand as the good jam, cross the bottom hand over the top, place it into the crack but rest it on top of the good jam for support (so skin is touching skin). The same technique can be used if the bottom hand is the good jam; just bring your top hand down to rest upon it. Assisted jamming is a technique which can be used across the whole spectrum of jamming sizes and angles, not just finger corner cracks. They are very useful for resting or as intermediate holds on longer moves. You're in effect creating a secret hold for yourself!

Ring lock cracks: With ring lock corner cracks it can be tricky to use jamming techniques along with laybacking and it can often be easier to go pure layback style. However, if it suits, you should have the top hand thumb down in a standard ring lock. The bottom hand should be pinkie down and finger barring. Assisted jams can be useful on ring lock cracks as quite often the finger bars will feel poor.

FEET

Before moving on to the positioning of the feet it's important to know your inside foot from your outside foot, or things will become really confusing.

- *Inside foot:* This is the foot which is naturally closest to the crack in the style that you are climbing (layback jamming). If the left side of your body is scraping up the rock face, it will be your left foot that is your inside foot.
- *Outside foot:* This is the foot which is naturally furthest away from the crack in

the style that you are climbing (layback jamming). If the left side of your body is scraping up the rock face it will be your right foot that is your outside foot.

Techniques and options stay the same across the sizes (from tips cracks to ring lock cracks), however the bigger sizes will just feel a bit more secure. There are four basic techniques and three basic positions.

Foot Techniques

Pinkie rand smear: Place the rand of your shoe on the pinkie toe side (outside edge of your climbing shoe) into the crack. Always use the push and wiggle technique (push into the crack, wiggle your foot side to side) to get as much of the shoe rand into the crack as possible. The rest of the sole of your shoe should be smeared against the corner wall outside the crack and your heel should be dropped low. This technique is essentially a "supported" (by the crack) smear. (See figure 35.)

Big toe rand smear: This is exactly the same as the pinkie rand smear, but you are placing the big toe side of your shoe (inside edge of your climbing shoe) into the crack.

Smearing: A common climbing technique (figure 35), smears are used when there are no holds to stand on. The friction of the rock along with your weight transferred through the foot makes the sole of your shoe grip the rock. Two primary factors make a smear stick:

- Have as much surface area of the sole of your toe box touching the rock as possible. To do this place your heel low. When you push and move up on the smear it's important to keep that heel as

Figure 35. Smearing

Figure 36. Edging

low as possible to maintain maximum rubber–rock contact; try to be flexible in the Achilles tendon and bend your foot from the toes.

■ Have a high and constant pressure going through the foot. A smear will often feel bad until you're actually putting weight through it, so just being confident and putting all your weight on to it will make it stick more easily. Make sure the pressure you are putting through the smear is as constant as possible: don't jiggle about on it as this relieves the pressure, making your foot move and consequently slip. Remember: "a weighted foot never slips."

Edging: Another technique used in everyday climbing (figure 36), edging is using the edge of your shoe to stand on a rock feature. There are a few different types of edging: front pointing, inside edging, and outside edging. To keep things simple,

I'll refer to the standard front-point edging, which is using the front of your shoe around the area of your big toe. There are two primary factors to edging effectively:

■ Get as much surface area of your toe touching the edge as you can. To do this you need to have the sole of your shoe parallel with the angle of the edge. So, for example, if the edge is protruding at a 90-degree angle from the rock face, your foot would be placed completely flat. If the edge sloped down slightly, your foot would be angled with your heel lower and your toe higher.

■ Keep your foot as rigid as possible. This helps to stop the toe from either lifting or rolling off the edge. The more rigid and stiff your foot, the easier it will be to put pressure through the foot. Imagine you have a steel rod running from the tip of your big toe to the ball of your heel. Don't let your foot sag!

- Use your inside foot to pinkie rand smear and your outside foot to smear or edge. This is a good option if the crack is slightly wider and there are face hold options.
- Use your inside foot to pinkie rand smear and your outside foot to big toe rand smear. Useful if there are limited face holds.
- Use both feet when edging or smearing. A great option if there are good face holds.

CLIMBING MOVEMENT

Now that you've learnt how to place a finger jam, know which finger jams to use in different situations, and understand general body positioning, it's time to start moving! Because at the end of the day, if you can't move between the jams, you won't make it to the top of your route.

As I said at the very start of this chapter, finger-width cracks are a fickle size of crack and often require a specific sequence. With this in mind, this section is intended to give you direction on common finger crack movements which you can take away and apply to the sequences on your routes.

PACE

Finger cracks are the cracks that are most like sport climbing, so take a sport climbing approach: move quickly through difficult sections; pause and recover at the rest spots; try to read the sequence of locks from the ground or from a resting position below a difficult-looking section.

GENERAL MOVEMENT TIPS

Foot to hand distances: When on sections of climbing which require less focus and are not as sequence-specific (i.e., not the crux),

try to make your foot movements match your hand movements. So, if you're making small hand movements, then small foot movements will complement them (figure 37); if your hand movements are large, then make large foot movements too.

Foot movements: Using your feet on finger cracks is difficult. Always look for holds and edges around the crack itself; you will get a greater upward push by pressing down on a small edge than by trying to push down on a terrible toe jam.

Big moves: hands

- Try to make big moves off pinkie-down jams as you will be able to reach a greater distance (figure 38). (It is more difficult to make long moves from thumb-down jams, although it can be done—often with a bit of dynamism: your wrist won't turn in the direction you want it to and your forearm will start to move further away from the wall and this will create an outwards pull rather than a down-wards pull.)
- When making big moves from pinkie-down jams, push the little finger into the jam and try not to rotate your fingers out

Figure 37. Big moves off pinkie-down jams

Figure 38. Small moves off thumb-down jams

of the jam. Keep your fingers stationary and rotate from the wrist.

■ When making big moves off thumb-down jams, be sure to keep your forearm in line with the crack. As you pull on the jam, don't let your elbow rise up and out to the side as this reverses the twisting action you initially put through the jam to make it stick. If you do need to reach further then lifting your elbow can sometimes help you do this, however you should be very aware that this can really affect the quality of the jam and make it feel as if

you are pulling rather than jamming to stay in the crack.

■ Intermediate jams can help with big moves. They are especially useful if you have to make a long move off of a thumb-down jam, as you can use an intermediate hold to steady yourself, before bumping to the next jam. Even the smallest of tips jams can make a big difference, so don't rule anything out.

Big moves: feet

When pulling and pushing, use opposite hands and feet. So, if you are pulling with your left hand, push with your right foot. This is a common rule in regular climbing and also applies to crack climbing. You won't be able to do this all of the time, but if you can make it work on big moves, you will find you'll be able to reach further and rely less on strength.

Moves off poor jams

When moving off a poor finger jam try to move more dynamically. Focus on pushing with your feet and using your momentum, rather than on a slow static movement. It's not always the hands that can be poor. On steeper finger cracks, the finger jams can be very positive and the feet poor.

It's always important to focus on the feet, because as with any style of climbing, as soon as the feet come off, the number of moves you can execute rapidly drops. You should try to distribute your weight correctly through your feet to prevent them from slipping while still getting the most benefit from them. Try to put more weight through the other one, two, or three contact points you have with the rock, which could actually be your hands. It sounds counterintuitive to put more weight through your hands, but if it prevents your feet from slipping, it will have a positive impact for the subsequent moves. As soon as your feet slip, you suddenly shock-load the arms, disrupt the finger jams, and lose your climbing rhythm. Take your poor jams to the "stick slip" point (see page 22) to get the most from them, but don't go over the threshold and let them actually slip. It's a fine line, and only with practice and fine tuning will you find out where, when, and how much weight you can put through

poor jams to get the most from them without them slipping or failing.

Moves to poor jams

- When you are moving to poor jams, try to move more statically and be very precise with the finger placement in the jam you are moving to. Really work and nestle the fingers into the jam before you commit your weight to it.
- Use intermediate jams to help you move closer and more statically to the poor jam.
- When committing your weight to a poor jam, use the intermediate jams you have just used to get to the poor jam, but with the lower hand. This will help to reduce the pressure on the high poor jam you are trying to hold.

TRANSITIONING BETWEEN JAMS

Being able to transition between jams effectively comes from reading the crack and the rock around the edge of the crack well and being able to determine which type of finger jam to use. Will it be thumb down? Pinkie down? Ring finger down? Pin scar finger stack? And so on . . .

Learning to do this correctly will take time (just like learning to read any piece of rock). There are no clearly defined rules which say, "this type of jam suits this" and "that type of jam suits that." However, below I consider some rock features and give a general overview of what works best the majority of the time. Remember though, rocks form bizarre shapes, so you have to be your own judge, using sight and feel, to determine what looks—and is likely to work—the best for you.

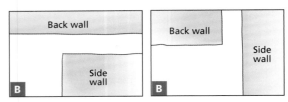

Figure 39. Left-facing corner (climbing left side in)
Figure 40. Left-facing corner (climbing right side in)

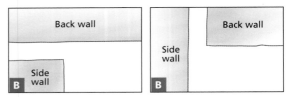

Figure 41. Right-facing corner (climbing right side in)
Figure 42. Right-facing corner (climbing left side in)

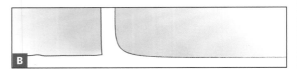

Figure 43. Crack with one rounded edge

Corners

A corner wall or offset produces a protrusion and therefore an obstacle which can prevent the palm of the hand from achieving the correct positioning for finger jamming to work well. Remember: when finger jamming you need to get your palm flat to the rock. The best way to achieve this is to place the backs of your fingers against the corner wall or offset, then cup your palm around the crack edge. This means that on long stretches of corner crack it can often be best to use one hand thumb down and one hand pinkie down.

- *Left-facing corner (climbing left side in):* left hand pinkie down, right hand thumb down (figure 39)
- *Left-facing corner (climbing right side in):* left hand thumb down, right hand pinkie down (figure 40)
- *Right-facing corner (climbing right side in):* left hand thumb down, right hand pinkie down (figure 41)
- *Right-facing corner (climbing left side in):* left hand pinkie down, right hand thumb down (figure 42)

Rounded edges

If one edge of the crack is rounded, rather than square cut (figure 43), it can be best to use your palm over this edge (more friction against the rock and more comfortable on your hand) and the backs of the fingers against the wall with the sharper crack edge. Although it can be disguised to the naked eye, in this situation the sharp edge produces an offset feature, which is why it often feels best to put the backs of the fingers against it (see "Corners," above).

Angle of crack

If the angle of the crack is not perpendicular to the wall (i.e., the crack goes into the rock face at an angle, like a big flake, creating one "sharp" edge and one "blunt" edge) it can often be nice to have your palm against the sharper edge. This will allow you to use a normal laybacking body position since the sharp edge of the crack provides a better hold to pull against, but you will also get the benefits of being able to jam with your fingers.

Opposite: *Mari Augusta Salvesen on* Ronny Medelsvensson *(Norwegian grade 9, F8b trad) at Jøssingfjord, Norway* (© Øyvind Salvesen)

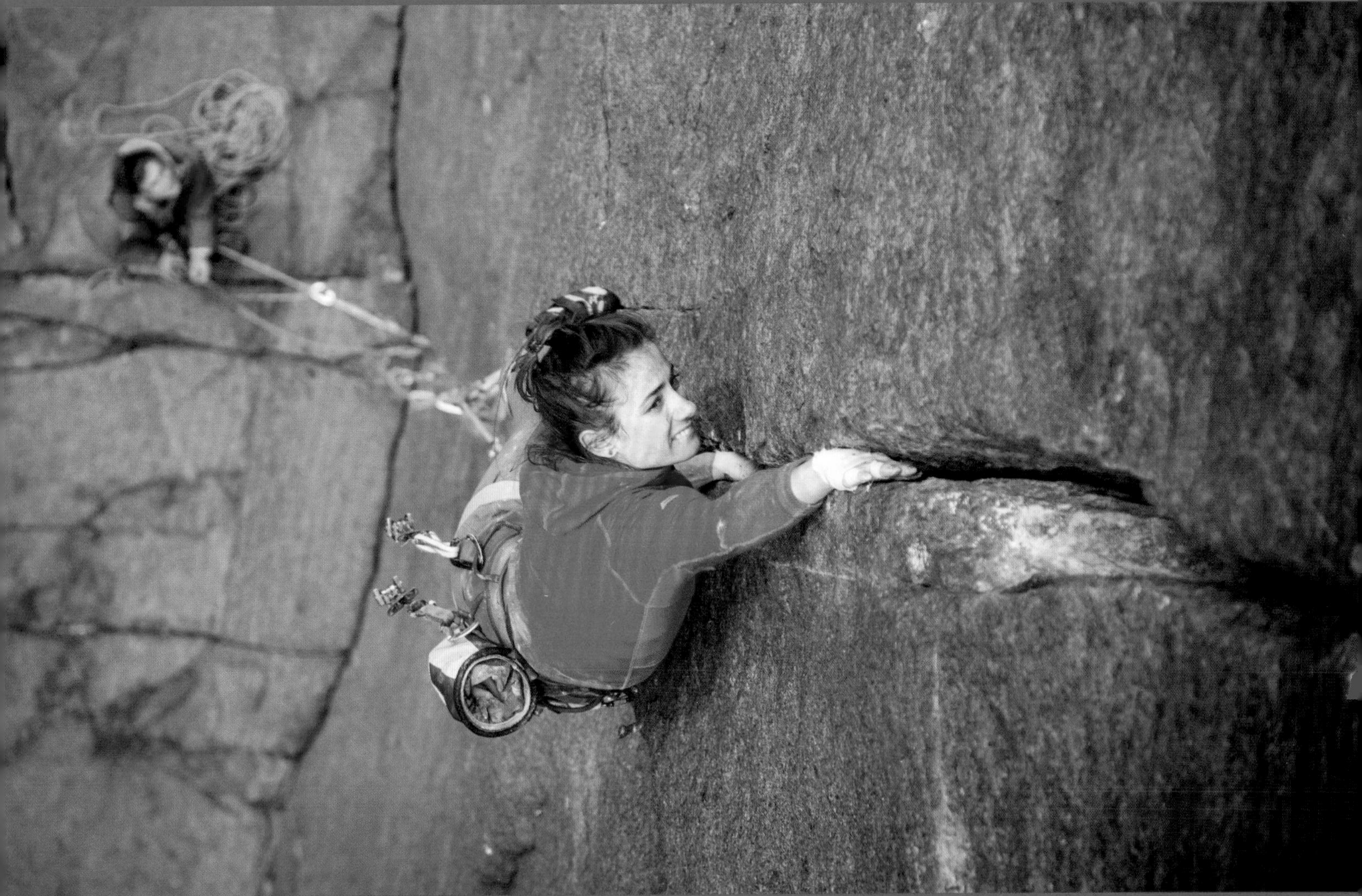

CHAPTER 3

Hand Cracks

Hand crack techniques are the staple jams in any crack climber's diet. Even if you don't necessarily want to climb cracks, the hand jam is a technique that every climber should learn, as when a hand jam is available it will improve your ability to rest, place gear, or move through a more difficult section of climbing without having to pull as hard.

This doesn't mean that hand jamming cracks can't be pumpy. After doing multiple hand jams, it might feel as if your thumb muscle is going to explode out of the base of your palm. When you hit astronomical pump in the thumb, even pulling the trigger on a cam or clipping a karabiner can be an utterly desperate task.

However, the hand jam is the foundation of many other jamming techniques, which is why it's such an important skill to learn. Whether you're trying to fight the pump on a continuous splitter or using a hand jam as an alternative to standard handholds, this is a technique that you'll want to learn the subtleties of.

The hand jam can be used across a broad range of sizes and in numerous different ways. They can start to be used when ring locks become too baggy, right up to when you can get a fist jam to stick.

HAND TECHNIQUES IN HAND CRACKS

STANDARD HAND CRACKS
Thumb-up jam
powerful jam, active expansion jam

This is the technique that everyone is taught when they first learn how to jam. The most simple of them all: the standard thumb-up hand jam. When you get this jam right, it will feel better than holding a massive jug.

1. *Starting position 1 (L-shape):* Create an L-shape with your index finger and thumb; this will move the thumb away from the palm of the hand, which will relax and decrease the size of the thumb muscle at the base of thumb.

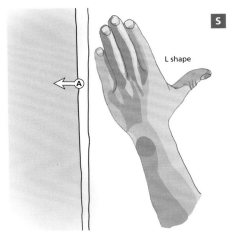

Figure 44. Standard hand cracks: hand jam starting position

Make sure the rest of your fingers are straight like your index (figure 44).

2. *Starting position 2 (hand orientation):* Now you have the hand and fingers in the correct position, adjust the orientation of your hand so it is in its thinnest dimension in relation to the crack. Have your thumb pointing in the direction of the crack and in the direction you are going to climb. Your palm and the back of your hand will be facing the crack walls.

3. *Starting position 3:* Don't lock your fingers together as this will slightly expand the tissue around the knuckles. Expanding your hand in any way before it enters the crack can mean that you can't insert as much of the body part, resulting in a poorer jam. It

may feel insignificant on bomber hand jams, but when it comes to thin hands, every millimetre counts. So, make sure your fingers are straight, but naturally relaxed.

4. *Starting position 4 (insertion):* Insert your hand into the crack fingertips or side of the hand first. As with any jam you should be looking to place the jam passively, so be sure to look for any constrictions in the crack which you can take advantage of.

5. *Thumb movement:* This action is the most important aspect of a hand jam. Rotate your thumb (in parallel with the crack) into the centre of your palm and try to touch the tip of your thumb to the base of your pinkie finger: don't move your pinkie finger. In most cases there won't be enough space for the thumb to touch the pinkie finger, and on thin jams the thumb won't even go into the centre of the palm, however, whether there is room or not, the action remains the same: thumb forced towards the pinkie finger. Moving your thumb this way expands the pulp at the base of the thumb against the crack wall, which keeps the jam in place. It's important to do this thumb movement before cupping (step 6) to ensure you can get the thumb as close to the pinkie finger as possible (figure 45). Cupping first will restrict this action.

6. *Cupping:* Even if you initially place your hand passively, you will need

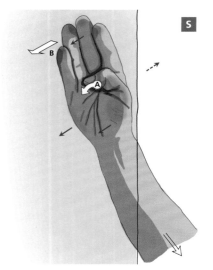

Figure 45. Standard hand cracks: thumb-up jam inishing position

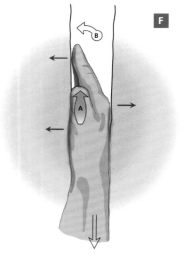

Figure 46. Standard hand cracks: thumb-up jam finishing position

to actively expand your jam to keep your hand in place. Keeping the fingers straight, push your fingertip pads and the heel of your palm against one crack wall, and the backs of your knuckles and hand against the opposing wall. You'll be making a cup shape with your hand and will have three contact points against the crack walls: fingertips, heel of palm, knuckles or back of hand (figure 46).

7. As you have used a thumb-up jam, your forearm will be nicely in line with the crack, so you will not need to move further to bring the rest of your arm in line.

8. Expansion created with the hand, along with an in-line downwards pull from the weight of your body, creates a solid jam, which works in a similar way to a camming device.

9. An exception to the "keep everything in line with the crack" rule can be used for resting. If you lean your body out of the line of the crack, you can get the front (or back) of your wrist to lie against the edge of the crack, which cams the back (or front) of your hand into the crack wall harder and relieves the pressure on the thumb muscle.

Thumb-down jam
powerful jam, combination jam (active expansion and twisting)

As you have two active parts within the jam, it can be a very useful technique when you're tired. If your thumb is getting pumped from using expansion you can

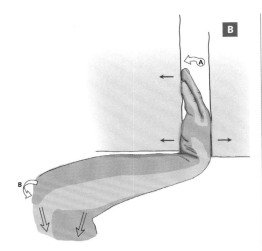

Figure 47. Standard hand cracks: thumb-down jam before elbow rotation

twist the jam more vigorously and relieve the pressure on the thumb muscle.

Starting position: The same starting position should be adopted with thumb-down hand jams as with thumb-up hand jams (so steps 1–4 of thumb-up jam should be followed). The only difference at this stage is you should orient your hand so that your thumb is pointing down towards the ground (hence "thumb down"), parallel with the crack.

Because you have rotated your hand into a thumb-down position it is likely that your forearm will be slightly out of line with the crack and your elbow will be pointing out to the side (figure 47). Don't worry about this for the moment: follow steps 5 and 6 of the thumb-up hand jam technique (thumb movement and cupping).

When your hand is in the crack and executing the correct active expansion jam (thumb movement and cupping) there is one more step which makes this jam work effectively:

Elbow rotation: rotate your forearm in a downwards motion so that your elbow starts to point towards the ground rather than out to the side. Bring it as in line with the crack as possible. Unless you have super-flexible wrists, it is likely that you won't be able to bring your forearm parallel with the crack. However, it is the motion of rotating your forearm down (and pointing your elbow towards the ground) that is the action you are trying to achieve. It's the same motion you would use when tightening or loosening a bolt with a wrench. Your forearm acts as a lever, which twists your hand inside the crack (figure 48).

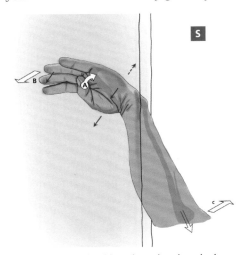

Figure 48. Standard hand cracks: thumb-down jam finishing position

When doing this rotation do not forget about the active expansion jam (the first part of the jam). Using both in combination will feel much more secure.

You will know if you are doing the twisting technique correctly if the "cupping gap" (the small gap on the side of the hand, which is created at the top of the palm and base of the pinkie finger when cupping) closes and can't be seen any more.

The higher you place a thumb-down jam above your head, the more in line your forearm will naturally become with the crack. In these cases, you may have to do less rotation with the forearm and a more subtle twist of the wrist to achieve the twisting action of the hand inside the crack. A good indicator of whether you are doing it correctly is if the back of your wrist is facing away from the crack.

CRIMPED HANDS
powerful jam, active expansion jam

A crimped hand jam can be used as an alternative to straight fingers in a standard hand jam—in either the thumb-up or thumb-down position. It should not be used instead of a standard hand jam, but it does come in handy in a couple of situations:

■ If you have slapped for a jam and haven't managed to get the whole of your hand seated within the crack, it can be useful to crimp your fingers inside the crack to help get purchase and then "bump" the whole of your hand in to a standard hand jam.

■ On long sections of a hand crack, the thumb muscle can become pumped and

very tired. By using a crimped hand jam, you can put extra pressure through the fingers which will relieve the stress on the thumb. If you really master this technique, you can actually untuck your thumb from the centre of your palm and give it little micro shakes within the crack—a cheeky little rest that no one will ever know you are taking! I've used this technique on long, pumpy roof cracks, so if you can do it correctly the steepness of the route shouldn't be a problem.

If you already have a feel for standard thumb-up and thumb-down hand jams, then this technique is easy to execute:

1. Start by following the same process for completing a standard hand jam; at the end, instead of having straight fingers bracing across the crack, crimp your fingers. This means that your fingertips and the heel of your palm will be touching one side of the crack wall (like in a standard hand jam); the back of your hand, knuckles, and the backs of your fingers (up to the second joint) should be touching the opposing wall.

2. It's important to complete a standard hand jam first and then crimp your fingers. If you try to adopt a crimped position with the hand before inserting it into the crack, you will not be able to insert as much of the body part into the crack, resulting in a poorer jam. Complete a jam, and then crimp the fingers.

3. When your fingers are in this position, it's important to pull down the wall with the fingertips (similar to

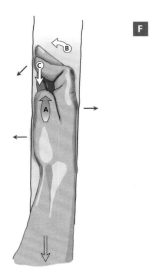

Figure 49. Crimped hands: thumb-up jam

if you were pulling down on a small edge): this will force the backs of your fingers into the opposing wall more vigorously, helping the jam to stick and maximizing the rest for the thumb muscle (figure 49).

THIN HANDS
powerful jam, active expansion jam

One person's thin hands is another's dreamy jam. But there should be no complaining from those with big hands, as things will even themselves out further up the scale when those cracks get wider! Thin hands often feel poor, but the keys to success are trust and maximizing the amount of friction. They are needed when the crack becomes too big to perform a ring lock, yet too small to get the whole hand inside.

They can be performed both thumb up and thumb down.

Thumb-down jam
When climbing thin-hand cracks the most common hand positioning should be the thumb-down position; when you execute any type of hand jam the most important parts of the hand to get inside the crack are the thumb and the thumb muscle. By orientating your hand thumb down, you will be able to insert this section of the hand first.

1. *Starting position 1:* The starting position of the hand should be the same as when performing a standard thumb-down hand jam (step 1, Standard hand cracks): the L-shape with fingers and thumb, along with a relaxed hand.

2. *Starting position 2:* The important part of a thin-hands jam is performing the insertion of the hand into the crack correctly. You should use the "chopping" motion.

3. *Starting position 3:* Place the base of your thumb/wrist against the crack entrance with the back of your hand and palm facing the crack walls. In this position it will look like you are in a thumb-up position, but your fingers will be pointing up and away from the crack.

4. *Chopping:* As you start to rotate your thumb down and into the crack, your fingers will start to rotate over the top of your thumb and enter the crack (figure 50). Imagine you are performing a really slow goodbye wave. It's important to first rotate from the

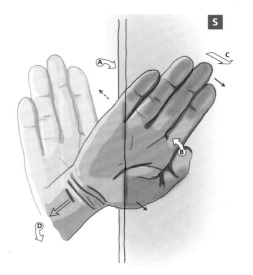

Figure 50. Thin hands: thumb-down jam

wrist, then when your wrist can't rotate any more, create more force and squeeze more surface area of the hand into the crack by rotating the elbow upwards.

5. *Thumb movement, cupping, and elbow rotation:* Now that your hand is inserted as far as possible into the crack, you are ready to perform the normal procedures of any other hand jam: thumb movement (standard thumb-up jam) cupping and elbow rotation (standard thumb-down jam). Elbow rotation must be performed as you will have moved the elbow up to get more contact area of the hand inside the crack, so this needs to be reversed so that everything comes back in line and you are pulling down on the jam rather than out.

Thumb-up jam

Thin hands thumb-up jams tend to feel worse than thumbs down. This is because it is hard to get the thumb muscle into the crack (the part of the hand that really helps with expansion). As a result, thumb-up jams feel more demanding as there is much more "holding power" going through the fingers. However, they can often be useful in corner cracks, roof cracks, and places where thumb-down jams might not fit.

1. *Starting position 1:* Put your hand into the standard starting L-shape position with your thumb pointing in the direction that you are going to climb. Your palm and the back of your hand should be facing the crack walls, and the tips of your fingers pointing into the crack.

2. *Starting position 2:* Insert your hand into the crack fingertips first. Your fingers should be at 90 degrees to the crack edge when you are inserting them.

3. *Starting position 3:* When the edge of the crack starts to come into contact with the top of your palm, give your hand a little wiggle and a push to get it further inside the crack. Remember the more friction and skin-to-rock contact you can get with this jam, the better it is going to feel.

4. *Thumb movement:* After you're convinced that your hand is inserted into the crack as far as possible, bring your thumb down inside the crack to sit on top of your index finger. Push down (and out against the crack wall) as hard as possible in the small gap between the index finger and crack wall; even

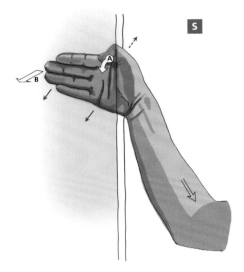

Figure 51. Thin hands: thumb-up jam

muscle being inserted into the crack and will feel much more like a finger bar (Chapter 2). A further solution to this is to execute the "chopping" action (see figure 50) but as an undercut motion. So, you will be rotating your fingers and thumb up into the jam, rather than down. This is quite useful if the jam is below chest level, however you'll need to have an incredibly flexible wrist to execute this motion effectively above this.

CUPPED HANDS
powerful jam, active expansion jam
Cupped hands are the awkward size between bomber hand jams and a solid fist and they cover a reasonably large range of crack size. The technique is simple, but because of the nature of the jam a lot of pressure goes through a very small surface area meaning that it can quite quickly become painful. Imagine someone standing on the back of your hand—a reasonably painful experience. But now imagine that same person putting the same weight across just the tops of the knuckles on your hand. Yes—ouch!

though the whole of the thumb muscle won't be inside the crack, the act of expanding it will keep what is inserted in there. The rest of the thumb muscle will mould around the edge of the crack, giving you slightly more friction.

5. *Cupping:* As with a standard hand jam, brace your fingertips on one crack wall and the back of your hand against the opposing wall. Push with your fingertips and apply opposing pressures on the crack walls (figure 51).

The important point to remember with this jam is to insert your fingers at 90 degrees to the crack edge: do not put the side of your little finger into the crack first and chop the other fingers over the top—this will result in none of the thumb

Now that you've been warned, let's dive in:

1. *Starting position:* The technique for this is easy—complete all the normal starting procedures of a standard hand jam. Now, this is the only hand jam where I recommend cupping before moving the thumb as cupped jams are wide; it's nice to get some friction from the crack walls straight away by cupping first. The thumb will then easily fit inside the cupped hand.

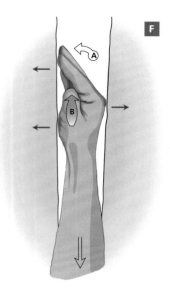

Figure 52. Cupped hands: thumb-up jam

Figure 53. Cup and twist: thumb-up jam

2. *Cupping:* When you get to the cupping stage, you'll notice that it is only the very tips of the fingers, the base of the palm, and the tops of the knuckles that are touching the crack walls. As there is minimal surface area touching the rock, it's important to focus on putting extra outwards pressure through these points. It may be slightly painful, but it will keep you in there. Reward doesn't come without a little sacrifice.

3. *Thumb movement:* The movement of the thumb is exactly the same as in other hand jams: rotate the thumb towards the pinkie finger. However, as your hand is nicely cupped you will be able to get the thumb right into the centre of your palm and possibly even

touching the base of your pinkie finger (figure 52). Because you will be really stretching your thumb across your palm it is common for the thumb muscles to get outrageously pumped very quickly!

While the hands may feel poor on this size of crack, the feet will be great (see next section) because the crack is slightly wider. Really use those feet to good effect.

Cup and twist
powerful jam, combination jam (expansion and twisting)

This is a great variation to the cupped hand jam and can be used when the "cups" get hideously cupped, i.e., just before you can seat a solid fist jam. It's a good way to make a terrible jam better as you are using active expansion and active twisting in combination.

1. *Starting position:* Complete a standard cupped hand jam.
2. Now turn your hand, as if you are turning a key in a lock. You'll feel an increase in pressure along your index finger and pinkie finger as they turn into the rock (figure 53). I find the best twisting directions to be:
   - right hand (either thumb up or down): twist clockwise
   - left hand (either thumb up or down): twist anticlockwise

OTHER TECHNIQUES
Forearm jam
resting or marginal jam, passive expansion jam

This is a passive expansion jam and a useful technique for resting rather than moving. It's very simple and requires minimal technique and is more about skin abrasion tolerance. Luckily you tend to use this technique only when you're tired, and when you're tired you tend not to feel pain as much. It works best when there is good rock friction and the crack is cupped hands size.

1. Complete all the normal starting procedures of a standard hand jam or cupped hand jam.
2. Put your hand into the crack, as deep as possible—until the crack becomes too narrow for your forearm to slip inside. As with any passive expansion jam, your forearm will want to

expand back to its original shape, and this expansion against the crack walls keeps the jam in place (figure 54).

3. You can wiggle your fingers and thumb to get a rest; the important thing to remember is to keep pushing inwards.

Forearm lever
powerful jam, active expansion jam

This technique is useful on face cracks and is extremely effective when layback jamming corner cracks. It gives a little extra support with a poor quality hand jam or if you are getting tired.

1. Complete the normal starting procedures of a standard hand jam (earlier this chapter). When you insert your hand into the crack, slide it in as far as it will comfortably go.
2. When your hand is in the crack in the desired position, complete all the stages of a standard hand jam.
3. Now press your forearm into the crack edge. It can be done either way—with both the top side and underside of your forearm. Pressing the underside of your forearm into the crack edge will usually feel more natural. So, if you are thumb-up jamming with your right hand, the underside of your forearm would touch the left crack edge (figure 55). If you were thumb-down jamming with your right hand, the underside of your forearm would touch the right crack edge.

You can use the position of your body to make this technique feel even better. Lean your upper body out to the side and use its

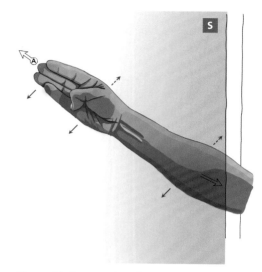

Figure 54. Forearm jam: hand-sized cracks

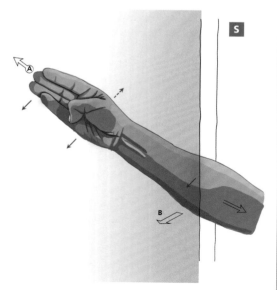

Figure 55. Forearm lever: hand-sized cracks

weight to force the forearm into the crack edge more vigorously. Useful for resting.

A forearm lever can be done using any part of the forearm. The crack edge could lie across the wrist, close to the elbow, or on any part of the forearm between these points.

FOOT TECHNIQUES IN HAND CRACKS

FOOT JAMS

Foot jams should feel absolutely bomber, like standing on a ledge. If you place a foot jam on a slab you should easily be able to stand on it no-handed. You will know you are doing it correctly when it feels this good.

Foot Jamming
powerful jam, active twisting jam

The starting position and execution of a foot jam are identical to that of a toe jam (Chapter 2). The only thing that differs is the placement of the foot in the crack. Instead of putting only your toes into the crack, you will now be able to insert a quarter of your foot (figures 55 and 56).

The key thing to remember with foot jams (aside from executing the standard procedure) is not to point your toes downwards when jamming. Point your big toe directly into the crack. You will get a greater surface area of your boot inside the crack and gain much more of a twisting action.

When you rotate your knee upwards so that your leg moves in line with the crack, it can then be difficult to slot your

Figure 56. Foot jam: starting position

other foot in above as your kneecap and lower leg will be covering the crack. To ensure you get the best placement for your next foot jam, stand up, straighten your leg, and let your lower leg and kneecap move away from the crack (but still keep your leg in line). As your leg moves away you will create a gap between your leg and the rock where you can place your other foot. Standing up, locking the leg straight and then moving it away from the rock is the key to making space for your next foot jam. If you don't create this space, your knee will start to drift out of line with the crack (to give you space to place your foot), reducing the twisting action needed and thus resulting in a poorer foot jam.

When climbing thin hand cracks, it's important to use the "push and wiggle"

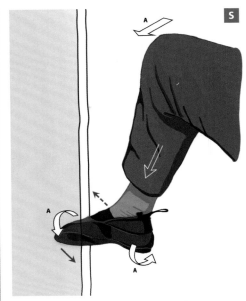

Figure 57. Foot jam: finishing position

technique to get the boot as far into the crack as possible. As you push your foot into the crack, give it a little wiggle up and down to help insert it further.

Cupped hand cracks are one of the best sizes of crack for feet. You can use a standard foot jamming technique or you can start to use the "heel down" technique (see Chapter 4).

CLIMBING POSITIONING

Positioning on hand cracks is all about whether you go thumb up or thumb down in the jams. Selecting the right option for the type of crack that you are climbing will make a route feel like a total cruise.

FACE CRACKS

Positioning on vertical cracks

A vertical crack is one which follows a straight line up the rock face. Vertical in this context does not refer to the angle of the rock: vertical cracks can be over-hanging, slabby or, in fact, vertical.

Bomber hand jams: When the crack has bomber hand jams the whole way, it is useful to use a combination of thumb-up and thumb-down jams. I generally climb with one technique (for example, thumb up) until it gets tiring, then rest and swap to the other technique (thumb down) until that starts to get tiring. Changing it around helps avoid becoming over-pumped and means you can do longer sections of climbing.

Thin hands: As highlighted earlier, a thumb-down jam in thin hand cracks will give the best purchase. You can get the whole of the thumb muscle into the crack and the jam will feel much more secure. So, where possible, use both hands thumbs down.

Cupped hands: a cup and twist jam in the thumb-up position for both hands is the most secure technique. However, cupped hand cracks can become very pumpy, so as with bomber hand jams, it is important to switch between both thumb-up and thumb-down jams to gain some respite in the thumb muscle.

Positioning on diagonal cracks

A diagonal crack is one that doesn't follow a straight line up the rock face, but instead trends across the face at an angle. For the following, imagine the crack is trending diagonally from left to right.

Bomber hands and cupped hands: In general, you want to position the top hand (right hand) thumb down and bottom hand (left hand) thumb up.

Thin hands: If the crack is not leaning too much, then keeping both hands thumbs down will be the best approach. Remember to keep executing the "rotation of the elbow" so that your forearm is in line with the crack. If the crack does start to lean aggressively, then it can become awkward and feel off balance to climb with both hands thumbs down, especially if there are limited footholds. You could instead go top hand (right hand) thumb down and bottom hand (left hand) thumb up. Remember, these are just options, and it's all about feeling for the correct positioning that works for the crack you are climbing. My feeling is, if things start to get awkward and I'm using strength and power to try to stay in balance, then there is probably better body positioning to be had. Crack climbing should feel as though you are locked in balance and only using your strength and power to do the moves.

Feet: The foot positioning is the same as is used in finger jamming (Chapter 2), but using foot jams (earlier this chapter) rather than toe jams.

Another technique can work for the foot that is being inserted into the crack. Place your toe into the crack like you would with a standard foot jam. However, instead of rotating your knee so that it becomes in line with the crack and twists the foot in place, drop your heel and let the top of your foot (the laces of your shoes), be levered against the upper crack wall. This is a very useful technique when the crack leans so much you feel like you are traversing rather than climbing upwards.

CORNER CRACKS

There are a number of different positions that can be adopted with the hands and feet that can affect the way you climb in a hand-width corner crack. What follows are a selection of different hand and foot positions, and then the type of climbing you'll experience by positioning yourself in this manner. No one position is right or wrong, it's just about picking the most appropriate one for a particular situation. Are you feeling tired? Do you need to move quickly? Do you want to climb securely? What's going to work best for the angle you're climbing? These are the type of questions you should be asking yourself to help select the most appropriate position.

HANDS

Before moving on to the positioning of the hands, it's important to know your inside hand from your outside hand (for description's sake), or things will become really confusing. See figures 39–42 for an illustration of different kinds of corners.

■ *Inside hand:* Imagine climbing a corner crack jamming straight in (like climbing a face crack). If the right side of your body is scraping up the corner wall, your right hand represents your inside hand. (See figures 40 and 41.)

■ *Outside hand:* Imagine climbing a corner crack jamming straight in (like climbing

a face crack). If the left side of your body is not touching the corner wall, your left hand represents your outside hand. (See figures 40 and 41.)

Whatever position is described below, the right and left side will always correlate with this description.

OPTION 1: OUTSIDE HAND THUMB DOWN (TOP HAND), INSIDE HAND THUMB UP (BOTTOM HAND)

This body position will produce a layback style of climbing as you are essentially laybacking the crack but with the added security of jamming (figure 58). It's a very

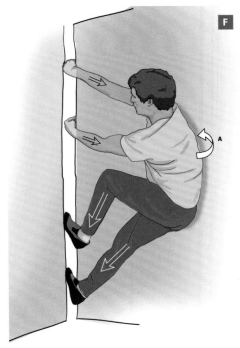

Figure 58. Positioning on corner cracks: option 1

Figure 59. Positioning on corner cracks: option 2

useful technique for moving quickly. Two extra tips apply when climbing in this style:

- Use your wrists: When leaning away from the crack, use your wrists on the crack edge for extra friction. If you gain enough friction you'll be able to release the pressure on the thumb muscles, thus preventing you from burning out as quickly.

- Use your forearms: If the jams are cupped, you can insert your forearms much deeper. You can gain more friction from your forearms in the crack, and you can also lean off them which will

really help relieve the pump and strain in the hands.

OPTION 2: OUTSIDE HAND THUMB UP (TOP OR BOTTOM HAND), INSIDE HAND THUMB UP (TOP OR BOTTOM HAND)

This body position will give you a sense of climbing the corner straight on (figure 59). You will be looking into the crack and directly at your jams, and will also be getting some friction from your body against the corner wall, which can act as a semi-rest. This is a useful technique if you want the security of being in the corner, yet still want to move at a reasonable pace—a happy balance.

OPTION 3: OUTSIDE HAND THUMB UP (BOTTOM HAND), INSIDE HAND THUMB DOWN (TOP HAND)

This body position will swing you into the corner and you will be getting lots of friction from the side of your body on the corner wall (figure 60). This position will give you a slow, solid yet slithering style of movement. If the corner wall (the wall your body is against) is slightly slabby and you are feeling pumped, tired, and need to shake out and rest, this can be a good position to adopt.

FEET

There are numerous different options for your feet in hand-sized corner cracks. When climbing the corner like a straight-on crack (options 2 and 3, above), then using the standard foot jamming technique will be the best option. However, when you start to use laybacking jams (option 1 for the

Figure 60. Positioning on corner cracks: option 3

hands), there are a number of different positions that can be used.

Before moving on to the positioning of the feet it's important to know your inside foot from your outside foot, or things will become really confusing.

- *Inside foot:* this is the foot which is naturally closest to the crack in the style that you are climbing (layback jamming). If the right side of your body is scraping up the rock face, it will be your right foot that is your inside foot.
- *Outside foot:* this is the foot which is naturally furthest away from the crack in

the style that you are climbing (layback jamming). If the right side of your body is scraping up the rock face it will be your left foot that is your outside foot.

OPTION 1

Use your inside foot like you are pinkie toe rand smearing (Chapter 2) but insert a larger surface area of your foot into the crack. Use your outside foot to either smear or edge outside of the crack. This technique is great for moving quickly and is more secure than smearing with both feet.

OPTION 2

Use your inside foot as described in option 1. Use your outside foot (as your top foot) like you would for a big toe rand smear (Chapter 2), but with a greater surface area of shoe in the crack. This will feel more secure, but progress and movement are likely to be slower.

OPTION 3

Use your inside foot as described in option 1. Use your outside foot (I prefer the top foot) as a standard foot jam. This is a useful resting position, and a position that benefits from feeling more secure, as both feet are nicely twisted into the crack.

OPTION 4

Use both feet outside of the crack, either smearing or edging. This is a great way to move quickly, however it can become strenuous if the feet are poor. On the other hand, if the feet are good, it can actually be quite restful.

Pop Quiz

1. Finger cracks or offwidths? Finger cracks
2. Stemming or roof cracks? Stemming
3. Hand jam or hand stack? Hand jam
4. Knee lock or chickenwing? None of those two!
5. Tape or no tape? Tape, if I want to climb longer than just a day
6. Cams or nuts? Cams
7. Sandstone cracks or granite cracks? Granite
8. Short and hard, or long and pumpy? Short and hard
9. Pressure wound or rock rash? Rock rash
10. Colour preference of crack climbing trousers due to unfortunate mistakes, red or brown? Brown

BARBARA ZANGERL

She's the best female all-round climber there is, so as you'd expect, "Babsi" is pretty handy at crack climbing too! From big walls to single-pitch beef-fests, she's squirmed, bridged, and jammed her way up some very tricky crack testpieces and has also established her own, including Gondo Crack (F8c trad / 5.14b R) *in Ossola, Italy. She made the second ascent of* Magic Mushroom (5.14a) *on El Cap in 2017 with Jacopo Larcher.*

FAVOURITE CRACK CLIMBING AREA?

The crags around Ossola! In northern Italy, just before the Swiss border, lies the village of Cadarese, nestled in a valley of steep granite and gneiss walls. The rock hides in a beautiful open beech tree forest, making the contrast between fallen leaves and laser-cut cracks, big layback flakes, and solid granite slabs appear. The rock is very compact, unpolished granite and offers perfect cracks. It is the closest crack climbing area to where I live so we spend quite a lot of time there. If this area was situated in Britain or in the US, there wouldn't be a single bolt to be found—but since it is in the middle of Europe, the trad climber's eye might water at the sight of beautiful cracks with shiny bolts. In recent years many routes have had their bolts chopped in a vendetta of crack lovers; the crag has seen a makeover and a pure trad sector has been established by a crew of north Italian climbers, adding huge value to the climbing there.

Cadarese is the main and most famous area for trad climbing in the Ossola valley, but there is of course much more to see. Within a short drive you can reach several other areas and every line you find in this valley has beautiful climbing; it is definitely worth a trip! Not only is the climbing great, also the people around Ossola and the small restaurants are worth a visit. Don't miss a cup of the greatest Italian coffee, and the food is delicious as usual in Italy.

BEST CRACK CLIMBING EXPERIENCE?

The Doors (F8b/5.13b) in Cadarese is one of the best cracks I have ever climbed. It is an outstanding-looking line with a varied climbing style (changing crack size). The first time I got on *The Door* I had almost no experience in crack climbing

so it was quite a challenge to climb this route. I got pretty pumped laybacking all the way up. Luckily there were some footholds next to the crack . . . It was such a great experience to hop on this route. Definitely five stars!

MEMORABLE CRACK CLIMBING EXPERIENCE?

Generator Crack (5.10c) in Yosemite Valley was the first offwidth I ever tried. I went there with Hansjörg Auer in 2010, just to test our non-existent crack climbing skills. We tried that route (an eight-metre-high crack line) to get a taste for the real business—El Cap.

After three hours without success we were pretty frustrated and totally trashed. We didn't find any kind of beta for this offwidth, and we really tried every kind of method—or so we thought. That was a really funny experience. We were pretty sure that we would not make it to the top of El Cap after that first taste. We needed three rest days for our knees and elbows to recover.

Our trip ended with Hansjörg's 20-metre fall on *Quantum Mechanic* (5.13a) on the last hard pitch near the top of Washington Column—and of course it was on an offwidth. He broke his wrist and we flew home. We had some really good days on that trip and enjoyed the time there, climbing on all the incredible walls that the valley has to offer, even if we did not make it to the top of El Cap.

THE KNOWLEDGE

Don't only use big shoes for cracks. In Ossola especially, you sometimes need tight shoes to stand on small footholds instead of squeezing your feet in the crack. And tape your hands if you want to climb for multiple days.

Opposite: *Barbara Zangerl on* Separate Reality *(5.12a), Yosemite National Park, California* (© François Lebeau)

Martin Kocsis climbing the immaculate thin hands and finger crack of Scarface (5.11a) on the Wingate Sandstone at Indian Creek, Utah (© Mike Hutton)

CLIMBING MOVEMENT

Hand cracks often follow less of a distinct sequence than, say, finger cracks. The jams are usually less specific, and in pure hand cracks they can be found in many places. That's not to say climbing hand cracks won't follow a certain sequence, but in general you can make the type of positioning and movement you use fit the sequence. What follows are some general movement rules and then some specific movement techniques.

GENERAL MOVEMENT RULES

There are a few basic rules which should be applied to general movement on hand cracks. These will make your climbing life less strenuous, enabling you to be more relaxed and therefore feel in greater control. You could be executing all the correct hand and foot techniques perfectly, but if you neglect these rules, the climbing will feel harder than it should.

Keep good body positioning when stationary: Hang off the joints, ligaments, and bones of your body, and use the skin friction from your jams—don't hang off the tendon and muscles or from bent arms. Place your top jam a reasonable distance above your head; by doing this you will bring your body closer to the wall, thereby putting more weight through your feet and less weight hanging out away from the wall through your arms. A common mistake is to place jams at chest and eye level: this becomes strenuous and forces you to pull your body in to the wall. Suddenly you're hanging from bent arms with both elbows sticking out to the side (out of the line of the crack), one of the most unnecessarily strenuous positions you can adopt while crack climbing.

Keep good body positioning when moving: When moving upwards, pull with the muscles and tendons. Don't roll on your joints or keep all your limbs straight. If you keep your elbow straight and try to roll around your shoulder socket to make upwards movement, you'll move out of line from the crack—you'll lean to the side and consequently start laybacking—and you'll look like a scarecrow trying to climb. Instead, bend at the elbow and pull your body up keeping everything in line with the crack (figure 61). Pull and push in straight lines, don't roll around your joints to move upwards.

Don't get too bunched up: If your feet and hands become too close together, you will find that your weight starts to hang out away from the wall resulting in the same problem as when you violate the first rule (above). Your knees can also start to flare outwards from your centre line as you try to provide room to place one foot above the other. However, when your knees move out of line from the crack, your foot jams inevitably get worse.

Don't get too stretched out: If you are too stretched out, you'll find that your weight gets close to the wall and hangs down rather than out (making it feel less strenuous than a bunched-up position), however you won't be able to execute the basic jamming techniques effectively. Becoming too stretched out on cracks limits the amount

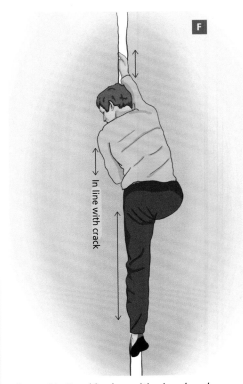

Figure 61. Good body positioning: hand jamming in line with the crack

of the body part you can insert into the crack for a jam, making the jam feel much worse. Becoming too stretched out can also lead to your bottom foot starting to point down in the crack, rather than staying at a level 90-degree angle which is what you want to achieve when foot jamming.

Apply normal climbing principles to your foot/hand sequences. Climbing with opposites is mechanically more efficient, i.e., pulling down with your left hand while

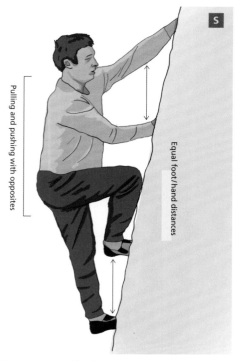

Figure 62. Good body positioning: opposite hand/foot movements and equal hand/foot distances

pushing up on your right foot. The same applies in basic crack climbing: pull with left/push with right, and vice versa. It is less strenuous, prevents the "barndooring" effect, and distributes your body weight across both sides of your body while you pull up.

Try to keep hand and foot movements equal as much as the sequences allow. If you make a long move with your hand, match the distance with your foot by

making a high step; or match a small hand move with a small foot move. This will prevent you from getting too bunched up or stretched out (figure 62).

Pace: Keep a steady constant pace on cracks that are very splitter. Go for a repeated rhythm of movement that keeps the pump at bay. One approach is to count a set number of moves, place some gear, then count a certain number of shakes on each hand, then repeat. By doing this you'll create a steady rhythm and will not over or under rest nor start to pump out.

Hand over hand

A common movement technique on hand cracks is to move hand over hand. This involves taking your lower hand out of the crack and passing it over the top of the other hand as you climb. Depending on the style, steepness, or angle of the crack, a variety of thumb-up and thumb-down jams are often used with this technique.

- *Hand over hand, thumbs up:* This is often used when you feel comfortable on the terrain and want to move quickly. If your aim is to move quickly, then making bigger moves will aid this (bigger or longer moves equals less time on the rock). See "Big moves" on the next page.
- *Hand over hand, thumbs down:* This technique is often used on thinner cracks. You can get better jams on thinner cracks by going thumbs down, however the size of move you will be able to make will be much smaller.
- *Hand over hand, one hand thumb up/ one hand thumb down:* This technique

is not commonly used as it can throw you off balance; however, if the crack is diagonal and the terrain is easy, it can be quicker to keep crossing your bottom hand (which would be thumb up), over your top hand (which would be thumb down). This is essentially the same hand positioning as the swimming technique (below), however you are crossing your arms each time to gain a little bit of extra height with fewer moves.

Swimming technique

Another common technique is the swimming technique. With this method, you don't cross your hands and you don't take them out of the crack: the top hand stays at the top and the bottom hand stays at the bottom. You move them together and apart, one at a time, in a scissoring motion. The movement is slightly slower and the moves you will make are smaller. This technique works well in the larger sizes of hand crack, from standard hand jams all the way up to fist jams.

You would typically use the swimming technique if:

- You are too tired to take one hand out of the crack to move it above the other. If you are tired, then leading with the hand that is least pumped is the best option. The leading hand takes the most weight, so this will help give respite to the following hand. You can keep alternating the leading hand to help the following hand recover.
- The jams are so poor that you can't take one hand out of the crack to move it above the other.

- The jams are really deep at the back of the crack and you are reaching a long way inside the crack to seat them.

There are three combinations that can be used with swimming technique:

- Top hand thumb down, bottom hand thumb up (most common). Useful if the crack is trending diagonally across the rock face or you want to make the most of wrist and forearm jams on the crack edge.
- Top hand thumb up, bottom hand thumb up.
- Top hand thumb down, bottom hand thumb down (useful if the crack is thinner).

A minor variation to this technique can be used on thinner cracks when you can't insert your whole hand. Stick to the swimming technique (scissoring your hands together and apart), but instead of shuffling your hands inside the crack at all times, take them out to help seat the jam on the edge of the crack. You are taking your hand out of the crack for each move to enable yourself to execute a better thin hands jam, but at the same time having the security of smaller movements and not overlapping your hands.

Big moves: moving off jams

Moving off a thumb-up jam: Try to make big moves off of thumb-up jams since your wrist and forearm will stay in the correct orientation and in line with the crack (figure 63). When making a big move, imagine there is a pin going through the centre of the palm of your jamming hand and, as you move, your

Figure 63. Big moves: moving off a thumb-up jam

hand and arm are rotating around this. If the move is really long, your fingers might end up pointing down and your thumb inwards as you move upwards.

Moving off a thumb-down jam: Sometimes you might have to make a long move off a thumb-down jam. The downside to making big moves from this jam is that when you pull up, your elbow will want to move out of line with the crack, making you feel like you want to layback the edge of the crack. The following two techniques can help prevent this from happening.

1. As above with thumb-up jams, imagine there is a pin through the centre of your palm. Keep your arm straight and rotate around this pin, so your torso and shoulders end up above the hand jam. By doing this you will keep everything in line with the crack, however it will feel strenuous in the shoulders and core as during the rotation your body will move away from the rock. When your body does move away from the rock, continue putting lots of pressure through your feet to keep yourself upright. You are not pulling through the jam, you are rotating around the jam. As it's a very strenuous way of moving, it usually works best on vertical to slabby terrain. You would need to have abs and shoulders of steel to make this work on steep terrain! In the finished position:

   - your fingers will be pointing down
   - your thumb will be pointing towards the crack entrance
   - your elbow, shoulder, and arm will be locked straight
   - your torso will be above your hand

2. Move dynamically so that you don't have to statically pull through the difficult position (where the elbow moves out to the side and you feel like you will end up laybacking). By moving dynamically through this position, you can effectively skip it, but you'll have to be precise at seating the next jam in order to stay on the rock.

Big moves: moving to jams
Moving to a thumb-down jam: If possible, when you've made a big move, go into

a thumb-down hand jam. As you will be reaching a long way, your fingers will be pointing upwards rather than inwards. If you reach into a thumb-down jam, the thumb muscle, which is the most important part of any hand jam, will be inserted into the crack first.

Moving to a thumb-up jam: When moving to a thumb-up jam, aim to get the thumb muscle into the crack as soon as possible.

Big moves: switching jams

If you have moved to a thumb-down jam and again need to make another big move, switching your hand to a thumb-up jam will help. A typical sequence might go something like this:

1. Big move from thumb-up jam to thumb-down jam.
2. Match hands by the thumb-down jam.
3. Switch the thumb-down jam to a thumb-up jam.
4. Make next big move from thumb-up jam.

MOVING OFF AND TO POOR JAMS

The same principles apply here as with finger jams (Chapter 2).

TRANSITIONING BETWEEN JAMS

It can be a blessing to have the option to use either a thumb-up or a thumb-down jam, and as you have this option, it is nice to be able to switch between the two. Here are a few situations in which it might be useful to switch and alternate.

■ *Fatigue:* The thumb muscles are likely to get pumped when jamming thumb up. The wrist and the forearm are likely

Richard Connors laybacking the initial section of The Strand *(E2 5b) at Gogarth's upper tier on Anglesey, North Wales; it's an endless 43-metre crack of the highest calibre that will eat your entire rack for dinner. (© Mike Hutton)*

to get pumped when jamming thumb down. By alternating between the two jams, you get to rest one set of muscles while using the others.

- *Crack features:* The crack features may lend themselves towards using one style of jam over another, for example, if there is a flare or an offset on one side of the crack. As a general rule, if the crack is offset, it can be nice to place the palm of your hand against it (especially if the crack is thin), as this means the pulp of your thumb and palm will sit against the rock. If the crack is flared, thumb-down jams work well as you can insert the pulp at the base of your thumb into the crack first to create a better jam. (Very similar principles apply to thin hands jamming.)

- *Crack width:* The crack width can determine the best way to jam. As a general rule, wider cracks suit thumb-up jams since you can cup your hand more effectively and also use cup and twist techniques. However, using only one technique on this crack width can become extremely pumpy in the thumbs, so you might consider combining it with thumb-down jams, even though they could feel slightly worse. Thinner cracks suit thumb-down jams as you can insert the pulp of your thumb into the crack first, exactly like doing a thin hands jam.

Opposite: *Rob Pizem fist jamming on* Willow *(5.11+) at Willow Buttress in Labyrinth Canyon, Green River Canyon, Utah* (© Andrew Burr)

CHAPTER 4

Fist Cracks

Fist cracks: the size of crack that most climbers hate. I'm a strong believer that most climbers loathe this size because they struggle to get fist jams to work effectively. The reason why they struggle to get them to work is due to the nature of the jam. When performing a fist jam very little expansion occurs from the fist, and on parallel-sided cracks this can make fist jams feel insecure and give the sense that you could slip out at any moment. If you are one of these slippery-fist-jam-type people and fear the fist, let's turn that negative into a positive right away.

Your fist jam feels like it might slip. Great! This is because a fist jam is hugely reliant on friction. If it's reliant on friction, this means you don't need much strength and power to execute it. And if you don't need strength and power, you'll need "feel" and friction to execute this jam . . . and if it's all about feel and friction, that means *everyone* can do it. Remember Chapter 1's Rule 4 of crack climbing: use structure not strength, and in this case structure comes largely in the form of skin friction.

Fist jams are also great because they are one of the least painful jamming techniques. They use the fleshy parts of your hand to jam against the rock rather than the thinner bony parts, making it feel as if you are jamming between two velvety, down-filled cushions . . . well, maybe not that luxurious, but you get the idea.

So, now that you know fist jams don't require strength and are comfortable, what are you waiting for? Let's delve in deep and learn how to fist jam.

HAND TECHNIQUES IN FIST CRACKS

STANDARD FIST CRACKS

As stated above, fist jams have a limited amount of expansion compared to, say, a hand jam, which is why with any fist jam, the first thing you should do is try to place it passively. This means looking for constrictions in the rock that will naturally lock your fist into place, rather than having to rely on expansion to hold it in there. This is obviously a very simple point and relates to almost every kind of jam, however it can't be emphasised enough with fist jamming: do this before anything else. Check the rock and look for the most suitable constricted placement with the most friction potential.

Before moving on to the mechanics and techniques of fist jamming, I've put together a list of features that you should look for in the rock before you even start to place your fist jam. These are relevant to most jams, but they're especially important when it comes to fist jamming.

■ *Look for constrictions.* The best will have a narrowing in the rock which pinches down to a point smaller than your fist so that your fist can't pass through. A constriction will help you place the jam passively, and you won't have to create as much expansion. Even if the constriction doesn't pinch to smaller than your fist, any narrowing is better than none.

■ *Look for where the crack narrows towards the edge.* The crack might widen on the inside, so as well as looking for constrictions to pull your fist down into, look for constrictions on the edge of the crack that you can pull out on and passively jam against (figure 64). You might, for example, slot your hand into the crack in the starting hand jam position (see figure 44) because the crack entrance is too narrow to insert a fist, then when it is inside you may have space to create a fist and pull back out against the constriction. A fist would never be able to fit into the crack where you have just managed to slide a hand, so when you pull

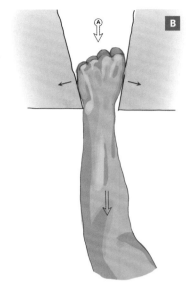

Figure 64. Standard fist cracks with crack narrowing towards the edge

back with a fist from the inside, it will not come out.

■ *Look for lumps, bumps, and edges.* These can act as small constrictions that will help prevent the jam sliding. Even the smallest of edges or bumps can create narrow spots which will help the jam stick.

■ *Look for crystals or pebbles.* These can work in much the same way as small constrictions, but you can also nestle them into the gaps at either side of your fist jam; this enables your fingers to wrap around something, creating a more solid jam.

■ *Look for rock with more friction.* Fist jams rely on lots of friction. If you can find areas or patches of rock which have higher friction, your fist jam will stick more easily. Look at the rock to eliminate the polished or slick areas straight away, then use "feel" to subtly find the areas with the most friction.

- *Look for a sharp edge to the crack.* A sharp edge can be useful to lean the wrist or forearm against, so you get extra "bite" from using another body part.

Palm-down (or in) fist jam
powerful jam, active expansion jam

The most common fist jam. The finished position has your palm facing towards the ground into the crack (figure 65).

1. *Starting position 1 (hand orientation):* With your hand outside the crack, rotate it so that your palm is facing down and in the direction of the crack, and the back of your hand is facing up. Your fingers should be straight (you'll be able to see the backs of them) and pointing into the crack.

2. *Starting position 2 (thumb movement):* It is in this hand orientation that you will insert it into the crack. First, you need to make it as thin as possible for better insertion. To do this, move your thumb into the centre of your palm and push it towards your little finger (see Thumb movement in "Standard Hand Cracks," Chapter 3).

   This will increase the depth of your hand; however, as you make this movement you'll notice that the knuckles of your index finger and pinkie finger drop and move inwards, reducing the width

of your hand. When you have moved your thumb across towards your pinkie, and your knuckles have dropped down and inwards thereby reducing the width of your hand, you are ready to insert your hand into the crack. Make sure you insert your hand into the crack with your fingers relaxed.

3. *Making a fist:* Once your hand is in the correct place inside the crack, wrap your fingers underneath your thumb and into the centre of your palm just above the thumb muscle, then wrap your thumb over the first joint of your fingers (usually your index and middle fingers). Essentially you are making the style of fist you'd use if you were going to punch something.

4. *Fist clench:* To make a fist jam work properly it's important to clench the correct part of your fist. It sounds straightforward, and it is, yet some people don't do it properly and this is why their fist jam starts to slide. You'll notice that the areas that are touching the rock are the fleshy parts down the index and pinkie sides of the hand; these are the parts you want to tense and expand. As you might have guessed, it is the index and pinkie fingers which have the greatest impact on this. When your fist is clenched, focus on pushing the tips of your index and pinkie fingers into your palm (imagine you are trying to push them through your palm). When you do this, you will notice that each side of your hand will tense up. If you stop pushing

into the palm with either finger, that side will relax. If either side relaxes, your fist jam will start to slide. So, it is important to simultaneously push with both your index and pinkie fingers into the palm to make sure that both sides of the fist expand and become solid.

5. *The thumb:* The thumb, which is wrapped over the tops of the finger joints, can help with the act of pushing the tips of the fingers into the palm of the hand. Just press your thumb into your fingers.

6. It's important to keep good form through the hand, wrist, and forearm when you use the jam. Imagine there is a steel rod running from your knuckles, down the back of your hand, over your wrist joint, then down the back of your forearm: this steel rod prevents any flexion of the wrist and keeps its rigid. Keeping your wrist rigid and straight gives a much more natural and strong position for pulling on. A common mistake is to have flexion in the wrist: when you then pull down on the jam, it feels less solid, which consequently means the elbow starts to lift up and out of line (trying to create some sidepull tension), and the jam feels worse still and could potentially slip.

Palm-up (or out) fist jam
powerful jam, active expansion jam

This is exactly the same as a palm-down fist jam; you are just flipping your hand 180 degrees so that your palm is facing up (or out) and the back of your hand is facing

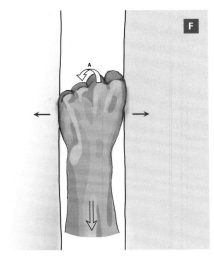

Figure 65. Standard fist cracks: palm-down (or in) fist jam

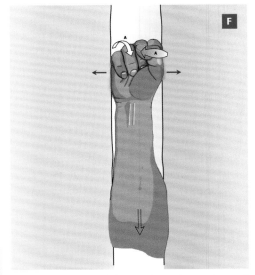

Figure 66. Standard fist cracks: palm-up (or out) fist jam

down, both in the direction of the crack (figure 66).

One thing to note when palm-up fist jamming deep inside the crack is that in the finished position your palm may look more like it is facing out towards you. The action when inserting your hand into this jam is similar to a boxer throwing an uppercut (a punch from below with an upwards motion intended to hit someone on the underside of their chin), but I suspect it doesn't hurt nearly as much!

ALTERNATIVE THUMB POSITIONS
powerful jam, active expansion jam

There are a couple of alternative thumb positions, where your fingers are wrapped over your thumb, which can be used to help span a slightly wider crack by just a few more millimetres. These techniques can be done either palm up or palm down. I'm personally not a big fan of these jams as I don't find them particularly secure; I prefer to use teacup jams (later this chapter) to help gain that extra width while fist jamming. Also, if you commit to burying your thumb inside the palm of your hand, you no longer have the option of freely moving it into different positions, which can impede transitioning into a teacup technique. That said, it never hurts to have a few more options at your disposal.

Thumb inside
1. Follow the same starting positions as for a palm-down fist jam. However, when you make a fist inside the crack, this time wrap your fingers **over** the top of your thumb so that your thumb ends up inside your palm.
2. Be sure to push your pinkie finger into your palm to tense and expand that side of your hand. Push the fingers that are resting on top of your thumb (index and middle, sometimes ring) into the thumb: this will push the knuckle at the base of the thumb into the crack wall. It is this knuckle touching the crack wall which enables you to span a slightly greater width of crack.

Thumb between the fingers
1. Again, follow the same starting positions as for a palm-down fist jam.
2. When you start to make a fist inside the crack, place your thumb into the centre of your palm with the tip pointing forwards (away from the wrist) and wrapped between your middle and ring fingers. You should be able to see the tip of your thumb poking out between your fingers. Remember to push the little finger into the palm. The fingers that are wrapped over your thumb (index and middle) should be pushing down on the thumb to help tense the thumb side of the hand and push the thumb knuckle out against the rock. As an alternative, the thumb can also be placed between the index and middle fingers.

MAKING FIST JAMS SMALLER
SQUISHED FIST
The squished fist jam is a very subtle size between a cupped hand jam and a fist jam. It's essentially still a fist jam, just a really

tight one. I find it a touch painful and awkward as it feels like it's rubbing the bones of my knuckles against each other. However, on a positive note, when it's in, it's in! The fact that you are trying to push something big into a small space means that it doesn't want to come out that easily. Bonus.

Once your hand is in the crack, the movement of the fingers and thumb and the clenching action of the fist are the same as with a standard palm-down fist jam, but the finished position will look distorted. It is primarily the insertion of the fist—trying to make the fist even smaller—which differs.

There are two options, depending on how much you need to squish your fist:

Squished fist in wider crack
powerful jam, active expansion jam

If the crack is only slightly smaller than normal fist size, only a subtle change to the position of the hand is required before insertion. All you need to do is emphasise the movement of the pinkie and index knuckles down and inwards to help reduce the width of the hand. To do this (having first completed step 1 of a palm-down fist jam) cross your pinkie finger under your ring finger so that the fingernail of your pinkie is under the finger pad of your ring finger. Do the same with the index finger under the middle finger. Remember to keep the middle and ring fingers locked together. Now move your thumb across the palm of your hand and touch the pad of your thumb to the fingertip of your pinkie. You should now be making a bowl-shaped feature with your hand. With your hand either in the palm-up or palm-down orientation, and with your hand as relaxed as possible in the position it is in, squeeze it into the crack (figure 67). Once inside, complete steps 3 to 5 of normal palm-down fist jamming to make the jam more secure.

Squished fist in narrower crack
powerful jam, combination jam (active expansion and twisting)

However much you try to collapse your index and pinkie fingers into the centre of your palm, your hand won't fit into the crack if it is too narrow. You'll need to use a different approach. Put your hand in the thumb-up hand jam position (Chapter 3) if the crack is very thin. Or into a fist position, with palm and back of your hand facing either crack wall if the crack is

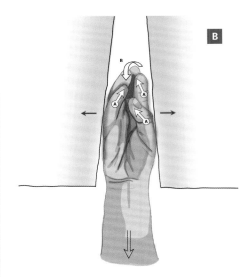

Figure 67. Squished fist: wider crack

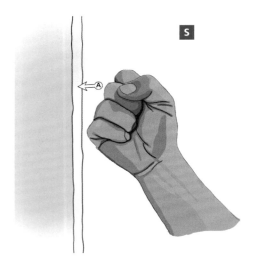

Figure 68. Squished fist: narrower crack
starting position

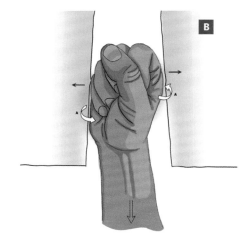

*Figure 69 Squished fist: narrower crack finishing
position*

slightly wider (figure 68). Insert it into the crack in this orientation (it should fit very easily). When your hand is inside the crack, rotate it either clockwise or anticlockwise depending on whether you would like to execute a palm-up or palm-down jam. As the crack is narrow, you will really have to force and wiggle your hand into position. It will probably feel like a bit of a bone cruncher. When you've rotated your hand as much as possible, follow steps 3 to 5 of the standard palm-down fist jamming technique. You won't be able to make a fist or clench your fist quite as much, as the fit of your hand inside the crack will already be so tight. It will likely look like a distorted fist jam (figure 69). This is normal, but just going through this process will make the fist stick more solidly.

PSEUDO FIST

marginal jam, active expansion jam

Pseudo fist can be used as an alternative to the squished fist jam when the crack is still too narrow for a standard fist jam. It can also give you pain relief if you've used a lot of squished fists and your knuckles are crunched and sore. However, while less painful, the pseudo fist jam is not as secure. It is a donut jam but with four fingers (Chapter 2), and as such it essentially levitates on the edge of the crack which means there isn't as much skin in contact with the rock.

To perform a pseudo fist jam, complete the steps of a donut jam but using all four fingers (figure 70). As this jam is marginal, you should look for small lumps, bumps, rugosities, crystals, or pebbles just inside the crack (on the crack walls) which you

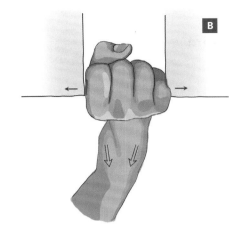

Figure 70. Pseudo fist

can wrap the first and second joints of your index or pinkie fingers around. Unless you are able to find a good finger wrap around a feature, it is unlikely you will be able to make a powerful pull on these jams, so climb with care.

MAKING FIST JAMS BIGGER
TEACUP JAM
powerful jam, active expansion jam

The teacup jam is a great way to enlarge the size of your fist jam so you don't have to progress to offwidth techniques so soon and you can keep moving your hands independently of one another. The downsides of this jam are that it can feel less secure, and on the extended sizes it can become very painful. So, sometimes progressing to offwidth techniques sooner can be more beneficial, as they might feel more secure and, surprisingly (if you're doing them

correctly), less painful. It's all about analysing the climbing and the condition of your body to see what is most appropriate.

All this being said, the teacup jam is my go-to method for making my fist jam bigger and it's a technique that I use a lot. There are two types of teacup jam:

Teacup jam, flat thumb

Follow steps 1 and 2 of a standard palm-down fist jam. However, when you start to make a fist, instead of wrapping your thumb over the top of the fingers, slide it around the side of the fist so the pad of your thumb rests against the side of your index finger between the knuckle and second joint (figure 71). The depth of your thumb will give extra width to your fist. Make sure you keep your thumb flat and

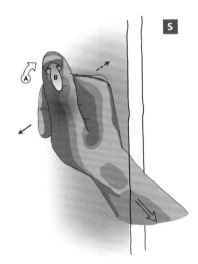

Figure 71. Teacup jam: flat thumb

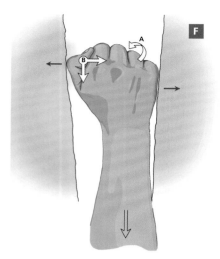

Figure 72. Teacup jam: protruding thumb

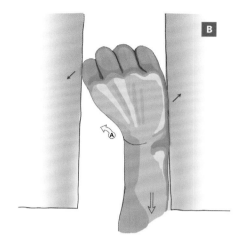

Figure 73. Twisted fist: twist from the wrist (side to side)

push the pad of your thumb down into your index finger to create an outwards force against the crack wall.

Teacup jam, protruding thumb

This is when teacupping can become very unpleasant; however it will give you an extra half inch to fill a void. Follow the same steps as for a flat thumb teacup, but as you move your thumb around the side of your fist, sit the tip of the thumb in the small indentation created by your bent index finger. This will make the joint of your thumb protrude out against the crack wall (figure 72). A lot of pressure will be going through a very small contact point which will make your thumb want to buckle back in. To prevent this from happening, push down and into the indentation with the tip of your thumb to help create

outwards expansion. You should tape the thumb joint for this jam or else it will very quickly become excruciatingly painful.

TWISTED FIST

balance jam, active twisting jam

An alternative to teacupping, twisted fist is less painful, but not as secure. You can't have everything! For example, you could definitely teacup jam in a roof crack, but trying to do a twisted fist jam on anything steeper than vertical would be extremely difficult. There are two variations of the twisted fist jam:

Twist from the wrist (side to side)

First complete all the standard steps for a normal palm-down fist jam. However, because the size of the crack will be too big for both sides of your fist to be in contact with both walls, you will need to twist either left or right from the wrist. The twisting action of the wrist is similar to the action of twisting the lid of a jar of jam. The base of your wrist will now be touching one crack wall, and either the index or pinkie side of your fist jam (depending on hand used and direction of twist) will be touching the other crack wall (figure 73).

It can also help to push the side of your forearm into the crack wall (the side that your wrist is against). This will create more friction, but you will also be able to apply a greater outwards pressure against the crack wall, making it easier to stay in the jam.

Twist from the wrist (up and down)

Twist from the wrist using the same motion as you would if turning a key in a lock. This twist will enable the two points on your clenched fist that are furthest apart from each other to touch the rock.

- If using your right hand, rotate clockwise.
- If using your left hand, rotate anticlockwise.

This rotation will make the thumb knuckle and pinkie knuckle come into contact with the crack walls (figure 74).

THUMB EXTENSION

balance jam, active expansion jam

This jam is for cracks that are too wide for teacupping, and it can only be used for balance. For example, you might need to shift your other hand into a different position or do a small foot swap. Trying to make a proper move or a powerful pull off

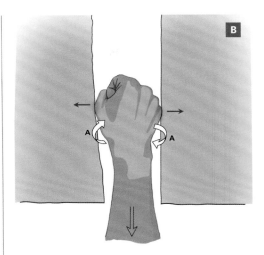

Figure 74. Twisted fist: twist from the wrist (up and down)

this jam won't work. However, when the space needs to be filled to help make a little adjustment and you only have one hand available to do it, then this technique could solve the problem.

There are two variations to this jam: which one you use will depend on the width of the crack.

Thumb extension, full extension

Put your hand into a position as if you were giving someone the thumbs up. Now rotate your hand into a palm-down position. This is the finished position you are looking to achieve inside the crack. The pinkie side of your fist will be in contact with one crack wall and the tip of your extended thumb will be touching the other crack wall (figure 75).

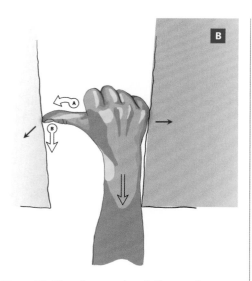

Figure 75. Thumb extension: full extension

For this jam to be at all useful, the stability and direction of push with the thumb is really important. Imagine smudging a chalk drawing on a blackboard: you would push into the chalk and then swipe across the board. The same principles apply with the thumb in the crack on this jam. While keeping the thumb as rigid as possible, push out against the crack wall with the thumb, but also smudge the thumb towards the crack entrance.

Thumb extension, half extension
Execute the first step from full extension, however, instead of having your thumb straight, bend it at the joint so that it becomes half the length. The finished position in the crack should have the nail and joint of the thumb in contact with one crack wall and the pinkie side of the fist touching the other crack wall.

Make sure to use the same smudging technique as with the full extension technique. As you will be trying to press into the wall with the back of your thumb rather than the pad, it will be noticeably more painful, so taping the thumb properly is a must!

Forearm jam
powerful or resting jam, passive expansion jam

The principles of forearm jams have been explained in the hand jamming chapter (Chapter 3), however you can make a slight variation to the orientation of your arm before you insert it into the crack to enable it to work with fist-sized cracks.

Rotate your hand in to the palm-up position (see figure 66). Relax your hand and fingers to ensure your forearm is not tensed. Insert your hand and forearm into the crack as deep as possible. Remember to wiggle and push it in. As climbers usually have larger than normal forearms, the edge of the crack will most likely lie a few inches down your forearm from the elbow.

By "overpushing" your forearm into the crack it will naturally want to expand, making it stick. If you feel like it is slipping you can curl your wrist up towards you, which will tense the forearm inside the crack, making it rigid (figure 76). When you do this, try to keep the hand relaxed so you can gain respite in the thumb muscle. Curling your wrist towards you will make the jam stick more easily; however, as with

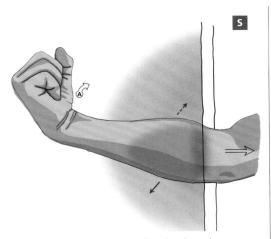

Figure 76. Forearm jam: fist-sized cracks

most crack climbing, there isn't a positive without a negative. In this case, a slightly tensed forearm will a mean slower recovery from pump.

Light bulb changer
balance jam, active expansion jam

A technique that is as easy to execute as changing a lightbulb.

1. Adopt the same starting position as you would when placing a standard thumb-up hand jam (see figure 44).
2. Insert your hand and forearm into the crack and place the top/back of your forearm against one crack wall (in this position the back of your hand will also likely touch the crack wall).
3. Now flex your wrist so that your hand starts to bridge the crack. As you flex your wrist, splay your fingers and thumb apart, then make them rigid

(either straight or with a slight bend, depending on the width of the crack) and finally reach each finger/thumb tip so that it comes into contact with the opposing crack wall.

4. The position of your fingers should resemble the position they would be in if you were to change a large light bulb.
5. You will have a single point of contact on one crack wall (the length of your forearm) and five points of contact on the opposing crack wall (the tips of each finger and your thumb—figure 77).
6. To keep this jam effective, it is massively important to keep rigidity through the fingers, whether they are bent or straight. To do this, tense your whole hand and imagine you're trying to grow longer fingers through the tips.

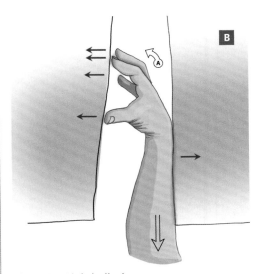

Figure 77. Lightbulb changer

7. This jam can also be used in smaller spaces. Instead of flexing the wrist so that your whole hand spans the crack's width, flex at the base of the fingers so just the fingers and thumb move across the gap. You will still end up with your five finger/thumb tip points of contact on one crack wall; however, on the opposing crack wall you will now have a single point of contact running from the knuckles, all the way down the back of the hand, across the back of your wrist, and then down your forearm.

It is worth noting that this technique can be used with your hand at any depth in the crack. You could have your hand close to the crack entrance, in which case the crack edge might run across your wrist. Or if the crack is deep enough you could have your whole arm inserted and the crack edge may well run across the back of your tricep or upper arm.

FOOT TECHNIQUES IN FIST CRACKS

Fist cracks are great for the feet. The size of the crack means you don't have to do that much twisting, yet your feet will still stick convincingly. Limited twisting means less pain, and, generally speaking, less pain means greater success!

Platform foot

powerful jam, passive expansion jam

As with any passive expansion jam, this technique is really simple as there is little technique required to make it work effectively. The key to this jam is less about *what* you do with your foot, and more about *where* you place your foot in the crack. The clue lies in the name: when you place your foot correctly, it should feel like you are standing on a platform. It should feel great.

The trick is to look for a place at the crack entrance which is slightly narrower than the width of your foot, but not so narrow that when you try to insert your foot it won't fit at all. You probably have around a centimetre to play with, which is why judging the crack's width and being able to compare it with the width of your foot is the secret to getting this technique to work properly.

1. Orient your foot so that the sole is facing down in the direction of the crack, and the top of your foot is facing up. Your toes should be pointing directly into the crack. In short, your foot should be in the same position as if you were just standing normally on flat ground.

2. Push your foot into the crack. If you have judged the width of the crack correctly, the sides of your climbing shoe should squeeze inwards as you push your foot inside. You may have to go for the push and wiggle technique—push into the crack with your foot and wiggle your heel from side to side—to get it to go in far enough. In the finishing position, the widest part of your foot should be jammed, the arch of your foot should be in line with the edge of the crack and your heel should be outside

the crack (figure 78). It is tempting to put your foot further inside, but the deeper you put your foot into the crack, the steeper you will make the climbing feel. A good platform foot jam is actually better with your foot closer to the edge of the crack.

3. You might consider putting your foot further into the crack if the jam feels as if it is sliding because the width of the crack is slightly too wide for your foot. In this case, slide the whole of your foot into the crack, so that your Achilles tendon is in line with the crack edge. When in the correct position, twist your toes either left or right so that the side of your heel touches the crack wall. This subtle twist and contact of the heel

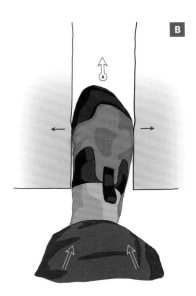

Figure 78. Platform foot

against the rock will stop the foot from sliding. Again, don't push your foot further into the crack than it needs to go, as this will make the climbing feel steeper than it actually is.

Heel-down technique
powerful or resting jam, active twisting jam

This technique can be used to good effect from wide hand cracks all the way up to fist cracks, and it feels less painful than a lot of twisting foot techniques. It can be useful on steeper ground, and when you are fully standing up and putting weight through the jam it can create a brilliant resting stance.

1. Adopt the same starting foot orientation that you would use to execute a toe jam (Chapter 2) or foot jam (Chapter 3).

2. Put your foot into the crack in this orientation, to a depth where the edge of the crack is in line with the arch of your foot. Place the top of your foot (the laces of your shoe) against one crack wall and the arch of your foot against the opposite crack edge. Once in this position, drop your heel down and inwards towards the centre of your body so the ball of your heel faces the ground. The arch of your foot should slide a short way down the crack edge and the top of your foot should be forced (twisted upwards) into the opposing crack wall (figure 79).

3. An easy way to help drop your heel is to straighten your leg and apply pressure through the foot jam. Straightening your leg also brings your knee

Figure 79. Heel-down technique: before heel drop

inwards and keeps everything in line with the crack.

4. If the crack is wider, push the inside edge of your climbing shoe down the opposing crack wall; this will bring your foot into a position halfway between a platform foot (earlier this chapter) and the heel-down technique, and will feel incredibly solid. Keep pushing down through the heel to ensure that the top of your shoe is continuously forced into the crack wall.

CLIMBING POSITIONING

Positioning on fist cracks is very similar to positioning on hand cracks. A palm-down fist jam translates to a thumb-down hand jam, and a palm-up fist jam translates to a thumb-up hand jam. I recommend reading the section in Chapter 3 about positioning on hand cracks as there are major overlaps. The following covers the slight changes you can do while fist jamming that aren't possible when climbing hand cracks.

There is one general piece of advice about positioning on fist cracks: for continuous movement, try to avoid having the top hand palm up as it will feel rather strange and inefficient. This doesn't mean to say you can't place your top hand palm up, rather that this position is usually used as a one-off to position yourself for a big move, or if the sequence leads you to do this.

FACE CRACKS

On vertical cracks the same positioning principles can be applied as on bomber hand cracks (Chapter 3). On diagonal cracks, one subtle change can be made: because you can insert your arm deeper into the crack, you will be able to rest your forearm on the lower crack edge, rather than just your wrist. This will help with extra friction and will enable you to rest the pump in your hand more effectively. In some cases you can actually gain so much friction from your forearms that you can release and rest your hands within the jam completely. On occasions, I've certainly been able to shake out both hands inside the crack while just hanging from the friction of my forearms.

CORNER CRACKS

Again, the same positioning principles can be applied on corner fist cracks as on corner hand cracks (Chapter 3), you just need to swap thumb down for palm down, and thumb up for palm up.

HANDS

The one difference between fist corner cracks and hand corner cracks is how deep you can place your arms inside the crack. If you are climbing in a layback style, you are able to insert more of your arm into the crack and are gaining more friction from the forearm. You can also start to lever the side of your fist jam against the crack wall inside the crack wall, and the bulk of your forearm over the crack edge that you are laybacking (as if you are trying to lever the crack open) very much like a forearm lever. This is a fantastic technique to aid recovery.

FEET

The feet can have two different positions, depending on whether you are laybacking or climbing straight in (Chapter 3). Before moving on to the positioning of the feet, it's important to know your inside foot from your outside foot or things will become really confusing.

- *Inside foot:* This is the foot which is naturally closest to the crack in the style that you are climbing (layback jamming/straight-in jamming). If the left side of your body is scraping up the face/corner wall, it will be your left foot that is your inside foot.
- *Outside foot:* This is the foot which is naturally furthest away from the crack in the style that you are climbing (layback jamming/straight-in jamming). If the left side of your body is scraping up the

face/corner it will be your right foot that is your outside foot.

CLIMBING IN A LAYBACK STYLE ON CORNER CRACKS

- *Inside foot:* This should be placed as your lower foot in the crack. The same technique as pinkie rand smear is used (Chapter 2), except the whole of your shoe should go into the crack, right up to the ankle. Push the sole of your shoe into one crack wall. Leave it solidly in position then pull the leg back so that the top of your foot, close to your ankle, makes contact with the crack edge. If the crack edge is sharp, this can become a little painful after a while: wearing high-top climbing shoes can help with this. (Figure 80).
- *Outside foot:* This should be placed as your top foot. The heel-down technique can be used as an effective jam in this position. And, of course, edges or smears can also be used if more appropriate.

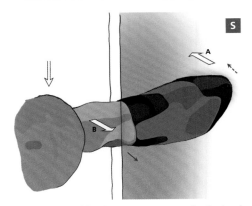

Figure 80. Positioning on corner cracks: layback style—inside foot

PETER CROFT

A legend of Yosemite climbing, Peter's outstanding free solos and free-solo link-ups were ahead of their time. He was the first person to free solo The Rostrum *and* Astroman *(both 5.11c) in Yosemite in a single day.*

FAVOURITE CRACK CLIMBING AREA?

I have to say Yosemite for variety, volume, and very big routes—oh, and very nice weather. I know some people will argue for Indian Creek because (1) you can lower back to the ground, and (2) you can place so much protection. I would argue back for the Valley because you can't and you don't need to (it is granite, after all).

FAVOURITE CRACK CLIMB?

Yeah . . . got a stack of them. I'd say the *Rostrum Roof* for single-pitch wonderfulness (although it does start 250 metres above the ground). Five metres off the belay you pull the lip, lose sight of your belayer, and you're all on your own. Supreme position, perfect splitter-ness and at the end, a summit big enough to party on!

MEMORABLE CRACK EXPERIENCE?

Again, I have a bunch running the range from embarrassing to heroic (at least in my head). Random pick: one day in Yosemite I went down to Cascade Falls to solo a finger crack called *Tips* (5.12a). Perfect, no one there—or so I thought. Roughly 30 metres long I was perhaps 12 metres up when I heard a high-pitched chirping/buzzing sound. Looking inside the crack I saw a bat wiggling his way towards my fingers—which had to look to him like an all-you-can-eat buffet of man flesh. I put it into high gear, but so did he: me finger jamming and him wing-barring—and keeping up. It was a classic contest of contrasting styles! After about 10 metres I left him behind, breathing a sigh of relief. *Tips*, though, is one of those Yosemite pitches that dead-ends at an anchor, requiring a rappel to get off. With no rope in the first place, I chalked up, psyched up and then speedily downclimbed. Sure enough, he was waiting for me and the race, this time down, was on again. Safe on the ground I inspected my hands. After any crack climb it's a point of pride to come away without a scratch. After inspecting all ten digits I could afford to smile—not even a nibble.

THE KNOWLEDGE

I'd say the most important piece of crack advice applies to finger and hand cracks—and it is this: thumbs up. Whenever possible, go thumbs up: it allows you to reach further with less effort.

Pop Quiz

1. Finger cracks or offwidths? I think that offwidths are a gateway technique to caving so I'd pick finger cracks every time.
2. Stemming or roof cracks? Now you're talking! It's a tie.
3. Hand jamming or hand stacks? Is that a serious question?
4. Knee lock or chickenwing? What is this, a book on spelunking?
5. Tape or no tape? Tape is for first aid not recreation. Same goes for drugs—within reason.
6. Cams or nuts? Cams when you can and nuts when you can't
7. Sandstone cracks or granite cracks? As sandstone is half stone and half sand I prefer granite—100 percent hard rock.
8. Short and hard, or long and pumpy? Long and pumpy—size matters
9. Pressure wound or rock rash? If the choice is between rashes and wounds, I'd pick a day on the couch with an enormous TV.
10. Colour preference of crack climbing trousers due to unfortunate mistakes: red or brown? White—own up to your mistakes!

Opposite: *Peter on* The Prow *(5.12b) on Cardinal Pinnacle, Eastern Sierra, California* (© Kevin Calder)

CLIMBING STRAIGHT-IN STYLE ON CORNER CRACKS

Inside foot

■ If using this foot as your top or bottom foot, both heel-down and platform foot techniques work in this position.

Outside foot

Platform foot techniques are most effective. Heel-down techniques can also be used, you will just not achieve as much of a camming action as the side wall will prevent the ball of your heel from twisting down as effectively.

You can also use the corner wall to your benefit. This technique can be used whenever there is a corner wall, but is especially useful when the crack is becoming very baggy for your feet to jam.

1. Place your foot in the crack in a platform footstyle.
2. Twist your foot so that the outside edge of your shoe makes contact with the crack wall and the inside edge of your heel makes contact with the corner wall (figure 81).

This technique can also be done with the other foot. In that case, your inside edge would be twisting into the crack wall and the outside edge of your heel would be in contact with the corner wall.

CLIMBING MOVEMENT

Like hand jamming cracks, fist jamming cracks often follow a less distinct sequence. Therefore, the same principles apply to climbing movement with fist jams as with hand jams (Chapter 3). The one area that is worth exploring separately, however, is big moves.

BIG MOVES

Because there is no twisting of the forearm when executing a fist jam (your arm is already in line with the crack), big moves can easily be done off both palm-up and palm-down jams. The same principles apply as with big moves off thumb-up hand jams (Chapter 3); however, this time imagine that your fist is wrapped around a pin (rather than a pin going through the centre of your palm) and you are rotating your fist around this to help make the big move. For example, your fist might rotate

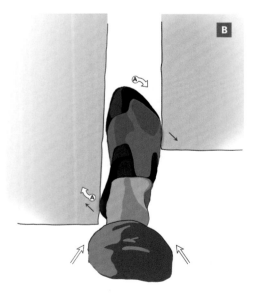

Figure 81. Positioning on corner cracks: straight-in style—platform foot with heel twist

from a palm facing up position to a palm facing in position, as you stretch and reach up from it (see figure 82).

BIG MOVES: MOVING OFF JAMS

Moving off a palm-up fist jam: Using your hand in a palm-up orientation can generate greater power and stability through the move (since you can engage the bicep more easily with your hand this way around). For example, imagine doing a bicep curl with a dumbbell—it's much easier with your palm facing towards you, rather than away from you. As you can generate more power through the move with your fist jam this way around, it can be a useful orientation when you have to lock off and stay stable through the move in order to reach the next hold with precision.

Moving off a palm-down fist jam: Using your hand in this orientation doesn't give you as much stability if you have to lock off on the jam to make a long move, but it can be surprisingly useful if you are able to rotate around the fist with a completely straight arm (i.e., hanging from the joints—structure not strength). You can lock the joints of your arm out and lean off and away from this jam with more ease than if your palm is facing up. This can be really useful if you are making a long reach from a vertical face and out into steeper terrain such as a horizontal roof. You can hang on the joints, lean out, and reach as far back as possible.

So, generally speaking, if you need to lock off and have stability through a big move, go palm up (figure 82). If you need to

Rob Pizem on Vesteggen *(Norwegian grade 6—roughly E1) on Stetind, the national mountain of Norway* (© Andrew Burr)

113

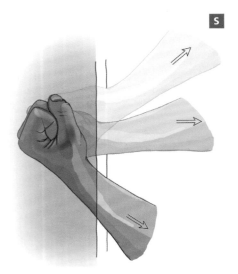

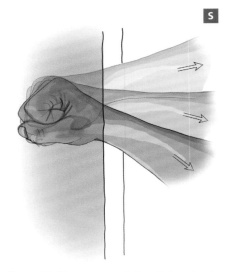

Figure 82. Big moves: rotating fist, palm up

Figure 83. Big moves: rotating fist, palm down

lean off and away from the jam while executing a big move, go palm down (figure 83).

BIG MOVES: MOVING TO JAMS

Moving to a palm-down fist jam: When you are making a big move to a fist jam, your hand will naturally want to position itself in a palm-down orientation, so this should be your first option.

Moving to a palm-up fist jam: It will probably feel unnatural and slightly awkward to make a big move into a palm-up fist jam, so only do this if the hold or sequence forces you to.

Opposite: *Caitlin McNulty hand/fist stacking on* Hypertension *(5.11a) in Squamish, Canada (© Irene Yee)*

CHAPTER 5

Offwidth Cracks

As soon as a crack is wider than the width of a fist it is classed as an offwidth: it is "off" the width you can move on comfortably. Many climbers dislike offwidth climbing; it's so far removed from the styles of climbing they first learnt, and it can be disheartening for them to feel as though they're back at square one. They try to crimp around the edge and inside of the crack. They try to layback or gaston the corner. They try to apply normal climbing techniques to a form of climbing which requires a very different approach. This is why offwidths can feel hideous.

Imagine how a road cyclist would feel if they went downhill mountain biking for the first time. They would obviously know how to ride a bike, but if they applied road cycling principles to downhill mountain biking they wouldn't stand a chance. In order to be successful, they must learn a completely new set of skills, and if they don't, they will really hurt themselves! Exactly the same principle applies with climbing and offwidth climbing: you have experienced climbing before, but you must accept that you are going back to the beginning and need to learn new skills in order to be successful.

Offwidth climbing isn't as nasty, hard or painful as is commonly perceived . . . *if it is done correctly*. If it's not, then you can expect to have a hard time getting off the ground, and if you do make it off the ground, you will most likely be heading home looking like you've tried to wrestle an alligator while blindfolded.

Here is a great quote from Bob Scarpelli, an old-school American offwidth climber:

You'll hear people call boxing the sweet science. Offwidth climbing is very much the sweet science of climbing because what happens is the brutality of the act disguises the craft. Good professional boxers have an incredible craft and really good offwidth climbers have that same craft. The brutality of it, the struggle of it, makes it seem like there's no art to it. But if you think that, you're on the wrong path.

I totally agree with Bob and believe offwidth climbing can be broken down as 50 percent technique, 35 percent physical aspects, 10 percent stubbornness and the

OFFWIDTHS: WHICH SIDE IN?

Before we dive into specific offwidth techniques, we need to consider the one question which is always asked before starting an offwidth crack: which side in should I go? In other words: should I insert the right or left side of my body into the crack? This will only truly be revealed when you start climbing, however you can generally make an accurate presumption from the ground before you set off.

Here are a few things to look for, in order of preference, before setting off:

1. *An offset:* Placing your back against an offset often results in the correct side of your body being inserted into the crack.

2. *A sharp crack edge:* A sharp edge can be useful as you can guppy the edge of it with your outside hand. You can also lean body parts against it to gain extra friction.

3. *A diagonal lean in the crack:* Putting your back against the slab side of the diagonal will usually result in the correct side of your body being inserted into the crack.

Obviously, you might have an offwidth with multiple features; I would prioritise them in the order listed above. For example, using your back against an offset trumps a sharp edge or a diagonal crack.

Sam Hamer following in the footsteps of the legendary crack master Joe Brown as he does battle with the surprisingly awkward offwidth Right Eliminate (E3 5c) at Curbar Edge in the Peak District, UK (© Mike Hutton)

ability not to give up, and 5 percent pain tolerance and the ability to suffer.

Notice how pain tolerance is only 5 percent; that's because if you master the techniques for offwidth climbing you shouldn't have to endure much pain. If you let your technique slip, it will have an effect on the other aspects. You will start to become tired, and tiredness further affects technique: poor technique results in thrutching, grinding, and scraping your way up the rock, which consequently makes for an unpleasant and painful experience. So, let's focus on that wide technique; before you know it, you'll be swimming with ease up these once-feared fissures.

HAND/HAND OFFWIDTH CRACKS

A hand/hand offwidth is a width of crack which requires two hand jams to be used in combination (along with other body parts to aid upwards movement) to fill the space efficiently.

At the start it will seem a bit alien to use your hands together as a single unit and then think about trying to move them, as we are accustomed to moving our hands independently in normal climbing. When you start climbing in this size of crack (and in hand/fist offwidths, covered later in this chapter) you'll begin to see the beauty of offwidth climbing.

To enable yourself to move your hands as a single unit, you have to be able to take them both off the rock at the same time. And if you can take both hands off the rock, you must have created a "no-hands rest." Thinking about it like this, offwidth climbing

at this size of crack should be a walk in the park as every move becomes a rest!

HAND TECHNIQUES

When you use your hands in combination with one another in the crack it is known as a "stack." Many different stacks can be used with the hands in this size of crack.

Butterfly jam: thumb up

powerful jam, active expansion jam, combination jam (two hand jams)

This is the most common hand/hand stack. It is called the butterfly jam because of the shape your hands make when you create it. It involves two thumb-up hand jams (Chapter 3) back to back with both palms in contact with the rock. To achieve this position, you have to cross your hands, with either your right crossed over the top of your left, or your left crossed over the top of your right.

Let's imagine you are crossing your right hand over the top of your left hand:

1. Place your left hand into the crack first, with your palm against the right crack wall. Your fingertips should be pointing up to the sky, and your forearm should be running down in line with the crack.

2. Cross your right hand over the top of your left and place the palm of your right hand against the left crack wall. Rather than pointing your fingertips up to the sky, point them into the crack. As you cross your hands, the thumb side (left hand) and pinkie side (right hand) of your wrists should touch.

3. When your hands are in position, execute standard hand jams with both

hands at the same time. Try to create a stack where both hand jams are the same size and are creating equal force; this will help the stack remain stationary and work more effectively. The main areas of contact will be your palms against the rock and the flats of the backs of your hands against one another. The index knuckle of your right hand might start to nestle between the knuckles of your left hand.

When you pull up using this jam, both hands should work in combination: they are both creating equal force against one another to keep them in position (figures 84 and 85).

You can use your hand jams to cater to the width of the crack. If the crack is slightly wider, you might have to cup the hand jams out a bit. If the crack is slightly narrower, you might have to hand jam against a flat hand: if this happens, remember to keep executing the hand jam procedures with the hand that is flat, i.e., keep trying to touch your thumb to your little finger even though you won't be able to get it into the palm of your hand. This helps keep rigidity and tension through the jam. Rigidity through the jam is important: without it the whole stack will slip out of the crack. Don't let that happen to your hand stack.

A final tip: although it is better to try to keep both hands equal in expansion size, you can deviate slightly from this if you notice that one hand is becoming more pumped than the other. A flat hand jam is less strenuous than a cupped hand jam, so you can use this to your advantage. Make

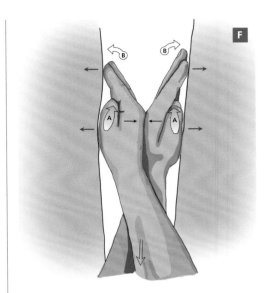

Figure 84. Hand/hand offwidth cracks: butterfly jam, crossed hands, thumbs up (combination 1)

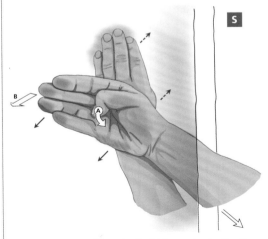

Figure 85. Hand/hand offwidth cracks: butterfly jam, crossed hands, thumbs up (combination 1)

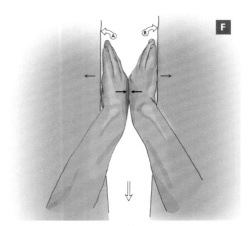

Figure 86. Hand/hand offwidth cracks: butterfly jam, uncrossed hands, thumbs down (combination 3)

your pumped hand flatter and take some of the strain through your fresher hand by cupping it out in the stack.

Butterfly jam: thumb down
powerful jam, active expansion jam, combination jam (two hand jams)

This is the least common hand/hand stack. I've seen some people use it, but I can't remember a time I've actually used it when another jam wouldn't have been more beneficial. Nevertheless, it does work, and if it works for you it's a good skill to have in your crack climbing repertoire.

This jam uses both hands, back to back, thumbs down (standard thumb-down hand jams—see figure 48). The palm of your left hand should be against the left crack wall, and your right palm should be against the right crack wall. Your hands do not cross. The fingertips of both hands should be pointing up and into the crack and your hands should be mirroring one another. As both hands are identical (just mirrored) in the crack, you should try to equate this back to the direction of pull, force, and expansion you create with them: make these equal.

The finished position (figure 86) might look like you are trying to prise open an elevator door: make sure you don't start to do this as your elbows will lift up and out which will make you want to gaston the crack edge rather than jam inside the crack.

Due to the position of your arms and elbows while executing this jam, it can be difficult to place the stack deep into the crack (unless the crack edge is flaring). To make sure it is done correctly, keep closer to the crack edge and don't try to over-stretch into the depths.

As I said, this stack isn't commonly used. The position feels unnatural and the orientation of your arms prevents good arm alignment with the crack. However, never say never to this jam: it is a solid position and can be useful in some situations. An example is when transitioning into and out of a crack: you might need to take the crack as a layback, pull into it, then layback out the other side of it.

Reversed butterfly jam
powerful jam, active expansion jam, combination jam (two hand jams)

This hand stack is the only double-handed jam which consists of putting the palm of one hand against the back of the other. One hand is always thumb up and the other

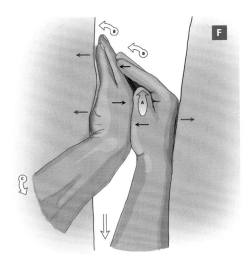

Figure 87. Hand/hand offwidth cracks: reversed butterfly jam, uncrossed hands, left and thumb down, right hand thumb up (combination 5)

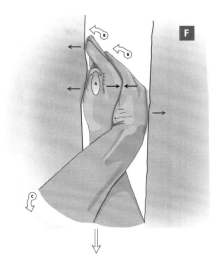

Figure 88. Hand/hand offwidth cracks: reversed butterfly jam, crossed hands, left hand thumb down, right hand thumb up (combination 6)

is always thumb down. I think standard thumb-up butterfly jams are more secure, but it can sometimes be difficult to place a butterfly jam since the nature of the crack can mean the jam is very deep inside or awkward to seat (for example on flared cracks or corner cracks).

Butterfly jams also force you into a position which is square on to the rock, which means your shoulders and elbows prevent you from reaching into the depths of the crack. If you feel like you can't seat the jam in deep enough, then the reversed butterfly could solve your problems. It places the forearms closer together—they lie on top of one another, rather than spreading apart from the wrist as in butterfly jams—and rotates the shoulders out of the square-on

position: both of which enable you to place your hands deeper inside the crack.

1. *First hand:* Place the hand which will be palm to rock first and complete a standard hand jam.

2. *Second hand:* Place the heel of the palm of your second hand against the backs of your first hand's fingers and slide this second hand back so both hands overlap perfectly. The palm of one hand should be against the back of the other. Now complete a standard hand jam with the second hand. Try to make the sizes of each hand jam identical.

3. It can be easy for the second hand to "collapse" out of the hand jamming position when it is on top of the other

hand. Try to keep good jamming form with this hand: brace with the fingers and push the thumb towards the little finger and brace with the fingers.

There are four combinations of the reversed butterfly which can have either uncrossed or crossed hands:

- *Uncrossed:* Right hand thumb down against right side of the crack, left hand thumb up
- *Uncrossed:* Left hand thumb down against left side of the crack, right hand thumb up (figure 87)
- *Crossed:* Right hand thumb up against left side of the crack, left hand thumb down crossed over the top (figure 88)
- *Crossed:* Left hand thumb up against right side of the crack, right hand thumb down crossed over the top

ARM TECHNIQUES
Bicep jam
powerful jam, resting jam, active expansion jam

As it's not too strenuous, a bicep jam (figure 89) is a great technique for resting an arm and your hands on this width of crack. If you want to use this jam for movement, then it is best used in conjunction with the upside-down guppy (step 5, below).

It should be noted that if you have either Popeye-sized biceps or twiglets for guns then this jam will only work on a larger or smaller size of crack.

1. *Orientation:* Turn your hand so that your palm is facing up in the direction of the crack and the back of your hand is facing down towards the ground.

2. *Insertion:* Insert your hand into the crack at just below shoulder height. When you insert your hand, make sure the rest of your arm is straight: do not bend at the elbow or tense or expand the tissue surrounding the elbow or bicep. Put your hand into the crack so that your whole arm is inside and the crack edge is against your armpit.

3. *Expansion:* Now imagine there is a pin going through the elbow joint. Keeping your bicep stationary, rotate your forearm up around this imaginary pin (i.e., flex at the elbow, like you would when tensing your bicep muscle), and bring your hand back out of the crack. The action of flexing the elbow will expand your bicep and the tissues around your elbow joint and produce an outwards force against the crack walls, jamming the arm into place.

4. *Resting:* If the bicep jam is tight, you will be able to keep your hand free and shake out any jamming pump that you may have.

5. *Hand technique (upside-down guppy):* If the jam is not quite as tight, the hand of the arm which is doing the bicep jam can perform an upside-down guppy on the crack edge (thumb pointing towards the floor). As well as giving a bit more security to the bicep jam, this extra technique can also twist the elbow in to the crack wall which adds a twisting jamming action to the expansion jam. If you can't perform an upside-down guppy, then extra twisting can be achieved by pushing

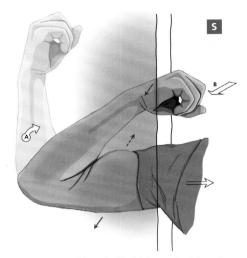

Figure 89. Hand/hand offwidth cracks: bicep jam

the side of the hand against the crack edge. Although this can be done in either direction, I find pushing the pinkie finger side of the hand into the crack edge to be the most effective.

6. Finally, there is one more trick which can help keep the bicep jam in place. Using your free hand, pull the hand of the bicep jam down so it touches the top of your shoulder; this will further increase the expansion of the tissues around the elbow and bicep. If you are going to use this technique, you have to be sure that the bicep jam is going to hold, as your free hand is no longer in use on the rock.

LEG AND FOOT TECHNIQUES

When describing techniques with the legs and feet in offwidth cracks, we look at both the inside leg and foot (those jammed inside the crack) and the outside leg and foot (those jammed on the edge of the crack).

INSIDE LEG AND FOOT
Leg (calf lock)
powerful jam, active twisting jam

1. *Orientation:* Insert your leg into the crack at waist height—your kneecap and toes should be pointing up towards the sky. The higher you can keep your leg, the less strenuous it will be for your core muscles to keep your upper body close to the wall. If your leg drops, your upper body will start to tip out from the crack and the climbing will become much more difficult, so keep that leg high. In some cases you can actually place your inside leg over the top of your hands—even on vertical terrain—at around head height or above, effectively putting you in a semi-upside-down position. This transfers some of the stress from your core to your leg and foot, and it is a good option if you have the strength and ability to place it that high.

2. *Insertion:* For the average person on this width of crack (and it obviously depends on how skinny or broad your leg is), your leg will be able to be inserted up to your knee; at this point it will most likely be too wide to fit any further inside.

3. *Twisting:* Now that your leg is inserted, you can twist it either clockwise or anticlockwise—as if your leg were a key in a lock. My preference is to twist

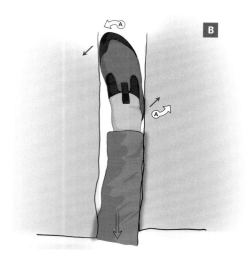

Figure 90. Inside leg in hand/hand offwidth cracks: calf lock and frogged foot

my left leg clockwise, and my right leg anticlockwise. When you twist your leg, your calf muscle should turn up against the crack wall and your shin will come into contact with the opposing crack wall and potentially the crack edge, creating a jam (figure 90). The remainder—and probably the most important part—of this jam is all down to the foot technique.

Foot

After twisting the leg inside the crack, there are two options for the foot.

Frogged foot

powerful jam, active twisting jam

This is the natural way to have your foot because it is the way it automatically moves and jams as you turn your leg into the crack.

1. Keep the sole of your shoe facing into the crack and your toes pointing upwards (how you have inserted your leg).
2. If turning your right leg in the crack (anticlockwise), the outside edge of your heel and the inside edge of your big toe should touch opposing crack walls (figure 90). It's important you forcefully twist the foot and ankle to make it stick.
3. Don't forget about the twisting of the leg: remembering to twist the whole leg will automatically put you into the starting process of the frogged foot jam.

Banana foot

powerful or resting jam, active rotational jam

This jam can be more awkward to seat properly; however, if you are able to get it in, it will feel much more secure and can sometimes even feel as if it's stuck.

1. This foot jam involves a whole 90-degree twist of the lower leg. Twist the leg so that your kneecap is no longer pointing towards the sky, but instead facing the crack wall. In order to do this, you will have to point your toes into the crack (or you won't be able to twist your leg enough). Imagine pointing your toes like a ballerina.
2. With your toes pointing into the crack, as you twist your leg you should be able to get the top of your foot (the laces of your shoe) and the ball of your heel touching the opposing walls inside the crack. When your foot is in

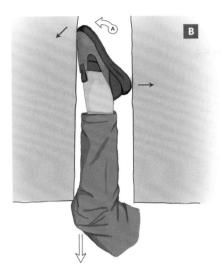

Figure 91. Inside leg in hand/hand offwidth cracks: banana foot

this banana position, your pointed toes will automatically want to flex back into their original position, forcing the two contact points hard into the walls and making the foot jam feel very solid (figure 91).

Outside foot

The "outside" foot is the foot which can feel as though it's flailing around on the outside of the crack and not being much use at all . . . *if it's not used efficiently.* If you feel like your outside foot is not working properly and you neglect it, this is when your offwidth troubles will start. You will begin to thrutch, grind, and pull hard with all the body parts that are inside the crack. If you do this, your body is going to get cut, squashed, bruised, and battered. I can't emphasise enough how important the outside foot is in offwidth climbing. Using it correctly or incorrectly can make or break you: incorrect, and you're likely to end up in a bloody heap at the bottom of the crag and have to get airlifted to the ER; correct, and you'll return home unscathed and successful—an offwidthing hero!

The outside foot can be used in a number of different ways. Some of the three techniques described below will feel better than others for different people, depending on their ankle and hip flexibility. Also, the nature of the climb might lend itself to one technique over another.

Frogged foot (or heel first)
powerful jam, active twisting jam

This is my preferred method for the outside foot; I probably use it 90 percent of the time. However, it is often neglected as you need reasonably flexible hips to get the correct positioning to make it work effectively. If you can make it work, it will feel totally solid.

1. *Orientation:* Rotate the hip of your outside leg outwards, so that your kneecap is pointing away from the crack. The sole of your outside foot should be facing the ground and in the direction the crack is travelling, your toes should be pointing away from the crack, and your heel should be the part of your foot which is closest to the crack entrance.

2. *Insertion:* Insert your heel into the crack first, deep enough that the edge

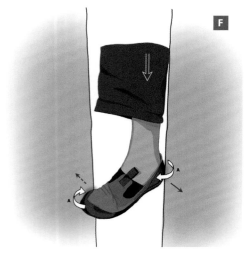

Figure 92. Outside leg in hand/hand offwidth cracks: frogged foot

of the crack lies just past the arch of your foot (roughly to where your foot is at its widest).

3. *Twisting:* Place the outside edge of your heel against one crack wall and point your toes slightly downwards. As you have opened up your hips, and placed your heel into the crack first, your outside foot will automatically want to turn back around into a normal position. Allow this to happen so that the inside edge of your shoe touches the opposing crack edge (heel on crack wall, toe on crack edge). You should aim to get the crack edge running across the base of your big toe. (This is why you need to point your toe slightly downwards, as the crack is still reasonably narrow for bridging

your foot across.) Placing your big toe on the edge of the crack gives you the pushing power that you can get from the toes (figure 92).

When using this frogged foot technique, the overall position of your whole body should have you looking sideways along the rock face outside of the crack (rather than looking into the crack). The hip of your outside leg should have opened up and you should feel like you are climbing the crack side on.

Twisted foot (or toe first)
powerful jam, active twisting jam

This is a jam I use only very occasionally in specific situations; it's not my preferred method. However, the majority of people prefer this jam as it is much easier to place than a frogged foot jam. It can also be a good option on this size of crack as it is very close to being platform foot size (Chapter 4), so a limited amount of twisting and rotation is needed to get it to work.

The downside of this jam is that it feels harder to maintain as you must actively perform the twisting motion, rather than your body automatically doing it, as in the previous technique.

1. *Orientation:* Position your outside foot so that the sole of your shoe is facing down towards the ground and in the direction of the crack, and your toes are pointing into the crack.

2. *Insertion:* Insert the whole of your foot into the crack, toes first, and place the inside edge of your heel against one crack wall. Don't place the foot too

deep—your heel should be just inside from the crack edge.

3. *Twisting:* Keeping the inside edge of your heel against the wall, point your toes slightly downwards and twist your foot outwards (away from the centre line of your body), so the outside edge of your pinkie toe makes contact with the facing crack wall. When you stand on the foot, maintain the outwards twisting pressure, but push through the heel rather than the toe to move upwards. By pushing through the heel, you will force your toe (which is pointing slightly downwards) up and into the opposing crack wall with significantly more pressure, gaining some "active rotational jamming" characteristics, helping the jam feel more solid (figure 93).

When using this twisting foot technique, the overall position of your whole body should have you looking into the crack, rather than sideways along the rock face outside the crack, as in the frogged foot technique. Your hips will be square on to the crack entrance.

Banana foot
powerful jam, rotational jam

I am unlikely to choose banana foot (figure 94) over the previous two methods, but I have seen people make progress with it when they have been unable to master the frogged foot or twisted foot techniques. It's worth noting and knowing.

1. *Orientation:* Orient your foot so that the inside edge of your shoe runs parallel with the rock face. Flex at your

Figure 93. Outside leg in hand/hand offwidth cracks: twisted foot

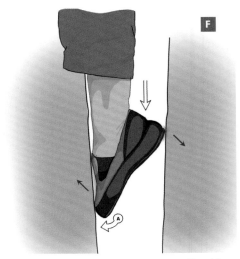

Figure 94. Outside leg in hand/hand offwidth cracks: banana foot

ankle so that your toes point down towards the ground. Imagine you were pointing your toes like a ballerina: the heel of your foot should be higher than your toes.

2. *Insertion:* Insert your foot into the crack in this position and place the heel of your foot against one crack wall.

3. *Rotation:* The flexion you have created in your ankle will automatically want to correct itself (mechanically) and bring your toes upwards. As your toes lift upwards, the top of your foot will be forced into the opposing crack wall. When you put pressure through this foot, make sure you stand through your heel, as this will force the top of your foot into the opposing wall more aggressively. It's very important not to stand through your toes in this jam as this will take pressure away from the heel and your foot will slide down the crack.

Hand/hand offwidth cracks can be quite tight for this jam (and of course it's all dependent on foot size), so you may find your foot doesn't fit that easily. If this is the case, bring your heel out of the crack and apply a heel-down technique (Chapter 4).

CLIMBING POSITIONING

Positioning on offwidths is all about using the correct hand stack for whichever side of your body is in the crack, or for the type of crack you are climbing. One stack could feel very awkward indeed and put your forearms (or whole body) completely out of position, whereas a different stack may turn

HAND/HAND STACK COMBINATIONS
Butterfly jam, crossed hands (thumbs up)
1. Right hand crossed over the top of left hand
2. Left hand crossed over the top of right hand
Butterfly jam, uncrossed hands (thumbs down)
3. Both hands thumbs down, no crossing of hands
Reversed butterfly jam, uncrossed hands
4. Right hand thumb down against the right side of the crack, left hand thumb up
5. Left hand thumb down against the left side of the crack, right hand thumb up
Reversed butterfly jam, crossed hands
6. Right hand thumb up against the left side of the crack, left hand thumb down crossed over the top of the right hand
7. Left hand thumb up against the right side of the crack, right hand thumb down crossed over the top of the left hand

your shoulders or body so that they sit much better. You should aim to get your inside shoulder (if climbing right side in, this would be your right shoulder) turned inwards and sitting closest to the crack entrance.

This section outlines all seven combinations of hand/hand stacks (see chart above). It then looks at different scenarios (or types of cracks) and which combinations will work to your advantage and turn that inside shoulder into position.

FACE CRACKS
Positioning on vertical cracks
(See Page 55 for a description of vertical face cracks.)

If climbing right side in:

- Combination 2: the best, most mechanical option for this kind of crack.
- Combination 3: as this jam is mirror imaged on both sides, you can use it right side in when climbing.
- Combinations 5 and 6: if you want to use reversed butterfly jams, then these are your two best options. Keeping your right hand thumb up automatically brings the inside arm in line with the crack (there is no need to twist the forearm, like in a thumb-down hand jam) and turns the shoulder against the crack entrance.

If climbing left side in:

- Combinations 1, 3, 4, and 7.

Positioning on diagonal cracks

(See page 58 for a description of diagonal face cracks.)
On diagonal cracks, reversed butterfly jams begin to have their advantages over standard butterfly jams. The undersides of the forearms lie comfortably across the lower crack edge and it feels like a more natural position to adopt.

Hands

If the crack is leaning to the left (and you are climbing right side in):

- Combinations 5 and 6: These combinations keep the palms of both hands against the lower crack edge, which rests the undersides of the forearms against the crack edge. Combination 6 (keeping your right hand as your bottom hand) has the slight advantage because you can release from the stack and still maintain

Figure 95. Positioning on vertical hand/hand offwidth cracks: combination 2

contact with the crack wall while you move your left hand along.

- Combination 2: If using crossed butterfly jams feels more secure, then this is the best option you can use because, again, you can release from the stack and maintain contact with the crack wall with your lower hand (right hand) while moving your leading hand (left hand).
- Combination 3: This can also be used if the crack lends itself to using this jam over another. However, for general positioning it can feel awkward.

If the crack is leaning to the right (and you are climbing left side in):

- Combinations 1, 3, 4, and 7.

Pop Quiz

1. Finger cracks or offwidths? Finger cracks
2. Stemming or roof cracks? Stemming
3. Hand jam or hand stack? Hand stack
4. Knee lock or chickenwing? Knee lock
5. Tape or no tape? Tape
6. Cams or nuts? Nuts (old habits are hard to break)
7. Sandstone cracks or granite cracks? Granite
8. Short and hard, or long and pumpy? Long and pumpy
9. Pressure wound or rock rash? Neither
10. Colour preference of crack climbing trousers due to unfortunate mistakes, red or brown? Brown

RANDY LEAVITT

A crack technician, Randy has helped push standards forwards by inventing new techniques—such as the "Leavittation" stack, the act of using leg and foot jams to progress stacked hands—that are still used today in many of the world's hardest crack climbs. In 1999 he made the first ascent of the stemming masterpiece Book of Hate *(5.13d) in Yosemite.*

FAVOURITE CRACK CLIMBING AREA?

The Needles is my favorite crack climbing area. In addition to the spectacular lime-green-covered rock and dramatic spires, the climbing itself is brilliant in a magical way. For example, if a crack runs thin, a foothold might magically appear. That happens over and over. If you need better texture for a smear, then often you will find the texture exactly where you need it. In other words, this place was made for free climbing—especially the cracks.

BEST CRACK CLIMBING EXPERIENCE/ FAVOURITE ROUTE?

Romantic Warrior (5.12b) takes an elegant, obtuse dihedral line up the spectacular south face of the Warlock Needle at the Needles, Sequoia, California. Unlike Yosemite—which always seems to have some heinous chimney, offwidth, or some type of unpleasant climbing—*Romantic Warrior* has no bad moves in nine pitches. Mostly 5.11+ and 5.12 finger jamming, with an insecure 12b stemming pitch for a crux, this route defines elegance with its singular line.

MEMORABLE CRACK CLIMBING EXPERIENCE?

In the late 1970s, I went to an offwidth climb in Yosemite with some Valley locals (including John Yablonski) called *Bad Ass Mama* (5.11d). After I watched the locals try to top-rope up this thing with chickenwing technique, I realised a new offwidth crack technique of hand stacking (with alternating foot or knee locks) might work "outside." This was a technique Tony Yaniro and I had been working to develop on a parking structure crack in Los Angeles. I cruised up the Yosemite offwidth in this fashion and I believe Yabo was the one who called it Leavittation. The other locals said it was an interesting technique, but you would not be able to lead *Bad Ass Mama* that way. I soon returned and led it using the Leavittation offwidth technique.

THE KNOWLEDGE

If you want to do well at crack climbing, you have to be committed. With sport climbing, it is much easier to talk yourself into climbing to the next bolt. But in crack climbing, there is usually nothing ahead except (maybe) an obvious hand jam, foothold, or an easy piece of protection to place. So, if you commit to climbing ahead to some goal (i.e., a hand jam or a stance), you won't pump out and spend way too much time on your jams. Spending too much time on a crack pitch is a good way not to succeed.

Opposite: Randy using a range of techniques somewhere near his home in San Diego
(© Brian Spiewak)

CORNER CRACKS

Positioning on corner cracks

There are two positioning options on corner cracks:

- *Swinging into the corner*: you might choose to do this if you want to climb more securely and use pure crack technique.
- *Swinging away from the corner*: you might choose to do this if you want to adopt a layback-style approach, if you think you might need to come out of the crack in order to layback in a few moves' time, or if you want to climb the crack straight in but with less friction from the corner wall.

Hands

If climbing a corner right side in:

- Combinations 2, 4, and 7: swinging into the corner.
- Combinations 1, 5, and 6: swinging away from the corner.

If climbing a corner left side in:

- Combinations 1, 5, and 6: swinging into the corner.
- Combinations 2, 4, and 7: swinging away from the corner.

If transitioning from swinging away from the corner to swinging into the corner: You might want to transition from a layback/bridged position (swinging away from the corner) to a straight-on position (swinging into the corner). If climbing right side in, for example, then using combinations 1, 5, and 6 to pull your body into the corner works well; your wrists are aligned correctly to let you pull your body forcefully into the corner. Once your body has been pulled into the corner, switch to stacking options 2, 4, or 7 to keep your body in a straight-on position and prevent it from wanting to swing away from the corner again. If you initially try to pull into the corner crack using the latter stacking options, you will find that your wrists aren't aligned properly and it will become awkward and you'll start disrupting the quality of the stack.

Legs and feet

- *Swinging into the corner:* If you climb in this style, then using your legs and feet with the techniques described in the leg and foot techniques section above will work well. One other technique that can be used with the outside foot is to bridge your foot across the corner (see "Offwidth Foot Technique" in "Feet in Corner Cracks" in Chapter 2) rather than across the edge of the crack.
- *Swinging away from the corner:* You might choose to climb in this style if there are more face holds or better bridging positions. Using bridging techniques in combination with stacking can give good respite from the offwidth techniques.

HAND/FIST OFFWIDTH CRACKS

A hand/fist offwidth is a width of crack which requires a hand jam and a fist jam to be used in combination (along with other body parts to aid upwards movement) to fill the space efficiently. It is therefore slightly wider than a hand/hand offwidth crack. When it comes to using both hands as a single unit, hand/fist offwidths are the easiest size of crack to climb. The body parts fit together nicely and they match up well. You are able to create a solid unit with the hands (hand/fist stacking), and also solid units with the legs and feet. If you can master this size of crack, then the stationary positions can start to feel very restful, which is not only functional but will also be very rewarding for your climbing.

HAND TECHNIQUES

When you use your hands in combination with another in the crack it is known as a "stack." This section looks at the technique for a hand/fist stack, where one hand is executing a hand jam and one hand is executing a fist jam, with both hands working together as a single unit. There are numerous different combinations of hand/fist stacks that can be used in this size of offwidth. I will first describe how to execute one of the most common combinations, and then look at all the different combinations possible.

Hand/fist stack
powerful jam, active expansion jam, combination jam, (hand jam and fist jam)

This is the description for the technique for a hand/fist stack with a left-hand hand jam and a right-hand fist jam (figure 96). The technique can obviously be reversed with the left hand as the fist and the right hand hand jamming (figure 97).

1. Place your left hand against the right crack wall in a thumb-up position. Your fingertips should be pointing up and into the crack directly up to the sky.

2. Cross your right fist (palm down) over the top of your left wrist and rest it in the crack next to your left hand (the wrists of your crossed hands will be touching). The thumb side of your fist should be touching the left crack wall and the pinkie side of your fist should be against the knuckles of your left hand (the hand jamming hand).

3. The key to getting this jam to work is lining up the hand and the fist correctly before you tense and make a solid unit. Aim to get the knuckles of your left hand in line with the indentation on the pinkie side of your fist. When you come to tense, the knuckles should sit in the small indentation of your fist.

4. Tense your right fist to create a fist jam (Chapter 4) and with your left hand create (and tense) a standard hand jam (Chapter 3). You should be forming an active expansion jam with both working parts. The knuckles of your left hand will expand and nestle into the indentation of your fist and help stop either part of the stack from sliding. Make sure you tense both the hand and the fist at the same time to create equal opposing pressures against the crack walls.

It is important with this stack **not** to create a chock with the hand jam and then slide the fist back on to it. If you do this, it is unlikely you will be able to get the hands to sit correctly in the stack (with the knuckles nestled into the fist indentation). Line the hands up, execute jams with the hand and the fist at the same time, lock them together with equal pressure, and pull through both the hand and the fist as a single unit.

The areas of contact when you have finished the jam will be:

- palm of hand jam touching right crack wall
- thumb side of fist touching left crack wall
- knuckles of hand jam and pinkie side of fist touching one another.

To accommodate for slight variations in the width of the crack, you can do two things to make your stack a little larger:

- *Alter the size of your hand jam:* Use cupped hand techniques (Chapter 3). This is the first thing to do, as altering the width of your hand jam is more secure than altering the width of your fist jam.
- *Alter the size of your fist jam:* Use teacup techniques (Chapter 4).

There are two common technique mistakes when hand/fist stacking. These should be avoided at all costs:

- **Never** put the palm of the hand jam against the fist, as this will collapse the hand jam and make it totally useless. Always think, "palm to rock."
- **Never** turn the hand jam into a sideways fist (i.e., tucking the fingers in rather than keeping them straight), as this will cut the backs of the fingers and be very painful. Always think "my hand jam should stay as a hand jam—fingers straight and thumb to little finger."

HAND/FIST STACK COMBINATIONS

There are lots of combinations when it comes to hand/fist stacking: crossed or uncrossed, palm up or palm down, thumb up or thumb down. It can all get very confusing and you can easily get lost in a whole world of fists and hands fondling cracks in many weird and wonderful ways. I've broken it down for you and looked at all the possible combinations. Firstly, you can do hand/fist stacks with both crossed and uncrossed hands; here are a few things to remember when using each.

Crossed hands

- Always have the hand jam thumb up.
- Using your fist palm down: cross your hands with your fist going over the top of your hand jam—as described in the example above (figures 96 and 97).
- Using your fist palm up: cross your hands with your fist going underneath your hand jam (figures 98 and 99). When you use your fist in a palm-up position, you will notice that the hand jamming knuckles will nestle into the indentation on the thumb side of your fist: this is fine, just follow the principles in the example above and apply it to this positioning.

Uncrossed hands

- Always have the hand jam thumb down (and remember: "palm to rock").
- Use your fist jam in a palm-up or palm-down position.

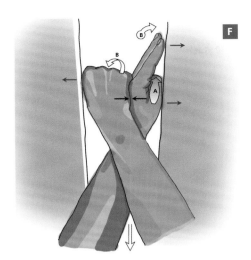

Figure 96. Hand/fist offwidth cracks: hand/fist combination 1

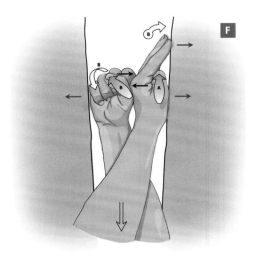

Figure 97. Hand/fist offwidth cracks: hand/fist combination 2

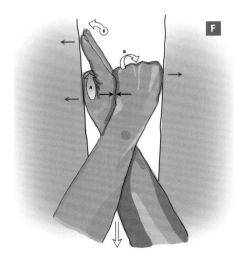

Figure 98. Hand/fist offwidth cracks: hand/fist combination 3

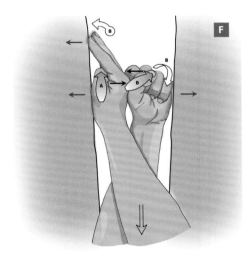

Figure 99. Hand/fist offwidth cracks: hand/fist combination 4

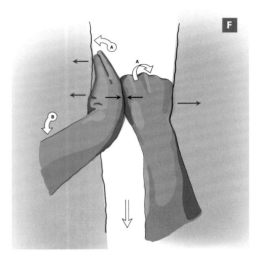

Figure 100. Hand/fist offwidth cracks: hand/fist combination 5

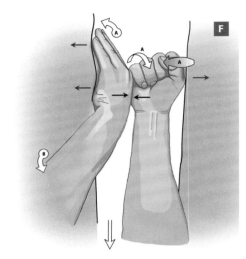

Figure 101. Hand/fist offwidth cracks: hand/fist combination 6

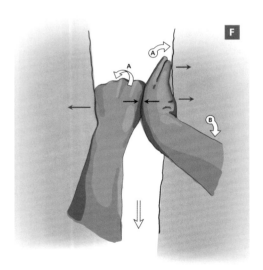

Figure 102. Hand/fist offwidth cracks: hand/fist combination 7

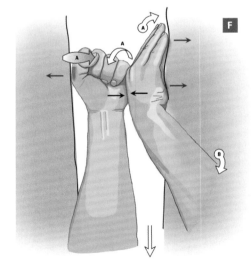

Figure 103. Hand/fist offwidth cracks: hand/fist combination 8

LEG AND FOOT TECHNIQUES

When describing techniques with the legs and feet in offwidth cracks, we look at both the inside leg and foot (jammed inside the crack) and the outside leg and foot (jammed on the edge of the crack).

INSIDE LEG AND FOOT
Leg (knee lock)
powerful or resting jam, active expansion jam

To use your inside leg effectively in this width of crack you need to use a knee lock. When a knee lock works it is one of the most solid offwidth positions. It doesn't rely on any form of strength to hold it in place; it is held in place purely by friction and expansion of the leg muscles and tissues. This means that if you can grasp the concept of how to do it, you should be able to execute it with ease.

1. *Orientation:* Insert your leg into the crack at waist height (same as calf lock, earlier in this chapter). Your toes and kneecap should be pointing up towards the sky, and the sole of your foot facing into the crack. Make sure your leg is as straight as possible as this relaxes the muscles in the leg and keeps it in its thinnest orientation. If your leg is bent, this will hinder how much of it will be inserted and will negatively affect the outcome of the finished jam.

2. *Insertion:* Put your leg into the crack past the knee and push it in as far as it will go—right to the groin if possible. It's important to push it as far into the crack as possible, so give it a really good shove. Go on—get it in there! It's a big body part and can handle a bit of rough treatment.

3. *Expansion:* Keep your thigh exactly where it is and—imagining there is a pin going sideways through the knee joint—rotate the lower half of your leg underneath your thigh and back towards the edge of the crack, so that your foot comes out of the crack all together. Think of it as trying to bring your Achilles tendon up to your bum. This action will expand the large muscle groups and tissues in the upper leg and around the knee, causing expansion and increased pressure against the crack walls, making the leg stick.

4. It is hugely important that when you rotate your lower leg out of the crack that you don't let your thigh drop down: keep it high and at waist level, exactly how you first inserted it. If you let it drop down, when you come to lower your body weight onto it (step 5) it will start to lever itself out of the crack. This will result in less surface area of leg in contact with the rock and suddenly the knee lock will feel very baggy and may start to slide.

5. Finally, lower your weight onto the leg that is in the crack (there may be an inch or two of "sagging" down—this is normal) and you will find that it sticks. (See figure 104). Again, when lowering your weight on to the leg, keep your thigh high and don't let it drop.

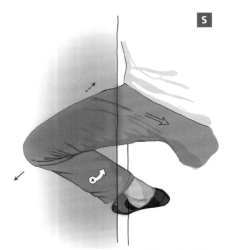

Figure 104. Inside leg in hand/fist offwidth cracks: knee lock and frogged foot

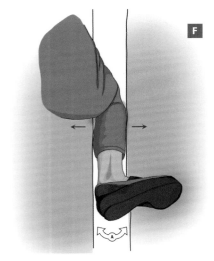

Figure 105. Inside leg in hand/fist offwidth cracks: knee lock and outside frogged foot

Foot (frogged foot)

After you have achieved a knee lock position you can gain extra purchase with your inside foot (which will now in fact be on the outside of the crack below your bum, but it is still known and described as the inside foot). There are two possible frogged foot positions:

Inside frogged foot: After finishing the knee lock your toes will be pointing towards the ground. To make more use of your foot, turn your foot up and inwards, so that your toes point in towards the centre line of your body. The top of your foot (so the laces of your climbing shoe) should be hooked round the crack edge and placed on the rock face outside of the crack (figure 104). If you are using your right foot, you should be twisting your ankle and toes in a clockwise direction.

Outside frogged foot: This is the same principle as above, but you turn your toes out and away from the centre line of your body. If you are using your right foot, you should be twisting your ankle and toes in an anticlockwise direction (figure 105).

Outside foot

The outside foot can be inserted and used in the crack in exactly the same way as the outside foot in hand/hand offwidth cracks (earlier in this chapter), either by using a frogged foot, twisted foot, or banana foot technique. As the hand/fist size of crack is a little wider than the hand/hand size, the frogged foot technique is very effective, and you don't need to be quite as flexible in the hips to make it work.

CLIMBING POSITIONING

As with hand/hand offwidth cracks, positioning on hand/fist offwidths is all about using the correct hand stack for whichever side of your body is in the crack. The aim is the same as on hand/hand cracks: try to get the inside shoulder (if climbing right side in, this would be your right shoulder) turned inwards and sitting closest to the crack entrance.

See the table below for all eight combinations of hand/fist stacks, followed by a list of scenarios (or types of cracks) and which combinations will work to your advantage and turn that inside shoulder into position.

Jason Kruk hand/fist stacking on Boogie 'til You Poop *(5.11b) at the Cirque of the Uncrackables in Squamish, Canada (© Andrew Burr)*

HAND/FIST STACK COMBINATIONS
1. Crossed hands: left hand thumb up, right fist over the top palm down (figure 96)
2. Crossed hands: left hand thumb up, right fist underneath palm up (figure 97)
3. Crossed hands: right hand thumb up, left fist over the top palm down (figure 98)
4. Crossed hands: right hand thumb up, left fist underneath palm up (figure 99)
5. Uncrossed hands: left hand thumb down, right fist palm down (figure 100)
6. Uncrossed hands: left hand thumb down, right fist palm up (figure 101)
7. Uncrossed hands: right hand thumb down, left fist palm down (figure 102)
8. Uncrossed hands: right hand thumb down, left fist palm up (figure 103)

FACE CRACKS
Positioning on vertical cracks
(See page 55 for a description of vertical face cracks.)

If climbing right side in:

- Combinations 2 and 5: These will bring the inside (right) shoulder really close to the crack entrance. These will feel secure and keep your body close to the rock (figure 106).
- Combinations 3 and 6: these will bring your shoulders more square on to the rock; the finished body positioning will be further away from the rock. These combinations are useful if you want to look down and see what you are doing with your feet, or for giving you the space you need to switch which side you have in the offwidth.

If climbing left side in:

- Combinations 4 and 8: these feel secure.
- Combinations 1 and 7: for a freer, more square-on position.

Positioning on diagonal cracks
(See page 58 for a description of diagonal face cracks.)

Hands

If the crack is diagonal there are three things you can do which will make your offwidthing life easier:

- *Place the hand jam on the lower crack wall:* By having the hand jam on the lower crack wall as you position the stack you will be able to hold on to the crack wall with the flat of your palm (like holding on to a sloper) rather than trying to hold on with the side of your fist.

Figure 106. *Positioning on vertical hand/fist offwidth cracks: combination 2*

- *Place the leading hand as the hand jamming hand:* By using the leading hand as the hand jamming hand, you can more comfortably reach further and you won't start to barn-door off to the side. So, if you are on a left-leaning crack then using your left hand as the hand jamming hand is the most efficient approach.
- *Place the fist in a palm-up position:* Using a palm up position forces the forearm and elbow to lie inside the crack. This helps gain extra friction, but is also a much comfier position as the side of your forearm doesn't lie across the crack edge.

So, the two most efficient ways would be:

- Left-leaning crack: uncrossed hands, left hand thumb down, right fist palm up (combination 6)
- Right-leaning crack: uncrossed hands, right hand thumb down, left fist palm up (combination 8)

Legs and feet

Only if the lean of the crack is very severe might you use slightly different techniques from the standard knee lock and outside foot techniques described earlier in this chapter.

The other option is to use your inside leg and foot how you would use them on an offwidth roof of this size (Chapter 9), and brace your outside leg and foot on the wall below you (see "Positioning on Diagonal Cracks" in Chapter 2).

CORNER CRACKS
Positioning on corner cracks

There are two positioning options on corner cracks of this size:

- *Swinging into the corner:* You might choose to do this if you want to use pure crack technique and climb more securely.
- *Swinging away from the corner:* You might choose this if you want to adopt a lay-back approach, if you think you might need to come out of the crack to layback in a few moves' time, or if you want to climb the crack straight in but with less friction from the corner wall.

Hands

If climbing a corner right side in:

- Combinations 2 and 6: swinging in to the corner

- Combinations 1 and 5: swinging away from the corner

If climbing a corner left side in:

- Combinations 4 and 8: swinging in to the corner
- Combinations 3 and 7: swinging away from the corner

Legs and feet

The same principles apply with the legs and feet as with hand/hand offwidths (see "Climbing Positions" earlier in this chapter).

FIST/FIST OFFWIDTH CRACKS

The fist/fist crack is a dreaded size. It is a width of crack which requires two fist jams to be used in combination (along with other body parts to aid upwards movement) to fill the space efficiently. While the body parts and the techniques that you use in a fist/fist offwidth crack will work, they will generally feel slightly less secure than those in hand/fist offwidths. So, while the techniques used in hand/fist-width cracks might feel like the components of a well-oiled machine with everything fitting and working together perfectly, the techniques in a fist/fist crack might feel more like an unserviced motor. You're fairly confident that everything works (as it worked last time), but you know that a little extra effort and care is needed to ensure you safely get from A to B. Bear this in mind when you are climbing this width and be aware that the techniques may feel less secure. However, be confident that they *will* work and get you to where you want to be—if used correctly and with extra care.

HAND TECHNIQUES

Fist/fist stacks

powerful jam, active expansion jam, combination jam (two fists jam)

Double-fist cracks require two fists to be used next to one another to form a single unit (a stack). If you have small hands in relation to the rest of your body, you might find that you have to resort to fist/fist stacks sooner than other people, which, if I'm honest, is an unfortunate offwidthing situation to find yourself in. Out of all the offwidth hand stacks (hand/hand, hand/fist, fist/fist), I find that fist/fist stacks are the most insecure. Personally, a baggy hand/fist stack trumps a secure fist/fist stack any day. That being said, there are subtle techniques which can make your life easier with double-fist cracks.

First, I will describe how to execute one of the most common combinations (combination 1: uncrossed hands, left fist palm down, right fist palm up), before looking at all the different combinations possible.

1. *Orientation:* Orient your left hand so that your fingertips are pointing up to the sky, your elbow is pointing to the ground and the back of your hand is facing towards you. Your forearm should be in line with the crack. This hand position should be much the same as the one you would adopt if you were stopping traffic. Now orient your right hand in a similar way but with your palm facing towards you (fingertips up, elbow down, forearm in line with the crack, palm facing towards you).

2. *Insertion:* Insert both hands into the crack in this position. Your left hand's pinkie finger will be touching the left crack wall and your right hand's thumb will be touching the right crack wall.

3. *Lining up:* When your hands are comfortably inside the crack, you can line them up to execute the jam. Getting the correct positioning of the two fists so they connect properly is the key to making this jam work. Rest the pulp of flesh down the side of your right hand (below the pinkie finger) in the groove that is formed by the index finger and thumb of your left hand. The fingertip pads of your right hand pinkie finger and left hand index finger should now meet.

4. *Active expansion:* Once in position you can form an active expansion jam. Simply execute two fist jams (Chapter 4) at exactly the same time. As with all stacks, the expansion and tensing of the jams should be done simultaneously and one should complement the other. So, try to make the fists equal in size and exert equal outwards pressure through both in order to form one solid unit. Your right hand should be palm up and your left hand palm down. The fleshy part of your right hand below your pinkie finger should nestle into the indentation on the side of your left fist.

The main contact points of the finished stack are:

- Thumb side of the right fist touching right crack wall.
- Pinkie finger side of the left fist touching left crack wall.

■ Pinkie side of right fist and thumb side of left fist connected in the middle.

To accommodate small variations in the width of the crack you can either place one or both thumbs inside or outside the fist. To make larger variations in width, use teacup techniques (Chapter 4) with the thumb that is touching the crack wall. It is possible to teacup with the fist, which is thumb against flesh, however it can start to feel less secure. If you use this technique, be sure to nestle the thumb joint into the indentation on the side of the other fist.

FIST/FIST STACK COMBINATIONS

As with all sizes of stack, many different combinations of fist/fist stacks can be used. All the combinations follow the same steps (above) to achieve the desired finished position: orient, insert, line up, active expansion.

It is possible to do fist/fist stacks with both crossed and uncrossed hands.

■ *Crossed hands:* One hand is crossed over (or under) the wrist of the other arm and your hands are placed side by side; your wrists will make an X shape.

■ *Uncrossed hands:* You will place your hands side by side; your wrists do not cross.

It is possible to do fist/fist stacks with hands either palm up or palm down.

■ Stacks which combine one fist in a palm-up position and one fist in palm-down position feel more secure as you are able to get effective nestling between the thumb and the pinkie finger. I tend to use these for powerful moves and general movement.

■ Stacks which use both hands either palm up or palm down feel less secure: there is either less surface area of the fists touching one another, or you don't get effective nestling between the fists which means the stack may feel like it wants to collapse in on itself. I tend to only use these if the sequence of the route forces me to.

It would be incredibly rare to use both fists palm up with crossed hands due to how awkward it feels, so I haven't listed this is a possible combination. However, never rule it out completely, and bear in mind that it could work on a rare occasion if the sequence forces you to do so.

Finally, when doing fist/fist stacks uncrossed and with both hands palm down, there are two slightly different and subtle ways you can position your fists together:

■ *Knuckles touching*: place the knuckles of your index fingers side by side, each fist being a mirror image of the other (figure 109). This will feel like bone is rubbing against bone.

■ *Knuckles nestled*: nestle the side of the index knuckle from the first fist (left hand) into the indentation of the second fist (right hand). Then nestle the thumb knuckle of second fist (right hand) into the indentation of the first fist (left hand). You will notice that the fists fit together more naturally, and that they are slightly staggered one above the other—in this case right is slightly higher than left. It can also be done with the left staggered above the right.

FIST/FIST STACK COMBINATIONS

1. Uncrossed hands: left fist palm down, right fist palm up (secure) (figure 107)

2. Uncrossed hands: left fist palm up, right fist palm down (secure) (figure 108)

3. Uncrossed hands: both fists palms down (insecure) (figure 109)

4. Uncrossed hands: both fists palms up (insecure) (figure 110)

5. Crossed hands: left fist palm up, right fist crossed over the top palm down (secure) (figure 111)

6. Crossed hands: right fist palm up, left fist crossed over the top palm down (secure) (figure 112)

7. Crossed hands: both fists palms down (insecure) (figure 113)

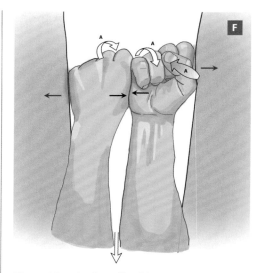

Figure 107. Fist/fist offwidth cracks: fist/fist combination 1

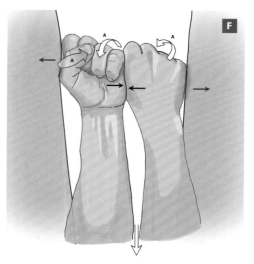

Figure 108. Fist/fist offwidth cracks: fist/fist combination 2

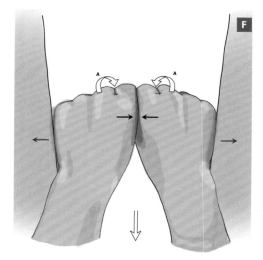

Figure 109. Fist/fist offwidth cracks: fist/fist combination 3

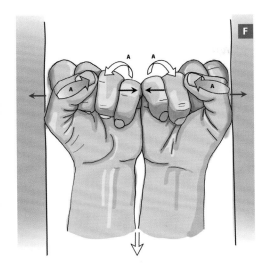

Figure 110. Fist/fist offwidth cracks: fist/fist combination 4

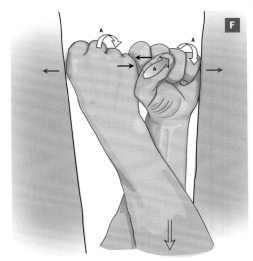

Figure 111. Fist/fist offwidth cracks: fist/fist combination 5

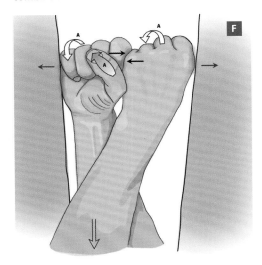

Figure 112. Fist/fist offwidth cracks: fist/fist combination 6

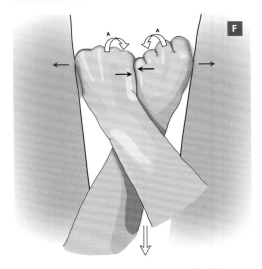

Figure 113. Fist/fist offwidth cracks: fist/fist combination 7

MASON EARLE

Mason Earle is an all-round crack master. He has climbed some of the hardest cracks on the planet across all styles—from the thinnest of tip seams to mindbendingly complicated offwidth puzzles. Perhaps his most outstanding crack achievement is the first ascent of Stranger than Fiction (5.14-) in Utah.

FAVOURITE CRACK CLIMBING AREA?
The Utah desert will always be my favourite crack climbing area. I learned to climb in Moab, and it's where I fell in love with crack climbing. The desert sandstone produces some of the most mind-boggling cracks on the planet.

FAVOURITE CRACK CLIMB?
My favourite crack experience was doing the first ascent of *Stranger than Fiction*, a 5.14- finger crack in the Utah desert. It took me many attempts to send this crazy, overhanging finger crack. On this route I used some wild beta, like taking my right shoe off mid-pitch to jam my taped toes in the crack.

MEMORABLE CRACK EXPERIENCE?
Once, as I was reaching for the last hold on my project, I realised there was a big scorpion perched on the hold. I jumped down and watched as the scorpion escaped back into the crack.

THE KNOWLEDGE
Always watch out for deer and cows when driving into Indian Creek.

Pop Quiz
1. Finger cracks or offwidths? Finger
2. Stemming or roof cracks? Roofs!
3. Hand jam or hand stack? I love stacking.
4. Knee lock or chicken wing? I've chickenwinged on sport routes.
5. Tape or no tape? Tape please
6. Cams or nuts? What are nuts?
7. Sandstone cracks or granite cracks? Mmm, sandstone
8. Short and hard, or long and pumpy? Soft for the grade
9. Pressure wound or rock rash? Occupational hazards
10. Colour preference of crack climbing trousers due to unfortunate mistakes: red or brown? Tie-dye

Opposite: *Mason on X-Factor (5.13+) at Harq il-Hamiem, Gozo, Malta* (© Andrew Burr)

OTHER FIST / FIST TECHNIQUES

There are three sneaky variations that can be used if the crack is too big for a cupped-out hand/fist stack yet too small for a standard fist/fist stack.

Golfer's grip, double fist

powerful jam, active expansion jam, combination jam (two fist jam)

Bringing golf to offwidth climbing! That's right, we are using the grip that some golfers use with their clubs on a pleasant 18 holes and applying it to one of the burliest forms of offwidth climbing. Who would have thought it?

1. Follow steps 1–3 of a normal fist/fist stack: orient, insert, line up. (See "Hand Techniques in Fist/Fist Offwidth Cracks" earlier in this chapter.)

2. Instead of tensing and creating two fist jams side by side, interlink the fingers: pass the little finger of one hand (your left, in this case) between the index and middle fingers of your other hand (your right, in our example).

3. Now simultaneously tense both fists as normal, using your thumb on the outside or inside of the fist to account for subtle variations in width (figure 114).

4. The stack should be a few millimetres thinner than a normal fist/fist stack and feel solid and secure as you now have an attachment point in the centre of the stack which prevents the stack from collapsing.

This technique works with combinations 1, 2, 5, and 6.

Golfer's grip, double fist thumb grab

marginal jam, active expansion jam, combination jam (two fist jams)

This is an even thinner variation of the golfer's grip technique.

1. Follow steps 1 and 2 of the golfer's grip technique above.

2. As you start to tense the fist jams, grab the thumb that is in the centre of the stack with the other hand (so in this case, right thumb is grabbed by left fist). Now simultaneously tense both fists as normal. One thumb (in this example, your left) will sit normally on the outside of the stack, and the other thumb (your right) will be grabbed and wrapped inside the other fist (figure 115). This stack should be another few millimetres thinner than a standard golfer's grip, however it will probably feel a bit less secure as the nestling process is disrupted.

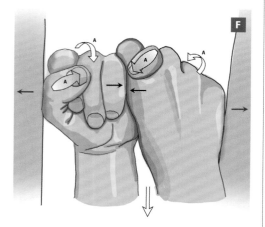

Figure 114. Fist/fist offwidth cracks: golfer's grip

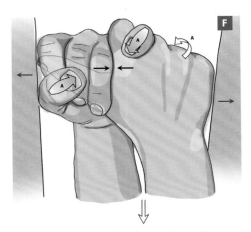

Figure 115. Fist/fist offwidth cracks: golfer's grip with thumb grab

This technique can work with combinations 1, 2, 5, and 6.

Double squished fist
powerful jam, active expansion jam, combination jam (two fist jams)

An alternative to the golfer's grip is to use a squished fist technique (Chapter 4) with either one or both fist jams. If you do use this method, make sure you use option 1 (wider crack) from the squished fist section as this will ensure that both fist jams line up correctly.

LEG AND FOOT TECHNIQUES IN FIST/FIST OFFWIDTH CRACKS

The leg and foot techniques in fist/fist cracks are very similar to those in hand/fist cracks. You should aim to emphasise the techniques to help them stick in a slightly wider crack.

When describing techniques with the legs and feet in offwidth cracks, we look at both the inside leg and foot (jammed inside the crack) and the outside leg and foot (jammed on the edge of the crack).

INSIDE LEG AND FOOT
Leg (thigh lock) and foot (frogged feet)
powerful jam, active expansive jam

In cracks of this width, the inside leg performs something called a thigh lock. This uses all the same procedures as a knee lock (earlier this chapter); the only difference is that you insert your leg a little bit further into the crack.

1. Follow step 1 (orientation) of the knee lock (see "Leg and Foot Techniques in Hand/Fist Offwidth Cracks," earlier this chapter).
2. When putting your leg into the crack you should be able to insert it further inside. It is likely you will be able to fit your whole leg inside, so the edge of the crack will run across your groin.
3. Now, follow steps 3, 4, and 5 of the knee lock procedure to complete the thigh lock.
4. You should use the frogged foot technique on the outside of the crack with your inside foot. The frogged foot technique is performed in exactly the same way as when using a knee lock.

Sometimes on this width of crack your thigh lock can feel a bit baggy even when you have executed the steps above. There is one extra little adjustment you can make to help it feel more secure. Lean your body off to the side of the crack: as well as getting expansion from the knee (through rotating your lower leg out), you can also twist the leg inside the crack (very similar to the action that you would use on a leg bar (See figure 120). The way you lean will depend on the direction you have decided to "frog" your inside foot on the crack edge: if you are using your right leg to thigh lock, and have frogged your foot/toes to the right, you will lean your body to the left (and vice versa).

Outside foot

To use the outside foot effectively on this width, a frogged foot (earlier this chapter) will be the most effective option, as this technique mechanically (automatically) twists your foot, rather than requiring you to forcefully twist it. As the crack gets wider, it's advantageous to use mechanical twisting, or things can become overly taxing.

If you have small feet, you may even find you start using your foot like you would in arm bar-sized cracks, (figure 128, later this chapter) as the length of your foot might span the crack width.

CLIMBING POSITIONING: FIST/FIST OFFWIDTH CRACKS

Positioning on fist/fist offwidth cracks follows similar principles to those in hand/hand offwidths (earlier this chapter). It is all about using the correct stack for whichever side of your body is in the crack: try to get the inside shoulder (if climbing right side in, this would be the right shoulder) turned inwards and sitting closest to the crack entrance.

See the table for a reminder of all seven combinations of fist/fist stacks, followed by a list of scenarios (or types of cracks)

FIST/FIST STACK COMBINATIONS
1. Uncrossed hands: left fist palm down, right fist palm up (secure)
2. Uncrossed hands: left fist palm up, right fist palm down (secure)
3. Uncrossed hands: both fists palms down (insecure)
4. Uncrossed hands: both fists palms up (insecure)
5. Crossed hands: left fist palm up, right fist crossed over the top palm down (secure)
6. Crossed hands: right fist palm up, left fist crossed over the top palm down (secure)
7. Crossed hands: both fists palms down (insecure)

and which combinations will work to your advantage and turn that inside shoulder into position.

FACE CRACKS

Positioning on vertical cracks

(See page 55 for a description of vertical face cracks.)

If climbing right side in:

- Combinations 1 and 6: these will bring the inside shoulder (right) really close to the crack entrance. This is good for feeling secure and keeping your body close to the rock.

If climbing left side in:

- Combinations 2 and 5

Combinations 3, 4, 7: try to avoid any of these for movement in fist/fist cracks—but have them in your offwidth arsenal as they can be useful if the sequence forces you into these positions.

Positioning on diagonal cracks

(See page 58 for a description of diagonal face cracks.)

Hands

When climbing diagonal fist/fist-width cracks, it is important to:

1. Keep the hands uncrossed: this stops you from barn-dooring and also helps you to keep your leading hand on the lower crack edge.
2. Keep one hand palm up and one hand palm down: this helps to bring one of your forearms inside the crack giving extra support and friction to make the climbing feel more secure.

If the crack is trending diagonally to the left (climbing right side in), use:

- Combination 1

If the crack is trending diagonally to the right (climbing left side in), use:

- Combination 2

When using these techniques on this width of crack it can be helpful to mix them in with arm barring techniques (see "Arm Bar and Chickenwing Offwidth Cracks" later in this chapter) to aid movement. You can use fist/fist stacks to help organise your legs and feet, and then convert to arm bars to shuffle upwards before repositioning the stacks a little higher.

Legs and feet

The techniques for your legs and feet in this width of diagonal crack are very similar to those in hand/fist-size cracks. If the lean of the crack is not that severe, then using standard thigh locks and outside foot techniques will likely be the most comfortable (see earlier this chapter). If the lean of the crack is more aggressive, you can use your inside leg how you would on an offwidth roof of this size (see Chapter 9): inserted straight into the crack, with your foot in the banana foot position. Your outside leg would adopt the braced position (see "Positioning on Finger Cracks," in Chapter 2).

Positioning on corner cracks

There are two positioning options on corner cracks of this size:

1. *Swinging into the corner:* You might choose to do this if you want to use pure crack technique and climb more securely.
2. *Swinging away from the corner:* You might choose this if you want to adopt a layback approach, if you think you might need to come out of the crack to layback in a few moves' time, or if you want to climb the crack straight in but with less friction from the corner wall.

Hands

If climbing a corner right side in, use:

- Combinations 1 and 6: swinging in to the corner
- Combinations 2 and 5: swinging away from the corner. When you are swinging away from the corner, it can become slightly awkward and painful across the side of your wrist. The most comfortable option in this situation is to use crossed hands.

If climbing a corner left side in, use:

- Combinations 2 and 5: swinging in to the corner
- Combinations 1 and 6: swinging away from the corner

ARM BAR AND CHICKENWING OFFWIDTH CRACKS

This is the size of offwidth where stacking hands together in a single unit will no longer work, yet the crack is still not wide enough for you to get your whole body inside. To fill the space efficiently you must use your arms and hands individually. If your technique isn't slick, it won't just be your hands which suffer from cuts and scrapes, your arms and shoulders will get torn to pieces!

HAND AND ARM TECHNIQUES

A number of different techniques can be used with this width of crack. Since your hands and arms are no longer stacked together inside the crack as one unit, as in the various hand stacking techniques, we must now look at each of them individually as an "inside" and an "outside" hand/arm.

Inside hand/arm

Some of these techniques are more effective with slightly narrower cracks of this size, while others work better with wider cracks. I'll start with techniques that work well with the narrower width and gradually work up to wider widths.

Narrower width
Arm bar
powerful jam, active expansion jam

The arm bar isn't as mechanical as some jams, meaning the twist or rotation won't automatically keep it in the crack. As long as you are aware that it does require a certain amount of push and power to make it work, then you will be on the right track.

1. *Orientation:* Rotate your hand into the thumb-up position (see "Standard Hand Cracks" in Chapter 3). The palm and back of your hand should be parallel with the crack walls and your fingertip ends should be pointing directly into the crack. Straighten your arm so there is no bend at the elbow. The position is very similar to reaching out to shake hands with someone.

2. *Insertion:* Insert your hand and arm into the crack so that the crack edge lies across the front of your shoulder. Place the flat of your palm against the crack wall (if inserting your right arm, your right palm would touch the left crack wall).

3. *Active expansion:* With your palm flat against one crack wall, bridge your forearm across the gap so that the bone of your elbow and the back of your upper arm touch the opposite crack wall. Now, push hard through the palm of your hand and force the elbow powerfully into the opposite crack wall to create equal and opposing pressures. It's beneficial to try to get contact with the elbow and whole of the

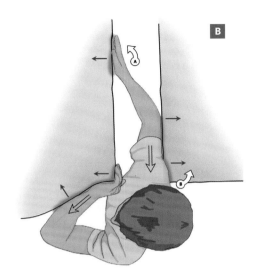

Figure 116. Arm bar and chickenwing offwidth cracks: arm bar and forearm scumming

Figure 117. Arm bar and chickenwing offwidth cracks: arm bar, different positions

upper arm on the opposite crack wall as this spreads the load over a larger and softer surface area (rather than just through the bony point of your elbow—ouch!).

4. *Positioning:* You can use your shoulder to make the jam feel even more secure. Turn your body so that your shoulder blade (of the shoulder of the arm you are arm barring with) turns towards and comes into contact with the crack edge. Turning the inside shoulder back towards the crack edge like this brings your body "side on" to the crack which puts your body into its thinnest dimension. This means you can get a greater body/rock contact area and achieve

a better jam (imagine climbing half a squeeze chimney—see Chapter 6). You will also find that by turning the inside shoulder back and in, your hips will turn out and your butt cheek will also come into contact with the crack edge. The desired position should have you looking sideways along the rock face rather than into the depths of the crack (figure 116). So, if you think about it, you can see that the arm bar is a catalyst for good body positioning on these types of cracks.

The arm bar can be used at different angles in the crack, depending on the steepness of the rock or whether you are resting or moving (figure 117). You can have your arm bar rotated anywhere from fingers pointing directly into the crack (like in the description above) to fingers pointing down towards the ground, but **don't** point your fingers up towards the sky while trying to arm bar as this is incredibly strenuous.

- *Fingertips pointing directly into the crack:* Useful for steeper arm bar terrain, or for when you need to hold yourself into the crack to rest or place gear.
- *Fingertips pointing slightly downwards:* Useful for general movement. The arm bar is high enough to hold you into the crack, yet your fingertips pointing slightly downwards helps with upwards movement (like squeeze chimneying; see Chapter 6.)
- *Fingertips pointing down towards the ground:* Useful when the angle of the offwidth is slabby.

Shoulder bar

powerful jam, active expansion jam

Shoulder bars can be used alongside and in combination with arm bars. It's nice to be able to switch between the two when doing long stretches of wide climbing as they provide respite from one another. I tend to find shoulder bars are less painful and give a better resting position than arm bars, but it is more difficult to make big shuffles and movements off them.

1. *Orientation:* Orient your hand and arm in the same way as you would for an arm bar.
2. *Insertion:* Insert your arm into the crack up to shoulder depth (like when arm barring) and place the back of the

Figure 118. Arm bar and chickenwing offwidth cracks: shoulder bar

upper arm against one crack wall (so if using your right arm it would touch the right crack wall).

3. *Active expansion and positioning:* Rotate your forearm up from the elbow so that your hand comes back towards the edge of the crack (but keep it inside). Your fingertips should now be pointing up and out of the crack (instead of pointing into the crack). This movement of rotating the forearm/hand up and out is very similar to the motion you would use when lifting a hammer to hit a nail. At the same time as you lift your hand, turn your shoulder blade towards the crack edge as you would do when arm

barring (arm bar, step 4). When you have lifted your hand into position, simply place the palm of your hand flat against the opposite wall. The same principles then apply as with an arm bar: push out with the flat of your palm against one wall and force your upper arm against the opposite wall (figure 118).

MEDIUM WIDTH
Chickenwing
powerful jam, active rotational jam

Imagine the shapes you would make with your arms to imitate a flapping chicken . . . that gives you a rough idea of the arm position you are looking to achieve in the crack with a chickenwing.

1. *Orientation:* Place your hand into the thumb-down position (see "Standard Hand Cracks" in Chapter 3). With your hand in this position, move it so that the back of your hand touches the front of your shoulder and your thumb touches your armpit. This action will fold your arm in half and stick your elbow out to the side (like a flapping chicken). Turn your body—not just your arm—so that you are side on to the crack and the tip of your elbow is pointing into the crack.

2. *Insertion:* Insert your arm into the crack elbow first and place the palm of your hand (which should be in a thumb-down position) against the crack wall. So, if you are inserting your right arm, the palm of your right hand will go against the left crack wall. Remember to look for bumps, holds, and friction on the rock for your palm to sit against which will help the jam.

3. *Rotational jam:* When your palm is securely in position, rotate your forearm so that the back of your upper arm connects with the opposite wall. The jam will probably feel pretty secure as you are using mechanical advantage rather than pure power. However, remember to push out on the crack wall with the palm of your hand and pull (using your body weight) out of the crack directly from the point where your elbow connects with the crack wall. Doing this creates a rotational jam where the harder you pull on it, the tighter it gets. This is the reason that chickenwings feel so secure.

Because "the harder you pull on it, the tighter it gets," it can sometimes be difficult to move on chickenwings. Below are suggestions for when it is best to use them:

■ *Narrow chickenwings:* If the jam is very tight, then it is best to use chickenwings for either resting or placing gear. Although they may feel very secure, trying to release and move off them will feel incredibly awkward. In tight jams, it is best to move on arm bars and then rest on chickenwings.

■ *Wider chickenwings:* When the crack gets wider and your chickenwing becomes more "tipped out"—i.e., the distance between your thumb and armpit increases—the chickenwing can be a great technique for movement: it can be easily released and moved upwards, yet when seated properly it will feel secure and less tiring than an arm bar.

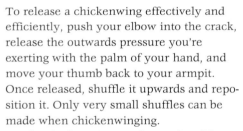

Figure 119. Arm bar and chickenwing offwidth cracks: chickenwing with elbow pointing directly into the crack

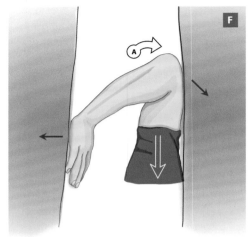

Figure 120. Arm bar and chickenwing offwidth cracks: chickenwing with elbow pointing up towards the sky

To release a chickenwing effectively and efficiently, push your elbow into the crack, release the outwards pressure you're exerting with the palm of your hand, and move your thumb back to your armpit. Once released, shuffle it upwards and reposition it. Only very small shuffles can be made when chickenwinging.

The chickenwing can be used at different angles in the crack, depending on the steepness of the rock or whether you are resting or moving. You can have your chickenwing rotated anywhere from elbow pointing directly into the crack (like in the description above) to elbow pointing up towards the sky, but **don't** point your elbow down towards the ground: remember, you have to put weight through the jam to make

it tighter. The more body weight you can put below the elbow, the more secure the jam will feel.

- *Elbow pointing directly into the crack:* This can be used on easier-angled terrain, or for movement. Your elbow isn't too high, so there is less weight going through it, making it easier to release and move (figure 119).
- *Elbow pointing slightly upwards:* This angle is useful for movement on steeper ground.
- *Elbow pointing up towards the sky:* A useful arm position if you want to rest or place gear (figure 120). If you're placing gear, remember it is likely to be easier to place gear underneath your jam rather than over the top of it.

WIDER WIDTH
Double chickenwing
powerful jam, active rotational jam

When the crack gets even wider (or flared on the edge), using both arms as chickenwings can be a great and secure way of moving. This technique is reasonably advanced, since to make it effective and be able to move, you have to be equally as secure with your legs and feet.

1. Execute a standard chickenwing, making sure your elbow is pointing into the crack rather than up to the sky. As the crack is wider, you will find that the chickenwing will be more open—i.e., your hand will be further away from your armpit. When you place this first chickenwing, be sure to keep your elbow pointing into the crack as this enables you to release and move the chickenwing easily and gives you space to place the other arm.

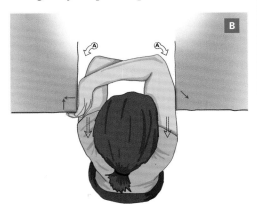

Figure 121. Arm bar and chickenwing offwidth cracks: double chickenwing

2. With the other arm, execute another chickenwing above and in opposition to the one you have already placed. Keep them relatively close together and make small movements with each so that you can make upwards progress with the arms (figure 121). It's easier to keep both your arms inside the crack and not take them out to overlap them—i.e., use swimming technique (Chapter 3) but with chickenwings.

Double chickenwing technique can be used for lots of different things:
- as a movement technique
- to switch sides in the crack, for example, from left side to right side, or vice versa
- as a stabilising position so that you can move other body parts

Outside hand/arm

With arm bar and chickenwing offwidths the outside hand can be used in a number of different ways, depending on the angle or steepness of the crack, the type of holds available and the style of the crack. Crucially, the outside hand isn't used in any type of jam, so the rules of jamming don't apply. It is used in what would be considered normal climbing positions. As a general rule, the first things you should look to use with the outside hand are actual handholds. And remember handholds don't necessarily have to be on the face outside the crack, they can be hidden inside on the crack wall. If you can find normal climbing handholds, things will quickly become a lot easier, so make sure you have a good look around.

Cupping

This is the standard go-to technique when climbing this size of offwidth. It is great on steep ground and feels secure and powerful on easier-angled terrain (figure 122).

1. Orient your hand into the thumb-down position at about eye level. The back of your hand should be facing towards you, and your palm facing the rock.

2. Place your hand on the edge/arête of the crack in this position and at about this height. Your thumb should be pointing towards the floor and your elbow out to the side.

3. The finished position should be a cupped hand position on the arête.

This cupping action should be pulling you into the crack to help prevent you from falling outwards. It can be tempting to reach much higher with this cupped hand so that you can look down and see what you are doing with your feet, however when you overstretch with the cupping hand, it becomes less and less useful for pulling you into the crack, which is the effect you need it to have. There are a couple of ways of ensuring that you keep your cupped hand at around eye level, while still seeing and controlling what is happening with your feet.

- Lift your elbow slightly upwards and tuck your head under your forearm to see what is happening below. This is useful if there are specific edges and footholds you have to make a conscious effort to stand on.

- Use "feel" with the feet to put them in place. This is useful if you are using your outside foot purely in the crack. You never have to look down, it can be much more efficient, and good form can be maintained with your hand and upper body. Being able to feel for solid foot jams does take some time to master, but when you do master it, you'll be shuffling with speed through those crux sections and you will never have to waste precious time and lose offwidthing form by looking down again!

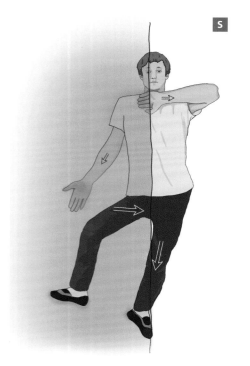

Figure 122. Arm bar and chickenwing offwidth cracks: arm bar and cupped hand on arête

Forearm scumming

This is a useful technique if the crack is rounded or flared on the edges.

To make this work, use the cupping technique (above), but lay the entirety of your forearm across the flare of the crack, as if you were trying to hold on to a huge sloping ledge (see figure 116). All you are doing is creating a greater contact area between you and the rock. This technique allows you to hold on to some surprisingly slopey crack edges, although if you've had to use this technique for long stretches of climbing on sharp rock, it might look as if you've had half your arm inserted into an alligator's mouth! So, wrap up well.

Downwards palming

This technique tends to work only on easier-angled terrain, as you can't hold yourself in to the rock effectively using palming techniques, so you have to be either tightly wedged into the crack or standing securely on your feet.

1. Use the palm of your hand on the rock face outside of the crack to help push yourself up and into the crack (figure 123). Place your hand so that your fingers are pointing down towards the ground and ensure that when you put your palm on the rock you do so with a bent elbow; if you don't, when you push up it will be totally ineffective. Always remember to look for the most effective areas to palm against to get the best support.

2. If palming on the rock face isn't an option, you can use downwards

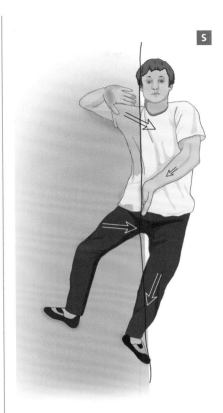

Figure 123. Arm bar and chickenwing offwidth cracks: chickenwing and downward palming

palming by cupping the arête/crack edge. Your fingers will still be pointing down towards the ground, however your hand will be upside down cupping the arête at about waist level. Using the corner of the arête can help give extra purchase to the outside hand.

The trout tickler

Tame and tickle the jam like you would a trout, but not so much that you laugh and fall off. The trout tickler is a very useful jam for resting, or to allow movement of other body parts.

Use any form of single-handed jam (finger, hand, fist) and jam it between another body part and the rock (figure 124). These three tips will help you get the most out of this jam:

- If using a finger jam, try to place it onto a bony part of your body (such as the top of your forearm), rather than a fleshy part of your body (such as the underside of your forearm). This will stop it from slipping straight through.
- If using a hand jam, putting the palm of your hand against the rock will feel most effective. It can also be done palm to flesh, but you might find your hand jam starts to collapse in on itself.
- Remember you can use any part of your body for trout tickling, it doesn't have to be your inside arm. It could be your leg, foot, chest or—if things are getting really funky—maybe your own head. Be creative.

If things are getting wide and desperate, then using a form of hand stack between another body part (commonly your legs, if you are inverted in a roof) can also be useful. This is often referred to as the Cod Tickler.

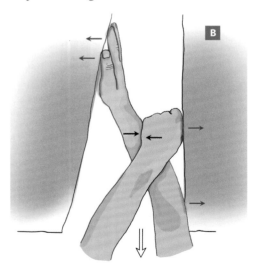

Figure 124. Arm bar and chickenwing offwidth cracks: trout tickler

LEG AND FOOT TECHNIQUES
INSIDE LEG/FOOT

The techniques used with the inside leg on an arm bar and chickenwing offwidth crack are secure but can feel a little strenuous. As long as you are willing to press, create some tension, and potentially have sore knees you will be fine. It's by no means brutal, but after a sustained period of using these techniques, you will experience some soreness—so be prepared. Knee pads are often useful. And as you are squeezing and tensing a lot with your legs in this size of offwidth, it can be a good idea to use a variety of techniques to help give some respite.

Leg bar
powerful jam, active expansion jam

This follows a very similar principle to the shoulder bar (earlier this chapter), but you are just using your leg instead.

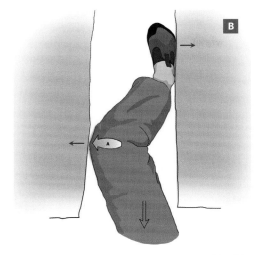

Figure 125. Arm bar and chickenwing offwidth cracks: leg bar

1. *Orientation:* Orient your leg so your toes and kneecap are pointing into the crack, and bend your leg to about 90-degrees.
2. *Insertion:* Insert your leg into the crack all the way up to the hip and place the whole of the outside edge of your boot against the crack wall (i.e., if inserting your right leg, the outside edge of your right foot should be against the right crack wall).
3. *Expansion:* Keeping your foot stationary, span the gap of the crack with your lower leg so that the inside of your knee (and possibly your thigh) touches the opposite crack wall.
4. Push out hard (and in opposite directions) with both the outside edge of your boot and the inside of your knee

(figure 125). After long periods of using this technique you will find it gets increasingly tiring in the top of your hip.

If the crack narrows towards the back, bridge your foot across the gap. Keep your heel on the wall where you placed your outside edge and turn your foot inwards so that your big toe connects with the opposite wall. Remember, in this situation the foot is only for extra support and is only useful if it can bridge the gap. If the crack is too wide, maintain full contact with the outside edge of your shoes.

Thigh bar
powerful jam, expansion jam

This is the leg equivalent of an arm bar.

1. *Orientation:* Orient your leg so that your toes and kneecap are pointing up to the sky and the sole of your shoe is facing into the crack. Your leg should be straight and as close to waist level as possible. This is exactly the same starting position you would use if doing a calf lock or knee lock (both earlier this chapter).
2. *Insertion:* Insert your leg into the crack all the way up to the hip.
3. *Twisting:* Now you are going to perform a twisting action with your leg. Twist the whole of your leg and your foot as one unit inwards through 90 degrees. Twist from the hip, rather than from the ankle or the knee. If you are using your right leg you will twist anticlockwise; if you are using your left leg you will twist clockwise.

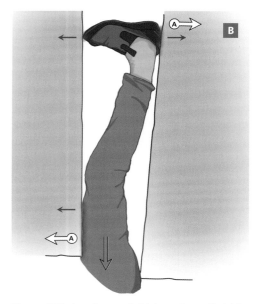

Figure 126. Arm bar and chickenwing offwidth cracks: thigh bar

4. The back of your heel should now be facing one crack wall and your toes and kneecap the opposite crack wall. To hold your leg in place, push the heel and knee out to their closest walls and apply opposing outwards pressures. If the crack is narrow you will find that you can also get a lot of friction against the crack wall with the top of your thigh (figure 126).

5. If the crack is narrow enough at the back, you can use your foot (which will now be bridging across the gap) to further improve the jam. The twisting movement with your leg will have automatically put your foot into a position

similar to the banana foot, so you can follow the procedures of that technique. Remember, if using this foot technique, it will feel "tipped out" due to the width of the crack; so it's important to maintain your focus on the tension between the knee and heel, and not be tempted to hang from your foot. Just use the banana foot for extra support.

Knee bar
powerful or resting jam, active rotational jam

Knee bars are commonly used in normal forms of climbing and are the leg equivalent of a chickenwing. They are rarely used for movement—although certainly they can be in specific circumstances—and are mostly used for resting. Sport climbers are notorious for using knee bars between features such as tufas or in large pockets. I'm always surprised by how many sport climbers seem to despise crack climbing, yet use crack climbing techniques such as knee bars all the time. You never know: when they discover that hand jamming exists, they might start finding things incredibly easy!

If you can find knee bars and make them work effectively, you can gain some mega-relaxed no-handed rests. Look for those wide openings and think like a sport climber (now there's something I never thought I'd write!).

1. Place your toes on one crack edge in a smeared position (Chapter 2). Either set of toes on either crack edge will work: just sense which foot feels the most natural or see which foot fits the sequence and pick accordingly.

2. Bend your knee so that the back of your heel and your bum move closer together. If the crack is narrow, you should aim to get them touching. If it's slightly wider, they can be further apart.

3. Now, keeping your toe securely where it is, insert your bent knee into the crack, kneecap first. If the crack is narrow, you may have to point your knee slightly upwards, insert it, and then make a small rotation downwards.

4. Keeping your foot on the smear and your knee pointing inwards, bridge the gap of the crack with your lower leg so that the top of your thigh comes into contact with the opposing crack wall. Your smeared toe and the top of your thigh will now be the contact points, with your lower leg acting like a lever bridged across the crack.

5. Pull your weight directly outwards (from the point where your knee touches the crack wall) to make the knee bar tighter (figure 127). Like with chickenwings, the more weight you put through the jam, the tighter it becomes. And although a knee bar is already very restful, if you can get a double knee bar in the crack then that's even better: just replicate what you have done already but with the other leg.

Knee bars work best in horizontal cracks or breaks as your body is upright and you have a massive foothold to stand on. The more vertical the crack, the more strenuous and core-intensive they become to hold.

Figure 127. Arm bar and chickenwing offwidth cracks: knee bar

If the crack is really wide and your lower leg only just bridges the gap, there is one little thing you can do to help with extra leg reach. Lift your heel (so you are no longer heel-down smearing) and stand on your tiptoes. This will give you some extra leg reach (like it would if you were standing on your tiptoes on the ground); however, be aware that the contact point with the foot may no longer be as good. Standing on your tiptoes will also become increasingly strenuous and pumpy for the lower leg.

OUTSIDE LEG/FOOT

How you use the outside leg/foot in arm bar and chickenwing offwidth cracks comes down to the angle of the foot in the crack. The technique is simple: bridge your foot between the two crack walls so that the back of your heel touches one crack wall and your toes touch the other crack wall. There are two distinct positions of the heel which affect how this foot is used.

Heel high

powerful jam, active rotational jam

Having your heel at the same level or higher than your toes releases a lot of tension and makes it easier to move your foot. If you're making quick shuffles, then keep a higher heel to prevent the foot from getting too jammed. Remember that when you have a high heel the jam will feel more tenuous: to keep it from slipping press hard with the toes into the opposing wall, and if possible keep the toes bent (even though your heel is high) so you can keep the largest possible surface area of boot rubber against the crack wall. You know you have the correct positioning when the angle between your toes and the top of your foot creates a V shape (figure 128).

Heel low

resting jam, active rotational jam

Dropping your heel below the level of your toes creates a solid and secure platform. In fact, it can be so solid that it can sometimes be difficult to release the tension in your foot and it can feel a bit stuck. This position isn't good for moving, however it's very good for stationary positions, for example, resting or placing gear. You know you have the correct positioning when the angle between your foot and lower leg creates a V shape (figure 129).

Figure 128. Outside leg in arm bar and chickenwing offwidth cracks: heel high

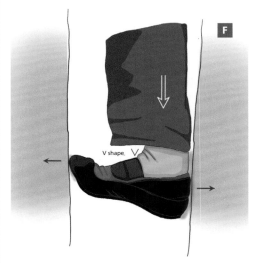

Figure 129. Outside leg in arm bar and chickenwing offwidth cracks: heel low

CLIMBING POSITIONING: FACE CRACKS
Positioning on vertical cracks
(See page 55 for a description of vertical face cracks.)

Positioning on this size of crack is very straightforward. Correctly applying the techniques outlined in this section will put you in the correct position to move. There are, however, a few little tips which will help emphasise the correct finished body position for climbing.

Arm barring/shoulder barring/chickenwinging: A common positioning mistake with these three techniques is to try to climb in a square-on position with your chest flat to the rockface. Remember when using these techniques that you want to be side on to the crack, rather than square on; by doing this your body will be in its thinnest dimension and you'll get a lot more friction against the rock from your shoulder and hip. To achieve this, you should be inserting your body into the crack shoulder first (so your chest and back are parallel with the crack walls). You will know you have the correct body position if you are looking sideways along the rock face outside of the crack, rather than looking into the crack itself. So, keep that shoulder opened out and don't look into the depths of the crack—take in the views!

Double chickenwinging: When you start to use double chickenwings, you will notice that when you place the second chickenwing, it will rotate your shoulders into a square-on position; this is correct and the position you should try to adopt. Your finished position should have you looking into the depths of the crack.

Positioning on diagonal cracks
(See page 58 for a description of diagonal face cracks.)

On diagonal cracks, the same techniques and positioning principles used on vertical cracks apply for the arms and inside leg. However, the amount the crack leans can dictate what you decide to do with your outside foot and which way you will face.

Gentle lean:

- *Facing down:* If the handholds on the lower edge of the crack are positive then it can be easier to face down, as you can pull down (and generate plenty of force) with the outside hand, preventing you from feeling unbalanced due to the lean. As the lean is gentle, using a standard outside frogged foot (figure 91) to generate upwards movement will work fine: it might just feel more awkward to get the foot in place because it won't be directly below you and you won't necessarily be able to see it all the time—using your sense of feel to place it in the crack is often the best method.

- *Facing up:* If the lower edge of the crack is flared, rounded, offset, or looks poor for holding on to with your outside hand, then putting your back against it and facing up can be an option. When you face up, keep your outside foot in a frogged position on the edge of the crack (like in standard offwidthing). Unlike with the facing down approach, you will be able to see, place, and push up on your foot more comfortably.

Steep lean:

■ *Facing down:* If the lean of the crack is steep, then placing your outside foot in the crack can be difficult as you will effectively be trying to place it behind you. This will feel unbalanced, and it is strenuous for your arms. If this is the case, brace your outside leg and foot as a rigid support on the wall below the crack and below your centre of gravity (see "Finger Cracks: Positioning on Diagonal Cracks" in Chapter 2).

■ *Facing up:* The same principles apply here as with gently leaning cracks. Only if there were very obvious and useful footholds outside the crack would you want to consider using them with your outside foot; the positioning would feel very awkward and impractical otherwise.

CORNER CRACKS

When climbing corner cracks of this size, the same techniques and positioning rules apply as with vertical cracks. The great thing about corner cracks is you can get a lot of the surface area of your back against the corner wall. As you will have turned your shoulder inwards, the whole flat of your back should be in contact with the rock; this means plenty of friction and things will feel more secure. A couple of extra techniques can be used with hands and feet on corner cracks because you can now use the corner wall as an extra feature.

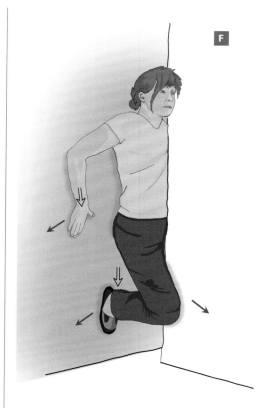

Figure 130. Positioning on corner cracks: backward palming and back stepping

Hands
Backward palming
Instead of using the standard cupping technique (earlier this chapter) with your outside hand, you can use a downwards palming technique (also earlier this chapter) but on the corner wall behind your back (figure 130). This is a really effective technique when the corner is slabby.

Legs and feet
Back stepping

The same principle can be followed with your legs/feet as with your hands. Lift your leg up behind you (heel to bum) and place the sole of your shoe flat against the corner wall; this can then be used as your normal pushing leg (figure 130). To make it even more effective, remember to look for little edges that you can rest the back of your heel on to make the foot placement more secure. If you are using this technique, be aware that your foot may slip and it is certainly not as secure as normal outside foot techniques. However, it does work well on easier-angled terrain and gives good respite when your outside foot becomes painful.

Knee clamping

Back stepping methods can be combined with knee clamping. With your outside leg, push your groin into the crack edge and the inside of your thigh into the rock face. A knee clamp with your outside leg in combination with a jamming technique with the inside leg will start to feel more secure; you will effectively be squeezing your legs around the crack edge.

Chicken leg
powerful jam, rotational jam

If the corner starts to become tighter than a 90-degree angle your outside leg can become really effective in a chicken leg position. The technique is the same as you would perform with the legs and feet in wide squeeze chimneys (hip thrust, Chapter 6). Imagine the tight corner is a flared chimney: place the sole of your shoe against the corner wall (like you would when back stepping), however place it a little further away from the crack entrance. Now bridge your lower leg across the corner so that your knee and the top of your thigh make contact with the rock face. Push out with your foot against the corner wall and put body weight down through your thigh as this will help the jam stick.

CLIMBING MOVEMENT IN OFFWIDTH CRACKS

Movement in offwidth cracks is something that all climbers struggle with. They can master the individual techniques and positioning, but the art of moving just seems impossible. They don't know how to use these techniques and positioning to generate upwards movement. All climbers run into this problem when they start offwidth climbing; it can feel demotivating and be painful on the mind and body when you realise you've only moved a few inches despite having made what feels like a thousand moves.

Offwidth climbing certainly isn't the quickest form of climbing as, unlike normal climbing, you can't make big long moves, step up high, or keep your body free from the friction of the rock. However, if you are moving at a pace of only a few inches a minute, you're probably doing something very wrong. The great thing about offwidth movement is that it is very repetitive, so once you get the hang of it, you can actually make very good progress in a short space of time and with minimal effort.

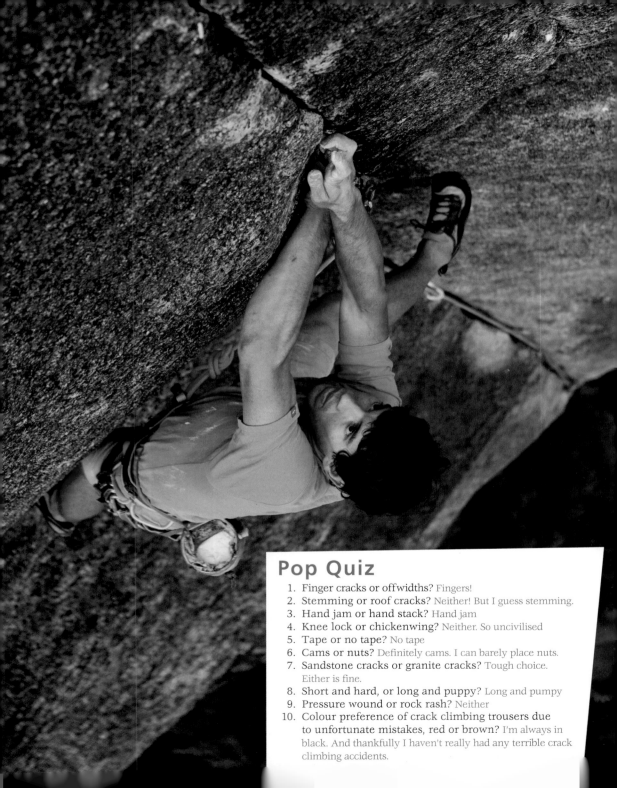

Pop Quiz

1. Finger cracks or offwidths? Fingers!
2. Stemming or roof cracks? Neither! But I guess stemming.
3. Hand jam or hand stack? Hand jam
4. Knee lock or chickenwing? Neither. So uncivilised
5. Tape or no tape? No tape
6. Cams or nuts? Definitely cams. I can barely place nuts.
7. Sandstone cracks or granite cracks? Tough choice. Either is fine.
8. Short and hard, or long and puppy? Long and pumpy
9. Pressure wound or rock rash? Neither
10. Colour preference of crack climbing trousers due to unfortunate mistakes, red or brown? I'm always in black. And thankfully I haven't really had any terrible crack climbing accidents.

MEET THE MASTER
ALEX HONNOLD

Alex is the master of free solo climbing. His achievements haven't just taken a step forward from previous generations, they have leapt out of reach. In a career of outstanding crack achievements, the highlight must be his free solo of El Capitan (via Freerider, *5.12d), Yosemite, in 2017.*

FAVOURITE CRACK CLIMBING AREA?
Yosemite, no question. The question is almost a joke. Where else in the world can you climb thousands of beautiful feet of perfect crack with easy access and great weather?! I think Yosemite is the most inspiring climbing area in the world. And you can't beat the cracks . . . The Salathé Wall or the *Nose* or the Muir Wall each have hundreds of metres of continuous cracks. Such great climbing!

FAVOURITE CRACK CLIMB?
Either the *Nose* or the Salathé—they're both great. Two of the most iconic routes in the world! But if you're asking about more conventional single-pitch splitters then I think that *Tricks are for Kids* (5.13b)—plus the extension—in Indian Creek is one of the most striking cracks in the world. I remember racking up below it with something like 10 or 15 0.75 Camalots. I couldn't even see the anchor—it looked like the route went forever.

MEMORABLE CRACK EXPERIENCE?
I had a pretty memorable experience on *Boogie 'til You Poop* (though I didn't shit myself). I distinctly remember learning how to hand stack on that route. I went up there to on-sight solo it on one of my first summers in Squamish and cruised up the initial squeeze chimney. Then I stalled out for a long time below the #4 crack not really sure how to climb it. Eventually I stacked two hand jams together and suddenly discovered hand stacking. It was a big moment for my crack climbing.

Another random crack story: when I climbed *Separate Reality* (5.12a) for the first time many years ago I fell out of the middle of the crack but my foot stayed jammed (the crack is slightly offset and my heel was on a little bump, which basically just held it in place). Anyway, I bat hung for a bit, depumped, and then finished the route. I still considered it an on-sight since I never weighted the rope!

THE KNOWLEDGE
I think that for people climbing cracks in Yosemite they should focus on their feet. Almost everything in Yosemite is slabby, even most El Cap climbing. So, it's all about footwork. Or at least good footwork can always help. It's not always about jamming harder or pulling; it's about standing on your feet and not having to jam too hard. Unfortunately, that makes you weak as well, which might be why I've always been a terrible sport climber.

But just remember, Yosemite is one big slab climbing area. So even though people think about it as crack climbing, it should really be thought of as slab climbing with a crack. My two cents . . .

Opposite: *Alex on* Leviticus *(5.12d) at Murrin Park in Squamish, Canada* (© Andrew Burr)

GENERAL MOVEMENT

The important thing when moving in offwidth cracks is to make a clear distinction between "outside the crack" and "inside the crack" body parts and their roles in the movement game. The common mistake that people make is to try to use the body parts that are inside the crack to gain upward movement. They concentrate so hard on these body parts inside the crack that they forget the most important body part for upwards movement: the outside leg/foot.

There are two important factors which will lead to success when moving up offwidths (rather than sliding back down them):

The inside body parts hold you in place. (The inside body parts are the leg, foot, arms, and hands that are inside the crack.)

- These body parts hold you in to the crack. They create solid, stationary positions which enable you to move the body parts outside the crack.
- They do not produce upwards movement (but can aid it), so don't try to make upwards progress using only these parts of your body: you will end up thrutching, grinding, and scraping your body.

The outside body parts produce upwards movement. (The outside body parts are the leg and foot that are on the outside or edge of the crack.)

- These body parts produce upwards movement. Lifting the leg up (bending it), putting it into a jam, and then standing up on it (straightening it) produces upwards movement. The art of

moving up in offwidths is all about the outside leg and foot.

- As well as upwards movement, the body parts on the outside of the crack can also be used for balance in the crack. They keep you upright, which helps stop your upper body toppling away from the crack. They give you something to stand on, and this relieves some of the strain on the body parts inside the crack as it stops all of your body weight sagging on to them.

HOW TO MOVE

When you start offwidthing it can feel like there is a lot going on. Stacks, inside leg, inside foot, outside leg, outside foot, pump, fatigue. It is hard to keep track of it all—you can be thinking about or trying to move one body part when you should be concentrating on another. The important thing is to be methodical: focus on one body part, execute whatever you have to do with that body part, then move on to the next part of the process. The moment you try to do more than one thing at a time, or you don't fully execute a jam before moving on to the next one, will be the moment you start moving back down the crack instead of up it.

There are four stages of movement in offwidth cracks.

Below we look at how you would move with your hands in a stacked position. It should be noted, however, that the same movement principles and stages also apply when you are in arm bar and chickenwing-sized cracks.

1. *Hold yourself stationary with a stack and inside leg/foot jam.* Place your stack and make sure it is good. Placing it just above eye level is a comfortable position. Don't over-stretch above your head as it will be difficult to seat the stack comfortably, but don't have it at chest level or your upper body will want to lean off away from the rock, moving your weight further from the wall and making the position more strenuous.

    Then place your inside leg and foot jam using the appropriate techniques for the given width.

    With these two jams (stack and leg/foot jam), hold yourself stationary and do not try to move upwards.

2. *Lift your outside leg and jam your foot on the edge of the crack.* While holding yourself in the stationary position, lift your outside leg and jam your outside foot in the crack using the appropriate technique. Your outside leg must be bent, as a bent leg will generate the necessary upwards movement.

    If you are tired, less confident, or the jams are insecure, you can make smaller steps with your outside leg, and vice versa.

3. *Push up on and straighten your outside leg.* Continue holding your stationary position and don't move any of the body parts inside the crack.

    Push up with force through your outside leg/foot—imagine you are doing a one-legged squat—until your leg is locked out and straight.

Use your inside leg/foot to pull your hips in and keep you in close contact with the rock as you stand up. Do not move this leg/foot jam.

Use your stack to pull your upper body close to the rockface so that your body weight doesn't sag away from the wall. As you push up with your outside leg you can also pull up and in with your stack to aid the upwards push from the outside leg. Do not try to move this stack.

When you have finished this process, your inside leg will be a little straighter and a little lower in the crack. Your stack will be at about eye level. Your outside leg will be locked out and straight and all you should have done is push up from a bent leg to a straight leg. There should have been no movement of the body parts inside the crack.

4. *Reset stacks and inside leg higher.* Now that your outside leg is straight you can reset your stack and inside leg/foot.

    To move your stack: Hold yourself into the crack with your inside leg and stand on your outside leg/foot like a platform. Release the tension in your stack, move it into a comfortable position above eye level and reset it. Remember that you don't have to completely take your hands out of the stacked position to move it, you can just release the tension in the jams, maintain contact with the crack wall and slide the stack up inside the crack.

To move your inside leg/foot: Hold yourself into the crack with your newly placed stack and keep standing on your straightened outside leg/foot like a platform. Release the tension in your inside leg/foot, slide your leg up, and reset it.

After resetting everything you should be back to the starting position in stage 1: your stack should be above eye level, your inside leg/foot at the appropriate height for executing the desired technique, and your outside leg locked out and straight. This position is the most comfortable and should be adopted when carrying out other stresses, such as placing gear, clipping, or having a rest.

REPEAT THE PROCESS

These four stages represent one whole cycle of offwidth movement. Depending on the size of step you made with your outside leg, you could have made anything from a few inches to a foot of upwards progress. Now all you have to do is keep repeating these four stages and you'll be shuffling your way to offwidth glory!

USING ARM BARS AND CHICKENWINGS

The above example of movement in offwidths describes the process if you are using stacked techniques. However, if you are using arm bar or chickenwing techniques, you should remember that the pushing up and straightening of the outside leg can also be aided with downwards palming and arm barring. Just be sure to only use this to aid the outside leg—don't

start neglecting this leg and put all your weight through your arms and palms.

PACE

When you can make multiple moves in a row, it's worth starting to think about the pace at which you move. Offwidth climbing uses a lot of the large muscle groups and after repeating the same move multiple times it can feel aerobic. You may get out of breath and start panting. This is OK and normal—just like if you went for a run, you would expect to start breathing more heavily. However, in offwidth climbing, you want to make sure you can control this breathing and stay below what I call the "red zone"—the zone where you are too tired to recover. You can do this by controlling the pace of your climbing.

You can pace your offwidth climbing by breaking it down into three sections:

1. *Base offwidth pace:* Controlled offwidth climbing. Do a sequence of five to ten offwidth cycles (stages 1–4, above) broken up by short micro rests (stationary positions in the crack) of 10 to 30 seconds. It's important to remember that even controlled offwidth climbing at a comfortable pace for your ability must still be broken up by micro rests. If you don't rest, you are likely to enter the red zone.

2. *Hard offwidth moves:* The extra effort you have to put in on a more difficult section or the crux of the route. Try to climb quickly through these sections and focus on keeping good form and technique.

3. *Resting:* Remain stationary in the crack in the restful starting position for several minutes. Although resting is good, it's important to monitor your rest time, as setting off after a prolonged rest can sometimes feel worse than if you'd set off sooner (and more tired), but with the blood still flowing. You might rest after a long phase of base offwidth climbing, or before and after hard offwidth moves.

TRANSITIONING BETWEEN JAMS (SWITCHING SIDES)

A common movement when climbing offwidths is switching from climbing right side in to climbing left side in, and vice versa. It's useful to be able to do this as the route might not lend itself to climbing one side in the whole way up. It can also be nice to switch sides as it works the other half of your body.

As transitioning can feel insecure and be difficult to execute, you should try to switch sides before you are too tired to do so. Don't think, "Argh, I'm totally pumped and going to fall off, so switching sides should make things better"—switching sides in this scenario will most likely result in you falling off. Pre-empt the fatigue and execute the switch while you still have the energy.

To switch sides:

1. Make sure you have a solid stack to hang from and a solid outside foot on the edge of the crack to stand on. Bring your inside leg/foot to the crack edge and place it as a twisted foot (see figure 97) just above your outside foot;

Patrick Kingsbury employing the "light bulb changer" on The Dentist's Chair *(5.11+) at Broken Tooth in Indian Creek, Utah* (© Andrew Burr)

this foot will be your new outside foot, so place it well.

2. Standing on your new foot placement, release the old outside foot and step it over the new placement, inserting it into the crack as the new inside leg.

3. Once composed on your new inside and outside legs, reorient your stack so it works with the side of your body that is now in the crack. (See earlier in this chapter for the combinations of hand/hand, hand/fist, and fist/fist stacks and which work best for right or left side in the crack.)

If you are using arm bars or chickenwings to switch sides there are a couple of options for the arms to help ensure a swift transition. (However, first remember to bring the inside leg to the outside of the crack and place it as your new outside leg/foot using the appropriate technique for the width.)

- If the crack edge is sharp and positive you can actually bring both hands on to opposing crack edges, rotate your body to the desired side which is going to be inserted, then dive back inside into either an arm bar or chickenwing. This procedure can be quite precarious and strenuous as you'll suddenly find yourself without much skin/rock contact for a split second while you make the transition. On the other hand, it can be quick and isn't that awkward to execute.

- Use double arm bars or chickenwings to switch. Turn so that you are looking into the crack, place a new arm bar/chickenwing above or below the first one, then slide the first arm bar/chickenwing out of the crack and into an outside arm/hand position. This can feel more secure, but is often more awkward than the first option.

Opposite: *Jay Anderson on* Offwidths are Beautiful *(5.10) at Potash Road in Moab, Utah* (© Andrew Burr)

CHAPTER 6

Squeeze Chimneys

As the crack becomes wider you'll find that you are able to fit inside it. You're now out of the dreaded offwidth climbing and into a new world of chimney climbing. As you can fully insert yourself in the crack this style of climbing is much more secure; however, in tight squeeze chimneys it can still be an aerobic full-body grind.

The great thing about squeeze chimneys is that you can get so much body in contact with the inside of the crack you can never fall off—you might just feel stuck—which is fantastic: you will never fail! Squeeze chimneys are therefore a great wide-crack confidence booster. They might look bigger, wider, and scarier than offwidths, but they are really the easier cousin. Although, if you suffer from claustrophobia, be aware that things are about to get pretty tight and enclosed. You will no longer be climbing on the cliff face, but in the belly of the beast.

This chapter describes three techniques which can be used on slightly different widths of squeeze chimney. Remember, with all of these techniques your whole body should be inserted inside the crack— don't leave anything behind, dive right in!

SIZE 1: NARROW SQUEEZE CHIMNEYS (BASIC SQUEEZE)

This is the most basic squeeze chimney technique. See figure 131.

TECHNIQUE AND POSITIONING

Overall body position: You should be in an upright position inside the crack, with the top of your head facing the sky and the soles of your shoes facing the ground.

Hands and arms: You should use arm bar techniques (Chapter 5) with both your right and left hands and arms. Place your arm bars so that your hands are by your side and your fingertips are pointing towards the ground. This will aid upwards movement (as you can palm down to move up) and also create a rotational jam (from the weight of your lower body) with your arm bar, making things feel really solid when you're stationary.

Back and chest: Your back should be firmly on the crack wall behind you (the palms of your arm bars will help push and force your back into the back wall). If the chimney is very narrow, then your chest will probably touch the opposing crack wall.

It might also be so narrow that you have to turn your head to the side or you'll risk grazing the end of your nose.

Legs and feet: Use leg bar techniques with both the right and the left legs (Chapter 5). If the squeeze chimney is incredibly tight and you have huge amounts of body–rock contact, you might not need two leg bars and one might be satisfactory to keep you in position. If this is the case, drop one leg and keep it straighter. (This leg can be used as a narrow thigh bar, i.e., back of heel against the back wall, knee and thigh against the front wall—see Chapter 5.) This will drop one hip which will narrow your

profile slightly, making it easier to move. It can also give you respite in one of your hips, which can be nice on long sections of squeeze chimney as your hips can start to scream with lactic acid after a while. Remember to keep swapping the dropped leg to aid recovery in the hip that is leg barring.

CLIMBING MOVEMENT

Climbing movement in the basic squeeze position is all about upper and lower body movement cycles and breathing patterns.

SEQUENCE OF MOVEMENT

Movement cycle 1—movement of the upper body (arms, shoulders, back, chest, head):

- Hold firm with your leg bars. Release the tension in your arms, and extend and shuffle your upper body up the crack—shrug each shoulder up individually to move your arms independently of one another.
- Use the back of your head to help keep some tension in the upper body as you release the pressure in the arm bars to move them up.
- When you've fully extended your upper body, reset your arm bars, back, and chest and hold firm in your new position. Don't expect lots of height gain; 6 to 12 inches is normal.

Movement cycle 2—movement of the lower body (legs, feet, hips):

- Push out with your arm bars to maintain a firm stationary position and then shift both your right and left legs independently so that your body returns to the original starting position.

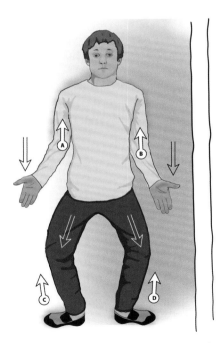

Figure 131. Narrow squeeze chimneys: basic squeeze

177

If you were to look at a sequence of many squeeze chimney moves in a row and from a distance, it would resemble the movement of a caterpillar: elongating and then shortening.

BREATHING

Using the correct breathing patterns is hugely important with all squeeze chimneys, however it is especially crucial with the basic squeeze. As the chimney can be very narrow, having lots of air in your lungs when you're trying to move can massively affect upwards progress.

Breathe in and keep as much inflation in the chest as possible when you want to remain stationary or at the end of a movement cycle. Fully exhale to decrease the volume in your chest and relax your muscles when you want to move upwards. If you get these breathing techniques the opposite way round, you'll probably give yourself a hernia when you try to move up.

As it's common to want to breathe in and tense when trying something hard, people often find it difficult to exhale and relax when they need to exert energy. However, by relaxing and breathing out, you will find that squeeze chimneys require less effort than you might have first thought. If it feels difficult, you're probably the cause of your own painful efforts. Are you pairing your breathing and movement patterns together incorrectly?

As you climb, elongate your breaths: nice, deep breaths in matched with long breaths out. Try to keep your breathing rhythmic and methodical. If you can manage to do this, you can then match your climbing to your breathing pattern:

- breath in: stationary in your starting position
- breath out: move your upper body until you need to inhale again
- breath in: hold your new position
- breath out: move your lower body until you need to inhale again
- breath in: you should be back in your starting position

OTHER TECHNIQUES: T-STACK

If you are using leg bars in narrow squeeze chimneys you will find that your hips become very tired. There is a unique technique that can be used for resting in this situation: the T-stack.

1. Place the whole outside edge of one climbing shoe against the back wall of the crack. The sole of your shoe should be facing the ground and your toes either pointing into or out of the crack, depending on which foot you're using and which way you're facing.

2. With your second foot, bridge the gap between the first foot you placed and the front crack wall. Aim to nestle the heel of your second foot close to the arch of your first foot, and have your toes touching the front crack wall. The position of the second foot should be somewhat similar to a bridged foot, low heel technique (see figure 129). When both feet are stacked together they should form a T shape (figure 132).

This technique is no good for movement, but a good T-stack should enable you to rest other body parts when on long sections of basic squeeze chimney climbing.

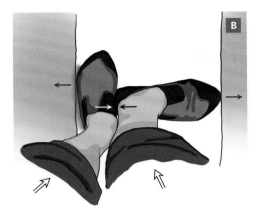

Figure 132. Narrow squeeze chimneys: T-stack

SIZE 2: MEDIUM SQUEEZE CHIMNEYS (THE SIDEWINDER)

When the chimney becomes a little wider, this is my go-to technique. It is a little more advanced; however, if you're confident with it, it can feel very secure and efficient. It can also be useful when you have to tunnel sideways in a chimney, for example out of a roof or to get deeper into a crack (figure 133).

TECHNIQUE AND POSITIONING

Overall body position: You should be in a sideways position in the crack, with one hip pointing towards the sky and one hip pointing towards the ground. The top of your head and the soles of your feet should either be pointing into or out of the crack, depending on which way you are facing.

Hands and arms: With your bottom arm (the arm closest to the ground) you need to use a downwards arm bar (see figure 117),

Danny Parker making good use of the sidewinder technique on Lucille *(5.12d) in Vedauwoo, Wyoming* (© Irene Yee)

179

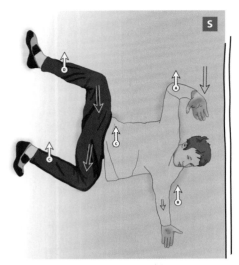

Figure 133. Medium squeeze chimneys: sidewinder

with your fingertips pointing towards the ground. As you are sideways in the crack, this arm should be your lowest body part. Do not let your feet drop below this arm. Your top arm (the arm that is closest to the sky) will be in a chickenwing position (see figure 120), with your fingertips pointing towards the ground and your elbow pointing towards the sky.

Feet and legs: Depending on the width of the crack, you can use either leg bars or thigh bars (see figures 125 and 126). Use leg bars if the crack is slightly narrower and thigh bars when it starts to widen. Always keep both legs high and don't let the top leg drop below waist level (often, the higher you can get the top leg, the better it will feel). If you allow your legs to drop, your

hips will also drop. If your hips drop, the technique becomes useless. So, keep your legs high as this will keep the hips engaged and maintain good body positioning in the crack.

Back and chest: Your arm bar and knees should be forcing your back onto the crack wall behind you. It is unlikely you will have any chest contact with the crack wall in front of you as the chimney is probably too wide.

CLIMBING MOVEMENT

Climbing movement in the sidewinder position is all about focusing on moving one body part at a time.

SEQUENCE OF MOVEMENT

1. *Starting position:* Gain a good starting position. If you are inside and at the bottom of a squeeze chimney, set your chickenwing above you, your arm bar below you and kick both your legs up and out to the side so that your bottom leg is at waist level and the foot of your top leg is at the height (or higher, if possible) of your chickenwing.

2. *Chickenwing:* To move your chicken-wing, focus on holding firm with all other contact points, release the tension (see "Chickenwings" in Chapter 5 for how to release tension), and move the chickenwing up elbow first.
   - Use your top leg to prevent you from losing any height.
   - Use your bottom leg to ensure your hips don't drop.

- Use your arm bar to help push your upper body upwards and then reset your chickenwing a little higher.

3. *Arm bar:* Use the same technique as for resetting the chickenwing to move and reset your arm bar a little higher in the crack.

4. *Legs:* Now focus on the lower half of your body and, applying the same techniques as for the arms, move each leg individually. As the bottom leg will be slightly "left behind," move this one first by matching it up to your top leg. Then reset the top leg nice and high at chickenwing level or higher.

5. *Hips:* Once you have moved all four body parts (in order: chickenwing, arm bar, bottom leg, top leg), you will notice that your hips feel low. To move them up use a "hip flick": release some tension from your back and bum and "flick" your hips upwards using one quick movement. To help flick the hips upwards, focus on pushing down with the arm bar. If you feel confident with the movement, a little trick you can use is to flick your hips and move your bottom leg all in the same movement. Then when you come to move your top leg again you can place it even higher in the crack so your hips aren't sagging behind you. An efficient sequence of movement would look like this:
    - move chickenwing
    - move arm bar
    - flick hips and move bottom leg
    - move top leg

SIZE 3: WIDE SQUEEZE CHIMNEYS (THE HIP THRUST)

This technique is useful just before the crack becomes wide enough to require chimney techniques. It is less advanced than the sidewinder and doesn't feel as energy intensive as the basic squeeze technique (figure 134).

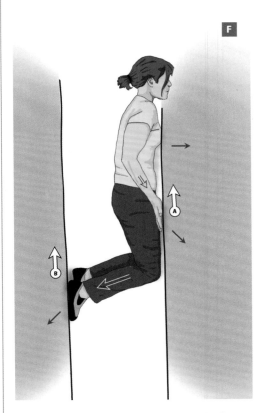

Figure 134. Wide squeeze chimneys: hip thrust

MEET THE MASTER
SEAN VILLANUEVA O'DRISCOLL

Sean is one of the most adventurous crack climbers that there is: the wider, the wetter, the greener, and the more esoteric, the better. He has established some of the most off-the-beaten-track crack routes in the world. From exquisite Patagonian body bridging to green Greenland thrutches, he's "been there, done that." Standout climbs include the first free ascent of Los Fabulos Dos on the east face of Cerro Catedral (1000m, F7c+), Patagonia, with Stephane Hanssens and Merlin Didier, and the second ascent of Hazel Findlay's Tainted Love (E8/5.13d) in Squamish.

FAVOURITE CRACK CLIMBING AREA?

Yosemite, Indian Creek, Joshua Tree . . . I can't really pick one area. Cadarese in Italy is pretty cool because it has a lot of high-quality single-pitch cracks very close to one another in a nice setting. Also, recently I went to Index, Washington, and I was blown away by the quality of the lines there. There is a place near my home town, Groenendaal, which has three 20-metre splitter hand roof cracks! It's an amazing setting: a concrete railway bridge with lots of impressive graffiti, and cars passing by which adds to the commitment!

BEST CRACK CLIMBING EXPERIENCE?

The Darbellay route on the north face of the Petit Clocher du Portalet (a 300-metre spire) in the Mont Blanc massif in Switzerland. It's a thin 80-metre crack which splits a blank, overhanging headwall. It starts off as a thin seam with some hard, delicate climbing with small precise feet. As you go higher it becomes a splitter finger crack with almost no feet and it finishes off with a diagonal, flaring hand crack.

The route was first aid-climbed in 1962 by Michel Darbellay himself! The crack was bolted and then free-climbed in two pitches (F8a and F7c+) in 1989 by Philippe Steulet (a legendary Swiss climber, who

died on the north face of the Eiger in 2002). In the early 2000s Didier Berthod, one of the best crack climbers in the world at the time, stripped the bolts and climbed the two pitches placing gear. His project was to link the two pitches in one monster pitch. He didn't manage to climb it before God called him and he stopped climbing to become a monk.

I first tried the line in 2006: it felt extreme, I took huge whippers on micro-nuts and didn't even manage to reach the top of the first hard pitch! Every three to four years I returned to it and each time I could feel my crack climbing progress. In 2014 I came very close to redpointing the first hard pitch, and I on-sighted the second (I had never tried it before as I had always gotten shut down by the first pitch). In the summer of 2017, I finally redpointed the first hard pitch and linked it straight into the second for a full 80-metre crack battle. As I clipped the anchor my belayer had taken off his belay device and was holding the end of the rope with the tips of his fingers. "End of the rope!" he yelled.

MEMORABLE CRACK EXPERIENCE?

I thought I was going to die a horrible death when stuck in a squeeze chimney up on the Citadel in

Opposite: Sean climbing out of the "Black Hole" on Impossible Wall, Sortehul Fjord, Greenland (© Ben Ditto)

Stewart Valley, Baffin Island, during the first ascent of *Catacomb* (5.12a OW, 900m). I was out there with Nicolas Favresse, we were completely isolated, far away from any other human beings. We had been there for almost two months after having skied in on the sea in early June with three Italian friends. Our Italian friends had left, and it was now just Nico and me. A sailboat was going to pick us up in the next few weeks as soon as the sea was clear of ice.

We had spotted this line of 900 metres of icy, wet, mossy offwidth cracks and squeeze chimneys. Close to the top and exhausted after about 24 hours of battles on hard offwidths, I was wiggling my way up the inside of a dark squeeze chimney. It became very narrow and I had to decide whether to get out and climb it as an offwidth or try to squeeze through. Mentally and physically drained from all the previous offwidths and with no possible gear placements, I decided to push through the slot. I exhaled completely, pushed as hard as I could, moved from left to right and just before the exit I got completely stuck! I couldn't go up or down! My head, chest and hips were totally jammed! I was there for about 40 minutes without moving an inch.

I hesitated to tell Nico to just cut the rope (I was stuck anyway, so I wasn't going to fall), rappel down, and get a rescue; but I knew that in the best case it would take at least a week for any rescue to arrive and even if they did manage to reach me what could they possibly do? I visualised how I was going to just die there, of starvation or hypothermia, stuck inside of this crack . . . Then I tried to relax and think. I remembered I had gotten into that position diagonally. All of a sudden I managed to get unstuck! I then climbed on the outside which turned out to be an easy offwidth as there were a lot of holds on the face. We finished the line in a 32-hour push.

THE KNOWLEDGE

Remember when you were a kid and you used to repeatedly bang on your head with a hammer? Everybody went through that phase, right? You whacked the hammer repeatedly on your head because it felt so good when you stopped whacking. Well, after a while, with life experience and vision you learn to appreciate even the part when you're whacking the hammer on your head! It's just a matter of how you look at things . . .

Pop Quiz

1. Finger cracks or offwidths? Offwidths
2. Stemming or roof cracks? Stemming
3. Hand jam or hand stack? Hand stack
4. Knee lock or chickenwing? Chickenwing
5. Tape or no tape? No tape
6. Cams or nuts? Cams
7. Sandstone cracks or granite cracks? Granite
8. Short and hard, or long and pumpy? Short and hard
9. Pressure wound or rock rash? Rock rash
10. Colour preference of crack climbing trousers due to unfortunate mistakes, red or brown? Definitely red! I hate when it's brown . . .

Josh Ewing on the classic Trench Warfare *(5.12+) in Little Cottonwood Canyon, Utah*
(© Andrew Burr)

TECHNIQUE AND POSITIONING

Overall body position: You should be in an upright position inside the crack, with the top of your head facing the sky and your toes pointing towards the ground.

Hands and arms: Place the palms of your hands in a downwards palming position on the crack wall in front of you. Have your hands down at waist level and point your fingertips towards the ground. The crack will be too wide to do any arm barring, so focus purely on the palms; look for sections of wall that will make palming easier— edges, indentations, high-friction areas. When you place your palm on the wall, ensure that you bend your elbow so that you can push and extend your arm to help upwards movement.

Back and chest: There are a few different positions for your back and chest. If you want the position to feel comfortable on the knees, then place your chest against the wall in front of you. This will spread the weight through your thighs and chest, however it can obviously be more awkward to see where you are placing your palms. Arch your back (but keep your thighs engaged) and look for palm placements in this position. The alternative is to sit down away from the front crack wall (so your bum moves closer to your calves); if the chimney is tighter then you might be able to rest your back against the back crack wall. This puts a lot more pressure through the knees, which can get painful, but you will be able to see palm placements more

easily and move upwards more freely due to there being less friction from your thighs and chest against the front crack wall.

Feet and legs: The soles of your feet should be on the back wall behind you. Point your toes down towards the ground; your Achilles tendon should be facing up to the sky. It is your lower leg that bridges the gap of the crack and therefore your knees and thighs will make contact with the front wall.

CLIMBING MOVEMENT

Climbing movement in the hip thrust position is just like walking. You make little individual steps with both the palms of your hands and the soles of your feet up the wall, moving one body part at a time to stay as secure as possible. Use the bend in your arms to push down so you can move up.

- To release the tension and move your palms: push with your feet into the back wall and thrust your knees, thighs and hips into the front wall.
- To release the tension and move your feet: push your thighs and hips away from the front wall by pushing with your palms.

When you move your hands and chest up the wall, your feet will become lower in the crack, meaning less pressure will go through them and there is a greater chance of slipping. To help prevent this, don't over-extend and leave your feet behind. If you do slip, the crack is now wide enough that you could actually fall down the chimney if you make a mistake.

Opposite: *Harrison Teuber makes* A Clean Getaway *(5.11+) at Sylvan Lake in Custer State Park, South Dakota.* (© Andrew Burr)

CHAPTER 7

Chimneys

Generally speaking, chimney climbing is one of the easiest forms of crack climbing. This doesn't mean that chimney climbs can't be hard—they definitely can, especially if they start to become open and flared or if the friction for the feet is poor. However, in the main, chimney climbs tend to be at the lower end of the grading scale.

Yet while chimney climbing does tend to be easier than other forms of crack climbing, it can also be more dangerous, which is something to be very aware of. Unless there are secondary cracks, such as cracks within the chimney walls, you will find it difficult to place protection, meaning if you make a mistake you could fall down the chimney. There have been times when climbers have made a mistake and have slipped and fallen all the way back down the chimney they were climbing. This isn't intended to scare you; it's just a warning not to become careless and nonchalant about the climbing being easy. Take one easy step at a time and walk the chimney safely.

The first thing to consider with chimneys is the best way to face while climbing. In order of importance, here is some guidance on how to decide which way to face:

Look for the best footholds: The only way you'll ever fall down a chimney is if your feet slip, so identify the side of the chimney with the most footholds and aim to put your feet on that side.

Look for any leans in the chimney: If the chimney has a steep side and a slabby side, aim to put your feet on the slabby side; a foot on a slab is better than a foot on a steep wall.

Look for the side with the least friction and obstacles: Aim to put you back against this side of the chimney, as when you move upwards your back will slide more easily across the rock and your clothing/rack will be less likely to get caught on obstructions.

Next, we will look at the techniques for the three sizes of chimney, from narrow through to wide.

SIZE 1: NARROW CHIMNEYS

Ascending narrow chimneys requires probably the most sequence-dependent chimney technique. People often get confused about which foot should be back-stepping and when they should be pushing up. However, if you are methodical about the technique—and literally make one step at a time—it will flow with ease and be very efficient.

TECHNIQUE AND POSITIONING

Overall body position: You should be in an upright sitting position.
Back: Your back should be against the crack wall behind you.
Legs and feet: Both your legs should be bridging the gap of the chimney. On this width of crack your legs will be bent. The more bent your legs are and the tighter the chimney is, the more secure the position will feel—but it will require more effort to move. Your feet should be smearing (see figure 35) on the crack wall in front of you and be slightly staggered, with one foot above the other.
Hands and arms: Place the palms of your hands on the crack wall behind you at waist level. Your fingertips should be pointing down towards the ground and your arms should be slightly bent: this will enable you to palm down, push up, and extend your arms for upwards movement.

CLIMBING MOVEMENT

Moving efficiently while back-and-footing is all about relieving the pressure on your back to enable you to slide it up the back wall with as little effort as possible. Rather than just pushing with your arms and hands to relieve the pressure on your back, you are going to use the help of one of your feet: arm/arm/foot is more effective than just arm/arm.

Back-and-footing

The above technique and positioning acts as the starting position for back-and-footing. Here we'll look at one full cycle of movement.

1. Adopt the overall starting position described above.
2. Take your lower smeared foot off the wall in front of you and place the whole sole of the shoe flat against the crack wall behind you. The more you can bend your leg and the closer you can get your heel to your bum, the greater the upwards movement you will make when you push—but the harder it will be to push out of that position. (It's like doing a squat: the further you bend down, the greater the upwards movement you can get, but the harder it is to push up from that bent position.) So, bend your back leg according to how fresh your legs are feeling, how good the footholds are to push up on, and how tight the chimney is.
3. You should now have one foot and two palms on the back wall. Use these three contact points to relieve the pressure on your back. Once the pressure

Figure 135. Back-and-footing in narrow chimneys: starting the movement

Figure 136. Back-and-footing in narrow chimneys: good pressure through the front foot

has been relieved, use both hands (in palm-down position) and both feet (one smeared in front and one back-stepping) to push upwards (figure 135). Push upwards until your front leg is straight and use it to push and reset your back into the back wall.

4. When you push upwards, it's incredibly important to maintain pressure through the front foot as it is now your only contact point with the front wall. If this foot slips, you may have the misfortune of toppling head first into the wall in front of you and then slipping back down the chimney—not good! The technique for maintaining good pressure on the front foot is to drop the heel as you push up (figure 136). This will keep good rubber–rock contact and ensure your foot is in a nice smeared position. Your Achilles tendon needs to be nice and flexible so that you can get a good V shape between your foot and your shin.

5. If the front foot is a poor placement and you think that it might slip as you push up, you can support your foot by transferring a hand from the back wall to the front wall. This will add more security. Try to use opposite hand to foot, although this isn't always possible if the chimney is difficult and there are specific hand and foot placements you need to use. When you transfer

your hand across you can use it in numerous ways depending on how far away the front wall is. If the wall is close, you can point your fingertips down towards the ground. If it's further away, you might just rest the tips of your fingers against the wall. Whatever you choose, don't over-stretch as this can affect the back foot and make that slip—so find a good balance point in the middle.

6. After pushing upwards and regaining a comfortable position, take your foot off the back wall to place it back on the front wall in a smeared position above the other foot. When you return your foot from the back wall to the front wall, always try to place it above the other foot as this helps to keep you moving upwards. You are now in the starting position but with the opposite foot in the higher position: this is half a cycle. Complete another half cycle—this time with the opposite feet—and you'll be back to your original starting position. The starting position and positions after completing the half and full cycles are the times to rest and place gear (if any is available), as these are the comfortable positions.

SIZE 2: MEDIUM CHIMNEYS

When the chimney starts to become wider, back-and-footing can feel precarious as there is an increased chance that your front foot could slip. Standard chimney technique is the easiest and safest option in this size of crack.

TECHNIQUE, POSITIONING, AND MOVEMENT

Standard chimneying

1. Adopt the same starting position as back-and-footing (above), although with this width of chimney you will find that your legs are a lot straighter in the crack (see figure 137).

2. From the starting position, use your palms to relieve the pressure on your back. Now, using both palms and both feet, push upwards and move your back up the wall. As your legs will be reasonably straight already, you'll find that the distance you can move upwards will be less than with back-and-footing.

Figure 137. Medium chimneys: feet on same wall

3. Now move your low foot and smear it above your high foot, then move both palms up together and reset them. Repeat the process.

Staggering your legs or keeping them low is less strenuous on the arms for pushing and moving upwards, however you must be careful to ensure that your bottom foot doesn't slip when you push up. If you have your feet matched level or placed high (figure 137), it will be more secure but also feel more strenuous.

If the chimney becomes very wide, you can lift your heels to give yourself some extra reach (as if you were standing on your tiptoes). This tends to work only if there are edges to stand on, and you have to be

Figure 138. Medium chimneys: stemming technique

incredibly careful not to slip. When the chimney becomes too wide, and the length of your leg is struggling to span the gap and your back is moving away from the back wall, the next option is to use stemming techniques in the chimney (figure 138; also see "Stemming in Chimneys" in Chapter 8).

SIZE 3: WIDE CHIMNEYS

When the crack is too wide for both standard chimneying and for stemming (next chapter), the last and only option is to body bridge. This uses the length of your whole body to span the gap of the crack. You'll need a strong core and stable shoulders or else you'll snap in the middle like a biscuit.

TECHNIQUE, POSITIONING, AND MOVEMENT
Body bridging

1. Place the palms of your hands against one wall. You can point your fingertips in any direction: I tend to go slightly out to the side as it helps with shoulder stability and also helps you to push upwards.

2. Walk your feet towards the opposite wall and place the soles of your shoes flat against the wall with your toes pointing down towards the ground; you should now be looking straight down at the ground. The higher your feet, the more strenuous but secure the position. The lower they are, the easier it is to hold the position but the higher the likelihood your feet will slip. I find that having your feet

ever so slightly lower than your hands works well (figure 139).

3. Now simply make little steps with both hands and feet up the wall. Remember to move only one body part at a time in order to stay secure.

The important thing with body bridging is to not let your bum sag down. If your bum and hips drop, the whole centre of your body will collapse inwards and you'll fall down the chimney—face first! Stick your bum up and maintain a good arched shape in your body. Think about an artificial bridge over a stream; they are often arched as this is a strong shape which stops them from collapsing inwards from the centre: apply this principle to your body.

Body bridging can also be done sideways, with the right side of your body lower than the left side, or vice versa. So, you'd either be looking into or out of the chimney, rather than down at the ground. This sideways position can be useful if you need to be more precise with your feet, as you can use your feet more effectively to stand on—and push against— edges when your body is oriented like this (figure 140).

For this technique to be a success it's all about your lower arm. As you will quickly find out when you are in this position, a lot of weight is transferred through this arm, so this should be your main focus point. If you lose form or focus with this arm, then it's likely to collapse and your body bridge will fail. When moving your feet or top arm, try to keep your lower arm locked out and

Figure 139. Wide chimneys: face-down body bridge

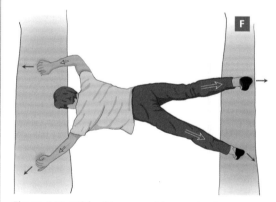

Figure 140. Wide chimneys: sideways body bridge

straight; this provides support and is less tiring. If your arm bends, your body drops, more weight is put through your lower arm, less pressure is put through your feet, and you'll probably fall out of the position.

193

Pop Quiz

1. Finger cracks or offwidths? Come on! Fingers, obviously . . .
2. Stemming or roof cracks? Stemming!
3. Hand jam or hand stack? Hand jam!
4. Knee lock or chickenwing? Chickenwing
5. Tape or no tape? No tape
6. Cams or nuts? Cams
7. Sandstone cracks or granite cracks? Both
8. Short and hard, or long and pumpy? Long and pumpy
9. Pressure wound or rock rash? Rock rash
10. Color preference of crack climbing trousers due to unfortunate mistakes, red or brown? Red (it's happened).

HAZEL FINDLAY

Hazel is one of the best technical climbers around, which is probably why she also excels at crack climbing. She is a master when the crack becomes a corner. Give her some palming and smearing on opposing walls and she'll make stemming on glassy granite look like walking up a flight of stairs. Check out her first ascent of Tainted Love *(E8/5.13d) in Squamish—stunning!*

FAVOURITE CRACK CLIMBING AREA?
Well it's not very original but it has to be Indian Creek. The landscape alone is worth a visit, but when you add in the absurd density of five-star splitter and non-splitter crack lines it blows your mind. The unique lifestyle of living in the desert under big skies and starry nights adds to the magic. It is also *the* school of crack. Pick a size you need to work on, pool your cams with your fellow dirtbags, and then attack—but be ready to sacrifice some skin, blood, and a large piece of your ego.

FAVOURITE CRACK CLIMB?
The Salathé headwall on El Cap. It sits 800 metres above the valley floor and overhangs so much there is only air from your feet to the trees. A 70-metre crack strikes through this headwall like a thunderbolt. You won't find a better protected trad route; for most of the headwall you can get a piece of gear in every inch. Even if you were to be a complete arse and fail to place any good gear, you wouldn't hit anything for a very long time. Despite this, the exposure is enough to get your bowels and stomach talking to your brain, telling you not to go. The headwall starts out with a very technical but brutal boulder problem up a shallow groove and into the main crack, then you have a 50-metre endurance pitch of flared tight hands culminating in a thin finger move to a rest. The final 10-metre boulder section finishes with very thin and powerful layback moves to a massive jug. Sticking this final move was one of the best moments of my climbing life.

MEMORABLE CRACK EXPERIENCE?
My most memorable crack experience was climbing the Monster Offwidth on *Freerider* for the first time. Rather than a climb it felt like a battle with a great granite monster. Halfway up I felt like I might be getting the technique, but in the next moment the crack would try to spit me out. I scraped around with my feet and shoulders, losing more and more skin. I got to the top and felt like I needed two litres of water and a three-course meal to even think about climbing the next pitch.

THE KNOWLEDGE
Getting good at crack climbing is like anything else; you need to practise. If it's not your forte, then it probably means you haven't practised it enough. If this sounds like you, then get your tape out and look for the crack lines in the guidebook. With the right mindset, crack climbs become very attractive because they tend to be safer than face climbs. Another attraction should be that many of the world's best routes and cliffs require crack climbing techniques. With motivation to practice, nothing can stop you.

Opposite: *Hazel on the* Salathé Wall *(5.13c) headwall, Yosemite National Park, California* (© Jonny Baker)

Imagine the lower arm as a strong straight post which you are leaning against while moving your other body parts. Moving this lower arm can be difficult if your other arm is on a poor placement. A couple of things can help you move your lower arm:

- Move it in small hops up the wall until it reaches the desired position.

- Place your top arm/hand a little bit lower down the wall (i.e., move it in an arching motion across the front of your chest) to provide some support for moving your lower hand. After moving your lower arm, aim to get it back into the straight, locked-out position as quickly as possible.

Opposite: *Tim Emmett levitates up* The Shadow *(5.13b) on the Grand Wall, Squamish, Canada.* (© Andrew Burr)

CHAPTER 8

Stemming

Put your biggest, strongest pair of legs on, zip up your fly, and make sure you've been to the toilet before starting to climb: you're about to open wide and things could get personal straight off the ground. You're out of the realm of "back of the hand" damage now, and into a new world of red-raw palms. It won't be necessary to tape the backs of your hands as it's your pads that will take a chafing. Squeaky shoes and rubber palms are a must!

If there is one important thing to remember about stemming, it's this: the style is back-to-front climbing. Push don't pull. Legs not arms. The opposite to most normal climbing. So slim down your arms and beef up your legs. Cycling might be good endurance training for stemming!

Stemming is used when the length of one leg isn't enough to bridge the gap of the crack using standard chimney techniques (Chapter 7). Instead you must use one foot on either wall and span the gap with both your legs. Stemming can be used on very easy terrain, such as wide chimney features with lots of footholds, through to some of the most difficult and technical climbing terrain, like flared open-book corners with only the friction of the rock to smear against. Regardless of the terrain, the same principles apply; but while in the first example you will feel solid, in the second you might feel as though you're sliding about all over the place like a slippery, wet salmon!

STEMMING IN CORNERS

Stemming in corners is where the real difficulty lies with this technique. You obviously want to stay on the rock, but the flare of the corner continuously wants to spit you off. As a general rule—unless there are lots of extra handholds and footholds—the more open the flare, the harder the climbing and the more the corner will want to push you out. We'll look first at general technique and positioning, followed by the basic rules of movement.

TECHNIQUE AND POSITIONING
HANDS
Use the heels of your palms on the rock (figure 141). Remember to look for edges or

Figure 141. Stemming in corners: standard stemming

smears for the palms, or anything else that might make a palming placement better for pushing up on.

Place your palms so that your fingertips are pointing away from the corner (so you are pushing your body into the corner) and down towards the ground (so you are pushing your body up the corner). It sounds simple, but your aim is to push yourself up and in to the corner, not down and out of it.

Try to keep your hands further out from the corner than the rest of your body. Their position should squeeze your shoulder blades together and open up your chest. Having

your hands behind you will automatically push you into the corner, which in turn will prevent you from falling backwards.

ARMS

Try to keep your arms below shoulder level; if they are too high you will struggle to push up on them. If the only option is to place them high, then look for holds to pull on rather than push on.

Locking the arms out straight will use skeletal strength—structure—rather than muscular strength (see "Rule 4" in Chapter 1), ideal if you are moving other body parts or trying to rest.

To push up on an arm, use muscular strength; place your arm in a bent position so that you can push up and extend it out.

Sometimes the features of a corner won't let you put your hands and arms behind you: there might be nothing to palm against and attempting to do so would just hinder you. In that situation, use your palm between your body and the corner. There are two options for how to do this:

- Right hand on the right corner wall (or vice versa): use a palm-down (mantel) technique. So, point your elbow up to the sky and point your fingertips down towards the ground; push up in this position (figure 142).
- Right hand on the left corner wall (or vice versa): use a chickenwing technique (Chapter 5). Place your arm into the corner like you would place a chickenwing (elbow first) and palm on the opposing wall with your fingertips pointing away from the corner. So, if

Figure 142. Stemming in corners: palm-down technique

Figure 143. Stemming in corners: chickenwing technique

using your right arm, the contact points would be your right palm against the left corner wall, and your right upper arm/tricep against the right corner wall (figure 143). It's essentially a flared and baggy chickenwing (see Chapter 5).

LEGS

The wider you can bridge your legs in a corner, the more secure the position will feel. A small bridging stance, with feet close to the back of the corner, will make it feel like a lot of your upper body is being pushed backwards out of the corner. A nice wide position with the legs, ensuring your upper body is leaning into the corner, is the most effective and relaxing stance. Have your legs bent so they can generate upwards movement.

As a lot of weight goes through your lower body on corner stems, your legs can get incredibly pumped. Two techniques help with this:

- Shake out your legs (like you would your arms when they get pumped during conventional climbing). You can do this one leg at a time or, if you find a good palming position or good enough hand-hold to hang from, you could even shake out both legs together.
- Lock your legs out and straighten them. This uses the structure of your body, and minimizes the muscular stress of having your legs continuously bent.
- If there are good enough foot holds, stand on the soles of your heels rather than the soles of your toes to relieve some strain in your calf muscles.

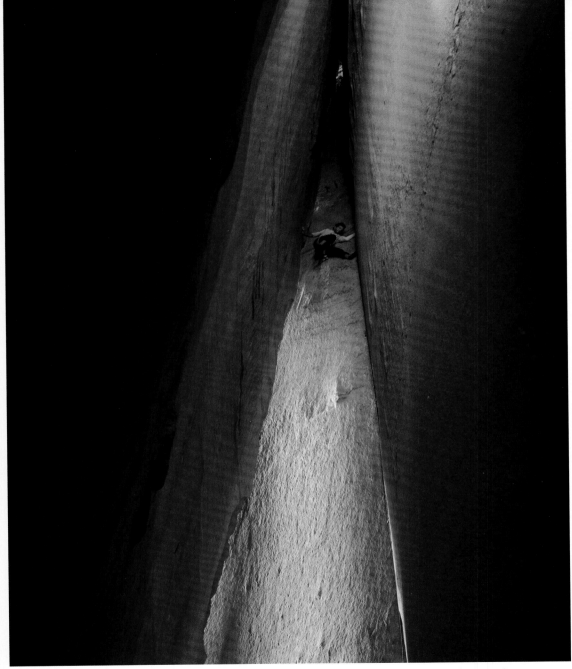

Andy Wyatt in The Cave Route *(5.10+) at Battle of the Bulge, Indian Creek, Utah* (© Andrew Burr)

NICO FAVRESSE

One of the strongest "artists" who has ever climbed, Nico climbs the hardest trad and biggest big walls in the world, with limited fuss and surprising ease. A climbing natural. In 2013 he made the first ascent of the incredibly difficult crack Recovery Drink *(F8c+) in Rogaland, Norway.*

FAVOURITE CRACK CLIMBING AREA?

For me it's definitely Yosemite because it is where I learnt how to crack climb and lived so many experiences. It is also the place where I get most motivated because the walls and the dirtbag climbing community in Camp 4 inspire me. And in terms of cracks, there are many of all sizes and it's not just cragging. You will find the best of them way up on El Capitan, which adds up to a great atmosphere.

FAVOURITE CRACK CLIMB?

Salathé headwall . . . it's a perfect crack located 800 metres from the ground in one of the most exposed locations on El Cap. This pitch is a beauty but doesn't go for free with a bloody hard F8a rating! It has a bit of everything: fingery boulder moves, stamina hand and finger jam, chimney, offwidths, all in one 60-metre pitch. I climbed it with my ex-girlfriend, leading and hauling and belaying (because she didn't want to jumar) every pitch. We spent seven days in total, four of which were spent hanging out in our portaledges in this super-exposed location just below the headwall. It was magical!

MEMORABLE CRACK EXPERIENCE?

While in Patagonia, I met Thomas Huber. For some reason we started talking about Yosemite and offwidths and he mentioned he knew no European climber who had onsighted *Ahab* (5.10b—the equivalent of F6a!). So, on my next trip to Yosemite I had to try it. While experienced Yosemite climbers would even solo it, I had the fight of my life on it! After 45 minutes of crawling, and giving it all like I had never done before on any climb, I finally reached the anchor but five minutes later puked. At the time I could redpoint F9a sport climbs but, still, a F6a could give me such a huge trouble! This is what crack climbing is all about—learning and humbleness—and that's why I love it.

THE KNOWLEDGE

Don't think too much about beta like you do with sport climbing, just shove your hands and arms inside as deep as possible and go for it full-on!

Pop Quiz

1. Finger cracks or offwidths? Impossible to choose
2. Stemming or roof cracks? Roof crack
3. Hand jam or hand stack? Hand stack
4. Knee lock or chickenwing? Chickenwing
5. Tape or no tape? No tape
6. Cams or nuts? Nuts
7. Sandstone cracks or granite cracks? Granite
8. Short and hard, or long and pumpy? Short and hard
9. Pressure wound or rock rash? Pressure wound
10. Colour preference of crack climbing trousers due to unfortunate mistakes, red or brown? Red

Opposite: *NIco Favresse on the crux pitch of* Eye of Sauron *(5.13a/b), Yosemite National Park, California* (© Drew Smith)

FEET

The first things you should always look for are good footholds such as edges.

If there are no obvious footholds, then smearing (see figure 35) is your only option. Remember, all the same smearing rules apply when using them in corners: don't overextend to a handhold and allow your heels to lift; keep your heels low, and make a few extra moves if necessary. If you do need to reach a long way, straighten your leg, be flexible in the Achilles tendon, and keep your heel low (make the V shape between your shin and foot).

CLIMBING MOVEMENT

Climbing movement while stemming is all about correctly distributing your weight to make it as easy as possible to move whichever body part you need to. In this section we'll look at the basic stemming rules and then use these in an example of how to make it easier to move while stemming.

THE RULES

Fifty percent of your body weight (or outwards pressure) is distributed through each (left and right) corner wall while stemming. This equals 100 percent of your body weight/pressure being pushed out.

If you are in a pure stemming position—pushing with both hands and feet—then you will be distributing an equal amount of weight/pressure through each wall. Remember this only applies if you are in a pure stem; as soon as you start pulling or pushing on holds (with either hands or feet), more weight/pressure will be transferred on to the corner wall that you are pulling/pushing on to.

If the weight/pressure through one corner wall drops below 50 percent, then things will start to feel insecure. You might start slipping, and then eventually you'll fall off.

If all four contact points (two hands and two feet) are weighted evenly, then 25 percent of body weight/pressure will be distributed through each contact point. However, it's unlikely that the pressure will ever be completely even because on stemming corners your feet often take a lot more weight/pressure than your hands. Let's look at how your weight/pressure might be distributed and how it could be shifted to enable you to make moves:

On the left wall:

- Your left foot is on a good smear: 45 percent weight/pressure is distributed through this.
- Your left hand is on a bad palm: 5 percent weight/pressure is distributed through this.

Together this equals 50 percent weight/pressure through the left wall.

If you were to lift your left palm off the wall in order to move it, the 5 percent of weight/pressure this was holding would be transferred to the left foot and now the whole 50 percent would go through this foot.

On the right wall:

- Your right foot is on a poor smear: 20 percent weight/pressure is distributed through this.

■ Your right hand is on a good palm: 30 percent weight/pressure is distributed through this.

Together this equals 50 percent weight/pressure through the right wall.

If you were to lift your right foot off the wall in order to move it, the 20 percent of weight/pressure this was holding would be transferred to the right hand and now the whole 50 percent would go through this hand.

This should illustrate how you must transfer weight and apply more pressure to other body parts so that you can move your feet and hands.

EXAMPLE

The following very basic example illustrates how you can make moving easier and less stressful on certain body parts. Start by making some choices:

1. From your four body parts (left hand or foot, right hand or foot), select the one that you would like to move.

2. From your remaining three body parts, select the most sturdy placement and put 50 percent of your weight/pressure through it, and then distribute the remaining 50 percent between the two other placements.

Let's imagine that you are in a basic stemming position—left hand and foot on the left wall, right hand and foot on the right wall—and you would like to move your left foot.

■ *If the left palm placement is good:* You can just transfer the weight/pressure from your left foot on to your left palm so that you can move your left foot up the wall.

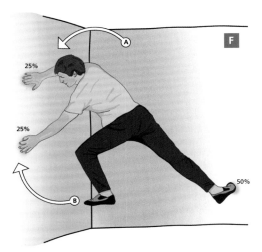

Figure 144. Stemming movement: matching hands to move foot

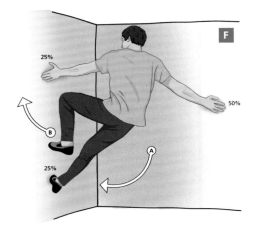

Figure 145. Stemming movement: matching feet to move foot

- *If the left palm placement is bad:* You might not want to transfer all the weight/pressure from your left foot on to your left palm. Instead, you could use a body part from the right wall and match it on to the left wall.
- *If the right palm placement is bad* (match-hands technique): You could bring the right palm over on to the left wall to support the poor left palm placement. This would split the weight and/or pressure equally (25 percent each) between the two hands and make things less strenuous and tenuous on the arms. You would then put a whole 50 percent of weight and pressure through the right foot (figure 144). By doing this you will have shifted the greater load from your bad left palm to your good right foot. The thing to be aware of when you have both hands on the same wall is that it can then be difficult to lift your leg high due to the position you have put yourself into, so this option is not good for high steps.
- *If the right foot placement is bad* (match-foot-to-hand technique): You could bring the right foot over to the left wall to support the poor left palm placement, meaning you will split the weight and/or pressure equally (25 percent each) between your left hand and your right foot. You will then put a whole 50 percent of weight and pressure through your right palm (figure 145). By doing this you will have shifted the greater

load from your bad left palm to your good right palm.

As you can see, stemming is all about working out which is the most solid placement and then applying the greatest weight and pressure through it, while simultaneously trying to even out the pressure on the poorer hand or foot placements. Don't be afraid to match different combinations of hands and feet together to help you transfer weight/pressure. Even the smallest of edges or the use of just your fingertips can help you spread the load more effectively so that you can move the body part that you want to.

STEMMING IN CHIMNEYS

Stemming in chimneys is a technique for use in the size of crack between standard chimney and full-width body bridging (Chapter 7).

The same technique and movement principles apply with stemming in chimneys as with stemming in corners. The only real difference is that the chimney won't be forcing you outwards like a corner would, and so it is not necessary to keep your hands behind your shoulder blades as you don't need to push your weight into any corner system.

Do keep your arms and hands below shoulder level so that you can push up on them, but keep them parallel to your shoulder blades and use the movement rules and techniques in the same way that you would on corner stems (see figure 141).

Opposite: *Mary Eden inverts on* Anal Flair *(V3) in Moab, Utah* (© Irene Yee)

CHAPTER 9

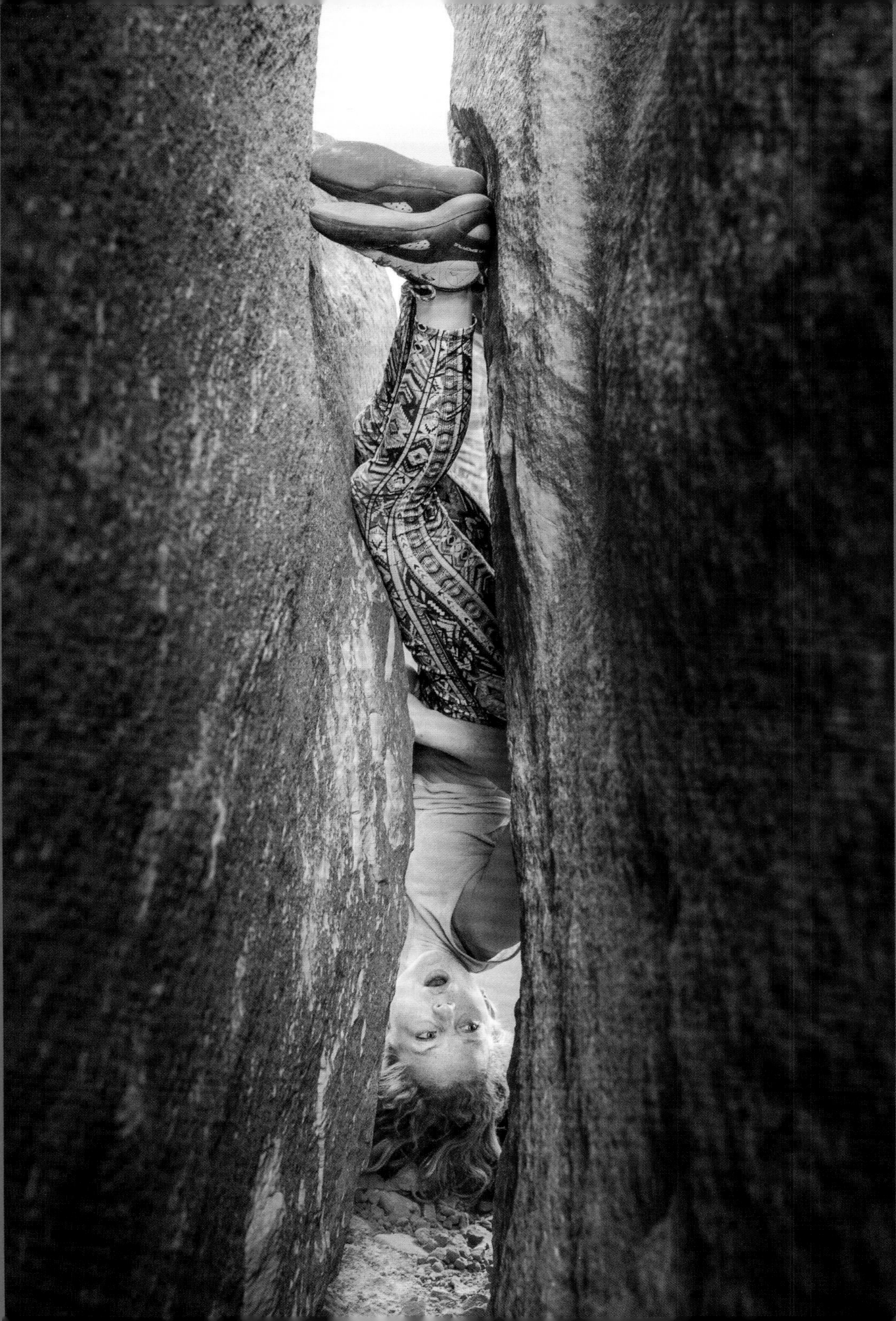

Roof Cracks

We're leaving the vertical world behind now and moving into a horizontal world of shuffling. Combine everything you have learnt from the previous chapters, add it to the extra tips and techniques in this one, and you'll start to get a feel for what it takes to succeed on steep cracks. You'll need to think in a three-dimensional way.

I've found that on roof cracks, good jams can act like jugs and the movement can contain some of the most gymnastic, sequence-dependent positions of any type of climbing. These factors mean you can often cover outrageous or impossible-looking terrain with a bunch of creativity and surprising ease, which—in my opinion—makes roof crack climbing one of the most interesting and satisfying forms of climbing. Surely nobody could deny that swimming easily through a huge roof on glorious hand jams wouldn't make you feel heroic! So, tighten up your core, get the biceps pumped up, and get your fingers, hands, fists, and feet wedged in to some horizontal cracks in some satisfyingly contorted manner.

This chapter looks at all the different sizes of jams from the previous chapters and how you can use the techniques that you've already learnt—along with some new ones—in the horizontal plane.

FINGER-SIZED ROOF CRACKS

Finger cracks in roofs are hard and on most routes it's unlikely you'll come across more than a few moves in a row. If you do, you'll be starting to climb some seriously tricky grades. (See Chapter 2, for specifics on techniques.)

Standard finger locks

Standard finger locks in roofs can be used in lots of combinations: thumb down, pinkie down, ring finger down. The difficult thing about executing these jams in a roof is that your forearm wants to drop down away from the crack rather than pull along the length of the crack. When your forearm drops, you lose the full twisting action and your fingers fire out. There are a couple of things you can do to help with this:

- Use your thumb like you would when doing baggy finger locks. Inserting your thumb into the crack like this creates more of a pinch grip, which will help support the jam if the forearm does drop.
- Keep your forearm as close to the roof as possible. This is easier said than done, and it's not as simple as just touching your forearm to the roof. The key is to have tension throughout your whole body. You need to be strong in the arms and shoulders to pull your upper body up and in to the wall, plus you also need to be strong in the core and lower back to prevent your hips from sagging down. If your body stays tight to the roof your forearm will automatically move closer to the roof and the jam will feel better. Unfortunately, there are limited tricks for "techniqueing" your way around this one; having strong tension throughout your body is the determining factor.

Donut jam

Donut jams can actually work very effectively in roof climbs as they take a downwards pull rather than requiring your forearm to pull along the length of the crack to make them stick. This means that you don't have to keep horizontal tension in your body to make them work. The downside to using these jams is you will most likely be hanging under a horizontal roof from monos—yuck!

Opposing jams

Opposing jams are standard finger jams used in combination with one another to make both of them stick. Use your leading hand to pull towards yourself and your following hand as an undercut finger jam. Finding constrictions to use makes this technique much more effective.

Your hands will still be completing the normal twisting actions, however the force you are trying to achieve is to push them together—much like compression moves used in bouldering. This can help a standard finger jam stick more easily: your forearm can drop away from the rock but the jam will still work because compression is keeping it in place. Opposing jams work best when your hands are slightly wider than shoulder width apart: the closer your hands are together, the less effective the compression element and the worse the jams become.

If there are suitable positions for the locks, then this technique can work very well for making multiple moves: it's a very similar movement to swimming technique ("Climbing Movement" in Chapter 3). They are also great for cutting loose and doing spin-throughs (later in this chapter) so that you can sort your feet out.

HAND-SIZED ROOF CRACKS

This is the dream size for roof cracks—perfect hand jams are just like jugs, enabling you to swim across exciting terrain with relative ease. Here we'll take a look at some of the alternative techniques, positioning, and movement skills that differ from hand jamming in face cracks.

HAND TECHNIQUE AND POSITIONING

Because hand jams work via expansion of the jam, you can pull on them in all directions and they will still feel good. When you climb roof cracks your body naturally wants to hang down, so by placing your fingertips directly up into the crack—rather than along the length of the crack, as you would on more vertical terrain—you will achieve a much comfier and relaxed position.

The most comfortable positioning for your body is to engage your shoulders but keep your arms straight—although obviously small bends and contractions are necessary for movement. Engaging your shoulders stops all the stress from going directly through the hand jam, and straighter arms use less energy which prevents you from pumping out as quickly.

It may sometimes be necessary to rotate your fingertips along the length of the crack or pull up into the crack to make big moves as this will give you more reach (see "Big Moves," later in this chapter).

THIN HAND POSITIONING

Pointing your fingertips straight into the roof crack will enable your whole body to sit better on thin hand jams. The downside to jamming like this is that you will struggle to get the pulp of your thumb muscle into the crack (remember this is the important part of the hand when it comes to hand jamming). So, when using thin hand jams in roofs, you need to focus on a couple of things:

- Pushing the pad of your thumb towards the little finger: as with any hand jam, this is the key element that keeps your hand inside the crack.

- Pushing the side of your thumb outwards against the crack wall

Keep in mind that it is possible to also use a crimped hand jam to give extra support (Chapter 3).

Sometimes on flared cracks it can be impossible to point the fingertips directly into the crack, in which case you can place your jam, thumb first. There are positives and negatives to this approach: positive—you now have the pulp of your thumb inside the crack making the jam feel more secure; negative—because you now have to pull along the length of the crack to get the jam to stick and stop it from rotating out, you must use more strength and tension through the rest of your body, much like when finger jamming in a roof (earlier this chapter).

BOXED CRACKS POSITIONING

If the crack is shallow (boxed), it is unlikely you will be able to insert your whole hand if you try to place it fingertips first. You have two options for achieving a positive and secure jam.

- *Place your hand thumb first (thumb side up).* This is much like the final point on thin hand positioning, the difference being you will be able to insert your whole hand, meaning you can actually hang down from the jam effectively, rather than having to pull along the length of the crack. You just have to be able to take a small amount of strain in your wrist as it will start to angle in a slightly strange manner. The finished position should have the thumb side of your hand facing up and into the crack, your fingers pointing along the length of the crack, and the pinkie side of your hand facing down out of the crack. Whether you are climbing feet first or hands first, you can orient both your leading and trailing hand so that your fingers either point away from or towards you. Let the route and moves dictate the combinations you use.

- *Place your hand pinkie first (pinkie side up).* This is essentially the opposite to the first option. The important thing is to ensure that the pulp of your thumb doesn't hang out of the bottom of the crack, or it will very quickly become a poor jam. The finished position should have the pinkie side of your hand facing up into the crack, your fingers pointing along the length of the crack, and the thumb side of your hand facing down out of the crack. If climbing feet first, your fingers will be pointing towards you and if climbing hands first your fingers will be pointing away from you.

It is worth noting that when climbing these styles of cracks you can mix and match the combinations to fit with the size of the crack and the direction that you are climbing. For example, climbing in a slightly wider hand crack feet first lends itself well to pinkie-side-up jams, as you can get the correct cup and twist motion, whereas climbing feet first in a thinner crack lends itself to thumb-side-up jams as the thumb pulp can be inserted. I am always changing and inserting my hands in different ways to suit the jams, style, fatigue, and the direction.

FOOT TECHNIQUE

Good footwork is as important as ever—if you don't use your feet properly in roof cracks you will suffer through your arms and very quickly pump out. To give you an idea of just how much weight you can take via your feet in a roof, in a positive hand-sized crack it is actually possible to hang no-handed from just foot jams!

OVERTWISTING

The techniques for foot jamming in roof cracks are the same as for normal foot jamming, although you can overemphasise one part of the process to create a better jam. When you twist your knee so that it comes in line with the crack, you can actually overtwist it so that your knee goes past the centre point. This is very effective when you are pushing off just one foot in the crack (and have the other flagged out in the roof) to make a move. This body position resembles the classic "drop knee" position.

Crossed heels technique

This is a new technique that only works in roof cracks. It is most effective when you use both feet in combination, and it is a useful tool when resting as it gives your feet, toes, and ankles respite from continuous twisting.

1. Insert your foot into the crack the way you would normally insert it when executing a standard foot jam in a hand-size crack (Chapter 3). So, sole and laces touching one of the crack walls, and knee out to the side and out of line with the crack. Now insert your other foot into the crack in the same

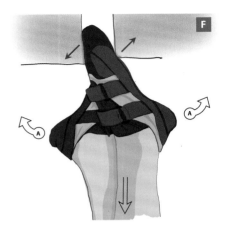

Figure 146. Hand-sized roof cracks: crossed heels technique

manner, either in front of or behind your first foot. Keeping the feet reasonably close together makes this jam easier.

2. Keeping your toes absolutely stationary, simultaneously push the ball of each heel up towards the roof—you will push them in opposite directions so that they cross and make an X shape. This will push the laces of your shoes into the crack walls; the arches of your feet should lie across the crack edges.

3. To bring your knees in line with the crack, push off the feet so that your legs become straight. Your bum should drop down, your legs become straight and in line, and your feet should be forced up in to the crack making them stick more easily (figure 146). Try to execute points 2 and 3 in one motion as this is more efficient.

4. If you have placed your feet close enough together, it is possible to push one foot into the other which helps to reinforce the jam and make it feel more solid.

5. Straightening your legs and dropping your bum is a useful position for resting and can relieve some of the strain that you will feel in your shins during intense roof crack climbing. However, keeping your legs totally straight when climbing can hinder your movement. When using this technique for movement, bend your legs (your knees may slightly flare out to the side) and lift your bum—remember to keep your heels crossed and lifted to keep the jam engaged. Your feet may not jam quite as effectively with bent knees, but this will prevent the "pushing away from the crack" effect that you get from straightening your legs when resting and you'll be able to move your hands more easily. Although this technique can be used to climb in a hands-first style, it becomes most effective when climbing feet first (later in this chapter), as you can move your hands towards the foot jams rather than having to push off and away from them. Pushing off the jammed feet to climb hands first does work, but you'll often find yourself blending the technique with normal foot jamming—twisting the foot and bringing the knee in line with the crack (Chapter 3)—to get the solid platform that is needed to push the body forwards.

OFFSET / CORNER CRACK POSITIONING

When climbing roof cracks your palms can obviously be placed towards the offset or away from it or be used in combination. Below are some of the advantages of going palm towards the offset.

- *Forearm friction*: your body will swing towards the offset, meaning your forearms will get pushed into it. You can use this to your advantage and essentially forearm scum (Chapter 5) and gain extra friction. If the offset is big, square cut, and angled as a slab, you can sometimes gain so much forearm friction that you can relax the hand jam entirely.
- *The use of face holds*: your body is automatically oriented in the correct position to use any available face holds on the offset.
- *Reinforcing the jam*: if the crack is thin, then having your palm against the offset (even if it is not entirely inserted inside the crack) will help to reinforce the jam, as the pulp of your thumb and palm of your hand will be in contact with the rock.

MOVEMENT SKILLS

Movement principles on roof cracks are very similar to those on vertical or less steep cracks. Both hand-over-hand and swimming techniques can be used to great effect (Chapter 3). Roof cracks suddenly become difficult when you have to use poor jams, so if you can make long moves between the best jams your horizontal world will be much more hospitable. Here we'll look at the techniques for effectively moving between the best locks and reaching past all the thin and dirty jams.

Big moves: lock and push (static movement)

This option is strenuous, but it gives you plenty of precision when executing the move. It is useful if you are making a long move to a jam which you must seat perfectly in order to be able to later move on it.

Pull your whole body towards the roof with both arms, lock off with your non-moving arm, and then push your body forwards with your feet in this locked-off position. Be sure to maintain your locked position to prevent your body from sagging down away from the crack (figures 147 and 148).

Big moves: swinging technique (dynamic movement)

This option is less strenuous, but it is also much less precise. It will only work if you are moving to a jam which is good enough that even when not seated perfectly your ability to move on it is not affected.

Keep a straight arm and use a backwards and forwards swinging movement in the roof to propel yourself forwards and up into the next jam. Using an intermediate jam or hold with the hand you are throwing forwards can often help with building momentum. If the jam you are moving from is good enough, it will hold you through a few swinging attempts to catch the next jam. Once you have caught the next jam, you can then make little bumps with the hand to seat it more solidly.

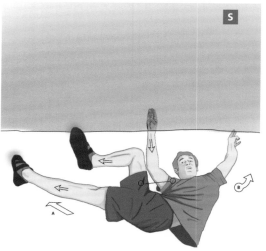

Figure 147. Big moves in hand-sized roof cracks: lock and push (opposite hand to foot)

Figure 148. Big moves in hand-sized roof cracks: lock and push (same hand and foot)

BIG MOVES: PUSH FROM THE CORRECT FOOT

The defining factor in whether a big move will feel easy or impossible in a roof is which foot you push off from in the crack. It's important to note that when you are making these big moves pushing off one leg is often a lot easier than trying to push off both—you will get more reach.

There are no strict rules to this as every jam and scenario are different, however here are some options and tips:

- *Lock and push, opposite hand to foot:* This is often the best hand and foot combination to use for lock and push as you are pushing through your body in a diagonal manner, much like in normal climbing (for example, right hand/left foot). Also, if the foot jams are a long way from the hand jams, using opposites will be less strenuous for holding the locked-off position. (See figure 147).

- *Lock and push, same hand, same foot:* If you have to push with the same hand and foot (for example, right hand and right foot), then it can be useful to do a deep flag with your spare leg across the crack and behind your pushing leg. (See figure 148).

- *A second same hand, same foot tip* which can help you to make a bigger move than if you were to use opposite hand to foot: Place your pushing foot close to

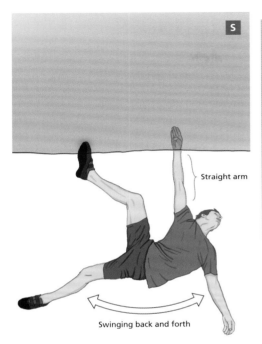

Figure 149. Big moves in hand-sized roof cracks: swinging technique

your pulling arm and twist your knee in line with the crack as you would when foot jamming. Now nestle and lock the elbow of your pulling arm into the fleshy part on the inside of your knee. With your elbow nestled in this position, it will be much easier to hold the locked-down position, you will be able to pull your body much closer to the roof, your foot will be placed close to you (so you can push off it very effectively), and you will find you can push and reach an incredibly long way—and very statically.

■ *Swinging technique, same hand, same foot:* This is often the best hand and foot combination to use for swinging technique, as everything can hang easily off a straight arm and leg directly below the crack and swing like a pendulum would do (for example, right hand and right foot). (See figure 149.)

■ *Swinging technique, opposite hand to foot:* Using opposite hand to foot (for example, right hand and left foot) can hinder your momentum slightly and you can often start a swinging motion and then find yourself starting to pull through the movement as you go for the next hold—and if you start to pull when you're supposed to be swinging you'll probably come up short of the prize. To help you gain extra swing in this position, push off the underside of the roof with your spare leg.

BIG MOVES: ROTATE THE FINGERS FOR MORE REACH

When climbing roof cracks, you'll often climb them with your fingers pointing directly up into the crack. However, keeping them in this orientation can lessen your potential maximum reach. To help gain maximum reach, point your fingers along the length of the crack rather than up into the crack. (See "Crack Positioning," earlier this chapter.) Move off a thumb-up jam and into a thumb-down jam. Moves executed in this manner will put your fingers, hands, and shoulders into a position that resembles a crucifixion.

Barbara Zangerl on Desert Gold *(5.13a), Red Rock Canyon, Nevada* (© François Lebeau)

FIST-SIZED ROOF CRACKS

Fist-crack climbing in roofs follows the same technique and movement principles as in vertical or gently overhanging fist cracks (Chapter 4). Note that it can be difficult to move hand over hand unless the fist jams are shallow, so swimming technique is often best for movement.

When making big moves, using a palm-up fist jam followed by a palm-down jam will usually give you the longest and most powerful reach, and movement with the greatest security (Chapter 4). All the techniques and movement skills for hand jamming in roofs (earlier this chapter) can also be applied to fist cracks.

OFFWIDTH ROOF CRACKS

Climbing offwidth cracks in roofs is all about inverting—placing your feet and legs securely above your head and then hanging from them like a bat. When you can use your feet like hands, things become a whole lot easier. Traditional vertical-style offwidth techniques can still be used, but you'd need shoulders and knees made in a forge in order to do long sections of steep offwidth climbing via straight-in arm bars and knee locks. So, get creative, flip upside down, and expect a rush of blood to the head if you want to succeed.

HAND / HAND-SIZED OFFWIDTH ROOF CRACKS

Body positioning is the key to climbing offwidth roofs of this size. The techniques used in standard hand/hand offwidths can be applied, however it's the positioning and movement skills that differ. There are two classic offwidth positions for this style of crack: the wide pony and trench foot.

Wide pony

With this technique, you are climbing with your hands between your legs, sideways, in a crablike style (figure 150).

Hands: Use your hands in the butterfly jam stack position (Chapter 5), so one palm is facing towards you. The palm that is facing towards you is used to aid your sit-up: use it to undercut the crack (and to keep your torso from dropping down) as you get your other hand in position.

It's important to have the correct hand facing towards you. If you are leading with your right leg, have your right palm facing towards you, and vice versa. This will give you greater reach in the direction you are moving, which gives options for other holds (undercutting, for example). It will also prevent you from stretching across your body to place the first hand of the stack, and this keeps the whole body more balanced. When you pull in on the stack, you'll also naturally pull slightly towards the direction you are moving, meaning you can then push your leading leg further along the crack, giving you greater progression in fewer moves.

Legs: Your legs should be inserted up into the crack at either side of the hand stack. On this size of crack, they can commonly be inserted to about mid-shin depth (depending on the size of your foot and leg). While it is difficult to insert them deep into the crack, the further you can insert your legs the

Figure 150. Offwidth roof cracks: wide pony

Figure 151. Offwidth roof cracks: wide pony feet

easier it will make things as it will be less strenuous to sit your torso up into the stacks. It can be worth enduring a little shin pain (by shoving your legs in further than you might want to) in order to save some extra strength in your abs for sitting up.

Feet: Once your legs and feet are inserted into the crack, a frogged foot technique (Chapter 5) can be used to make your feet stick (figure 151).

Overall position: The overall position of this technique has you hanging from the roof in such a way that resembles you riding a big upside-down pony (or hanging like a bat). Your stack should be in front of your face directly above you in the crack, and both legs should be frogged out on either side the stack. If you are able to open up your hips and insert your feet into the crack, the wide pony is generally the go-to technique for this width of crack as your body is in the most balanced position.

Trench foot

With this technique, you are climbing feet first.

Hands: Exactly the same hand position is used as for the wide pony technique above.

Legs: Both legs should be inserted ahead of you, past your hand stack and with the toes of both feet pointing back towards you—so you will be climbing feet first. As with the wide pony, and due to the width of the crack, you will be able to insert your legs to around mid-shin depth.

Feet: The foot that is closest to your stack should be using twisted foot technique and the foot that is furthest away from your stack should be using frogged foot technique (Chapter 5). Your closer foot will have the inside of the heel against one crack wall, and the outside edge of the boot (pinkie toe side) against the other crack wall. Your leading foot will have the outside of the heel against one crack wall, and the inside edge of the boot (big toe side) against the other crack wall. Both heels will be against the same crack wall and both toes against the other. (If you have large feet, you might be lucky enough to gain some extra friction from either the inside or outside edge which shouldn't be in contact with the other wall.) It's worth noting that I find this combination to be the most secure when using a trench foot style of climbing. However, depending on the width, style, or lean of the crack, different combinations

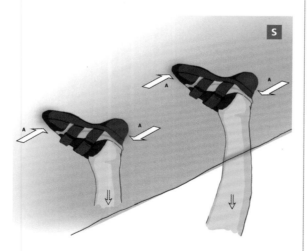

Figure 152. Offwidth roof cracks: trench foot feet

can sometimes trump it and feel more secure. If one combination isn't feeling secure, it's worth trying an alternative. Here are the different combinations:

- Both toes touching the same crack wall, both heels touching the other crack wall and both feet twisting in a clockwise direction (figure 152).
- Both toes touching the same crack wall, both heels touching the other crack wall and both feet twisting in an anticlockwise direction.
- The outside edges of both toes touching opposite crack walls (toes twisting outwards) and the insides of the heels touching opposite crack walls (heels twisting inwards).
- The inside edges of both toes touching opposite crack walls (toes twisting inwards) and the outsides of the heels touching opposite crack walls (heels twisting outwards).

Overall position: The overall position of this technique has you climbing feet first, toes pointing back towards you and with the stack following along behind your feet. Using your legs and feet in this manner can be useful on this width of crack if you don't have flexible hips and can't open them up into a wide pony position. It is also a good technique if you have large feet, as orienting your body in this way more easily puts your feet into their narrowest dimension. On the other hand, this technique can feel slightly out of balance, as whenever you try to move your stack you can feel as though you are swinging away from the crack and beneath your feet.

HAND / FIST-SIZED OFFWIDTH ROOF CRACKS

The same techniques, positioning, and movement skills can be used on this width of crack as with hand/hand-sized offwidth cracks. However, there are some subtle variations that are important to note:

Hands: Hand/fist stacks are most commonly done with your palm facing towards you, so that you can undercut the crack more easily when you are placing the stack. However, they can also be done with your fist at the front of the stack. Having all the variations in your toolbox of techniques is handy as using different combinations helps to spread the stress of stacking (using just one combination all the time can get tiring). Certain crack features or sequences might also lend themselves to having your fist at the front of the stack.

Legs: As the hand/hand offwidth crack is slightly wider, you will be able to insert your legs into the crack to a greater depth. You should always take advantage of this. Inserting your legs to a greater depth equals more leg friction (less stressful on the feet) and means that you don't have to sit up as far to reach the stack (less strenuous on the abs).

Leg levering: As you can now insert your legs into the crack up to the tops of your shins and just below your kneecaps, you will be able to start using a technique called leg levering. Push the heels of your shoes hard into the crack wall, straighten your legs and lever the tops of your shins against the opposing crack edge. This levering action can help to relieve a little bit of jamming stress in the shin muscles and feet.

Leg levering can be painful—especially if the edge of the crack is sharp—and cause pressure wounds, so kneepads that extend down over the tops of the shins are recommended if you know you will be using this technique a lot. Leg levering can also be done on thinner cracks, but the amount of pain you will experience directly across your shin bones tends to mean this technique is more detrimental than beneficial. It is from hand/fist offwidth size and up when leg levering becomes really useful.

Feet: *Franana jam* is a blend between a frogged foot and banana foot jams. The standard technique for the feet in this width of crack is frogged foot (Chapter 5). However, as the crack has become a bit wider, you can start to blend your frogged foot techniques together with banana foot techniques (Chapter 5). It's unlikely you will be able to achieve the full banana foot position, but if you start to twist them inwards from the frogged position and to the banana position, a halfway point can be achieved that feels very solid. This halfway position is often so solid that it's not very useful for climbing as your feet can feel stuck. The franana jam is perhaps most useful for resting.

POSITIONING AND MOVEMENT SKILLS ON HAND/HAND AND HAND/FIST OFFWIDTH ROOF CRACKS

POSITIONING ON DIFFERENT ANGLES OF CRACK

When climbing steep offwidths, it's important to conserve as much energy as possible. One action which saps energy is repeatedly having to sit your torso up

so that you can stack your hands into the crack. As the angle of the crack changes, you can make this easier for yourself by switching your positioning and altering where you place your stack in relation to your feet. The aim is to do the least amount of "sitting up" into the stacks as possible, and to alter the positioning of your feet/legs accordingly. A few example scenarios:

- *Roof:* The least strenuous and most balanced position for roof climbing is the wide pony. Your stack should be placed up into the crack directly in front of you.
- *45-degree overhang:* As the crack becomes less steep you might decide to move your stack more towards your trailing leg so that you don't have to do a really hard sit-up to place it an equal distance between both legs. More stress will be put through the leading leg, but the sit-up will be much easier.
- *25-degree overhang:* When the crack becomes much less steep, you will have to do an impossibly hard sit-up to get your stack between your legs; an alternative here is to actually stack behind the trailing leg so that you don't have to execute an extraordinary feat of sit-up strength. Using your feet in either a trench foot (see figure 152) or wide pony (see figure 153) orientation can now work.

An alternative foot positioning is to use a trench foot technique but switch the leg which you are leading with. So, place what would normally be the leading leg as the trailing (lower) leg with your foot in a frogged foot position. Then, cross your trailing leg behind your new low leg and place it into the crack toe first (trench foot style) as your new leading leg. Your new leading leg will be straight, your new trailing leg slightly bent, and your legs will now be crossed. A benefit of this position is that your feet will be placed close together, which gives a little more room for stacking hands behind your legs. Also, it can make setting up to execute a pivot (later this chapter) more straightforward; you'll be able to take the leading leg out with ease and pivot around the closer trailing leg as the trailing leg has the correct foot position around which to execute a pivot.

MOVEMENT SKILLS

Movement on these types of cracks is actually very simple as there are only three body parts to move: left foot, right foot, and stack. In order to move these body parts, remember to adhere to the standard off-widthing movement rule: "move only one body part at a time."

Because there are three body parts in these two sizes of offwidth climbing, this means there are three movement stages:

Stage 1: Hold a stationary position with your stack and trailing leg, then slide your leading leg forwards—your legs will now be spread further apart.

Stage 2: Hold a stationary position with both legs, then move your stack towards your leading leg.

Stage 3: Hold a stationary position with your leading leg and stack, then slide your trailing leg towards your stack. You are now back in your starting position. (See figure 150 for order of movement.)

Figure 153. Offwidth roof cracks: positioning on different angles of crack

This cycle of movement would resemble a "crabbing" style over a long section of repetitive roof crack climbing.

Remember, when moving any body part, you don't have to take it out of the crack: you can bump or slide it along inside the crack; this helps to keep some body/rock contact and makes staying on (in) the rock less strenuous. If you reach a narrower section of crack, however, it might be necessary to take the body parts out (one at a time) in order to move around the constriction.

FIST / FIST-SIZED OFFWIDTH ROOF CRACKS

When you start climbing fist/fist-sized off-width roof cracks you'll realise that you are becoming heavily involved with the crack. You'll be deeply inserted and be using a whole range of stacking, palming, and undercutting techniques to aid you through the steepness.

Positioning

Hands: You have some options for positioning your hands.

- *Stacking:* Double-fist stacks can be used with the hands on this width of crack (Chapter 5), but they can be difficult to place as your legs will be so deeply inserted into the crack (see "Legs," below) that there will be little room for your hands. Rather than trying to place, the stacks between your legs, a good alternative on fist/fist-sized cracks is to place the stacks *behind* your trailing leg. It won't feel like such a strenuous sit-up as you are so deeply inserted in the crack.

- *Undercutting:* Undercutting the edge of the crack works a treat for this width as your hands are in a perfect position to do it—by your waist, which is lying across the crack edge. Make sure you feel around inside the crack for any sneaky hidden handholds. As soon as you find any holds (even tiny ones), you'll find it requires less effort from the biceps and is significantly easier to move your legs.

- *Palming:* When one edge of the crack becomes sufficiently offset, or if the crack is in a cornered roof, then you will have a sidewall available to use and rest your bum on. This sidewall can be useful for downwards palming to help either push your hips up into the crack to more deeply insert them, or to push them along the crack for movement. As you won't be making huge shuffles with your hips (just lots of small ones), you don't need to push off a bent arm to gain extra movement. The majority of the time it's useful to keep your palming arm straight and locked out since this creates a strong and sturdy position (and doesn't use muscular strength), and use the movement you have in your shoulder to push yourself forwards. As you shuffle the rest of your body forwards, shuffle your straight palming arm forwards as well.

- *The "private pirate":* This technique blends downwards palming and undercutting together to make moving along the roof/steep crack easier. As you have to use palming, it will only work when there is a sidewall. Place your leading hand in an undercut position and your trailing hand in a palm-down position; push and pull in unison to release the pressure on your bum so you can shuffle it along the sidewall more easily (figure 154). A great technique to help kick your legs forwards in the crack is the "reversed private pirate." Reverse your undercutting hand so that your elbow points up to the sky and you are holding the crack in a gaston-style of grip—this grip actually works best behind the trailing leg.

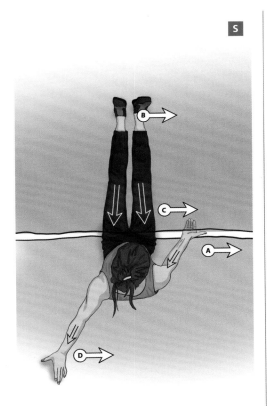

Figure 154. Offwidth roof cracks: private pirate

Legs: Your legs on this width of crack should be fully inserted into the crack so that the edge of the crack is lying across the tops of your thighs. Your finished position with both legs should be a thigh lock (Chapter 5), but obviously upside down. Getting the edge of the crack to lie across the tops of the thighs is the important factor and is what will make or break a successful ascent. As soon as your legs start to drop

out of the crack, it's game over. Remember in this particular crack, the deeper you can penetrate, the greater the satisfaction and likelihood of success.

Feet: The gap should now be wide enough that you can use banana foot technique (Chapter 5).

Movement skills
Movement skills on fist/fist offwidth roof cracks differ from hand/hand and hand/fist-width cracks only when you have a sidewall to contend with. You still need to stick to the process of moving each body part independently, but there are a few more body parts to shuffle. In this width of offwidth you have to move an undercutting hand, a palming hand, a left leg, a right leg, and your hips.

Moving the undercutting hand: Hold firm with your other body parts and move your undercutting hand forwards.

Moving your legs: To more easily move your legs, you need to put pressure through your bum to enable you to release the tension in your feet/legs. Use your undercutting hand to pull your bum in hard against the sidewall. Now you will be able to release the tension to move your legs. If you are struggling to create enough force with the undercutting hand, then using the "reversed private pirate" (above) can help to push your bum harder into the sidewall.

Moving your hips (the hip flick): To move your hips, you need to release the tension from your bum against the back wall. To do this, push down with the palming hand. Once the tension has been released, you should move your hips forwards in a "flicking" action—quickly and with force. If you try to move your hips slowly, by the time you are halfway through the movement your bum will have been out of contact with the sidewall long enough that you will start to feel yourself slipping out of the crack. If this happens, upwards movement will rapidly turn into downwards sliding. Remember, it's all about the hip flick.

Moving the palming hand: This is an easy movement. Hold firm with your feet and legs and bump your palming hand along the sidewall behind you.

ARM BAR AND CHICKENWING-SIZED OFFWIDTH ROOF CRACKS

With arm bar and chickenwing-sized roof cracks, you need to start thinking about the crack as a hanging chimney. It's all about getting fully inserted inside the crack and not letting any body parts hang out: let the crack eat you up. These widths can feel incredibly daunting—especially if they are flared—as they look dark, deep, and nasty. With practice, however, they're actually one of the most secure and easy styles of offwidth roof climbing as you have so much body/rock contact.

The techniques in this section are only really applicable if the crack becomes narrower deeper inside. If it doesn't get narrower, you can get fully inside, turn the correct way around, and shuffle across in a basic squeeze chimney position (Chapter 6). However, if it does become narrower, then it's very unlikely that you'll be able to

fit your head and shoulders inside (in an upright position); instead you'll be able to put your legs and arms up into the crack as they are narrower.

It's possible to use either sidewinder technique or a fully inverted technique to cross roofs of this width.

Sidewinder

The same body positioning is used as when executing standard sidewinder technique in squeeze chimneys (Chapter 6); the difference is you will be inching body parts and sliding hips along the roof rather than moving body parts and flicking hips upwards. You'll find that it is actually easier to move forwards in a sidewinder position than it is to move upwards, as you only have to maintain a constant height and not put any effort into moving upwards.

Full invert

If the crack becomes much narrower inside it might be difficult to place the top chickenwing that is needed to execute a sidewinder position. Instead you can use full invert technique. This offwidth position can look outrageously difficult, but again can actually feel much less strenuous than other roof offwidth techniques because you have so much body-to-rock contact keeping you in the crack and helping to spread the load. One of the more unusual problems with this method is that you get a massive rush of blood to the head because you are upside down, surrounded by rock, and can't sit up to move your head into an upright position!

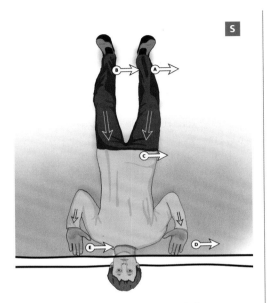

Figure 155. Offwidth roof cracks: full invert

Positioning

- **Arms:** Both arms should be in an upside-down chickenwing position, with the palms of your hands at around shoulder level. Gravity acting on your body to pull you out of the crack will make your chickenwings tighten, so unless the palms of your chickenwings slip (or your body slips when you are moving them), then it's mechanically impossible for you to fall out when you're stationary.

- **Feet, legs, and hips:** you will use counter pressure between all the remaining parts of your body to keep you solidly inside the crack. On the back wall of the crack you will be pressing outwards with the backs of your heels (if the crack becomes very narrow inside you can start using tipped-out banana foot techniques), your bum, and your back. On the front wall of the crack (the wall your nose will be touching), you will be pushing outwards in an opposite direction with your knees, thighs, and palms (figure 155).

Movement on this type of crack is simple; all you are doing is holding firm with your chickenwings while moving one leg at a time and doing a small hip shuffle. Then hold firm with your feet, legs, and hips to move an individual chickenwing. As with any kind of offwidth climbing, it's all about focusing on moving one thing at a time and making lots of quick, small shuffles, rather than big moves, to cover the terrain.

Getting inverted

Just getting into a sidewinder or full invert position in a roof can be the most strenuous part of these techniques, as you have to wriggle your whole body inside the crack. Every situation where you must become inverted is different, but there are some tricks which can help.

- *Look for single-handed jams or holds:* Make sure you look for other jams and holds to invert from to help pull yourself up into the crack.

- *Palm down:* Once you are partially inverted, any features that can be used to palm down against can help push you up into the crack.

- *Leg bar:* As soon as your legs enter the crack, start leg barring with them to keep inverted tension. If you fail to start jamming your legs immediately, you'll feel as though you're doing an inverted front lever, which isn't the easiest thing ever . . .

- *Chickenwings:*
  - As soon as the edge of the crack is past waist level, be aware that you will soon be able to fit your chickenwings into the crack. The sooner you can seat a chickenwing, the sooner you will get sucked up into the crack entirely and feel secure.
  - It can sometimes be possible to place a chickenwing before your legs are deeply inserted (you need either good foot jams or leg bars). To do this, hang by your legs/feet, do a sideways sit-up, and place the chickenwing to the left or right, rather than in front of you. When your chickenwing is in place, rotate your legs up so they are directly above you.
  - If you are inverting off a chickenwing, imagine your body and legs are like the hands of a clock. You want to rotate them upwards (either clockwise or anticlockwise) in a large circular motion until they reach twelve o'clock (fully inverted position).

SPIN THROUGHS

Spin throughs are a very useful technique which can enable you to pass difficult sections of climbing more easily. They can also create a feet-first style of climbing. However, they only work if you have a strong core, as you need to be able to move your legs and upper body without them being in contact with the rock. If your sit-ups or leg raises are poor, spin throughs, will be of little benefit to your climbing. So, get the abs ripped and you'll be cutting loose, spinning through, and discovering all the benefits of these techniques in no time whatsoever.

Spin throughs with the feet

This type of spin through involves cutting loose on to jams with the hands (fingers/hands/fists/stacks), flicking your feet ahead of you, and inserting them back into the crack so that you end up in a feet-first position. Climbing in roof cracks isn't always about leading with your hands!

1. Cut loose with your feet and hang from just your hands on your jams. If you are using finger jams, then opposing jams can work very well (earlier this chapter).

2. Spin your body through 180 degrees and place your feet back into the roof ahead of you. Staying locked off with your arms, tipping your back backwards, tucking your legs up towards your chest, and making sure your body remains close to the roof will all make the spin through with your feet easier. If you straighten your arms, straighten your back, and let your legs dangle below you, you'll only have to lift it all back up again. Don't let everything sag down; stay strong and tight to the roof. Ideally you should look for a foot placement

that is good and beyond your next hand placement as you want to avoid trying to reach around your foot. This movement can be very core intensive if your foothold is a long way away, as it can feel like you have to front-lever like a gymnast to have any hope of reaching the foothold. A solution to this—if footholds are available—is to initially place your feet close to you in the roof and then walk them step by step through to the foot jam you are aiming for.

There are two ways to walk your feet in the roof:

- *Foot over foot:* this is the same as hand-over-hand movement (Chapter 3), but with the feet—you are crossing your feet one over the other as you move them. You can make quicker movements like this, but it becomes strenuous and can be more difficult to seat the foot jams if they are poor as your closest foot can obscure your view of the next placement.
- *Swimming feet:* this is shuffling the feet along the crack while never overlapping them. It's a slightly slower but more secure method and useful if the crack is uniform as you can slide your feet along very effectively without having to remove them. If there are no intermediate foothold/jams to walk your feet on to reach your desired foothold, then make sure you have good form with your free leg. Keep your free leg tucked in tight to your body, then stretch your other leg out

Figure 156. Spin throughs: hand to foot movement

in front of you to the foothold, exactly like doing a half lever.

3. Once your feet are in the desired position, lock them in place and use them like a pair of hands so you can reach to the next handhold.

4. If you have to make really long moves, with the hands after spinning through, it can be easier to use one foot in the crack and dangle the other foot in space; this enables you to twist your body in a way that brings you closer to the roof and squeezes your shoulder blades together and opens up your chest (figure 156). However, your foot jam must be good, because if it slips, you'll be out of there.

Pop Quiz

1. Finger cracks or offwidths? Offwidth
2. Stemming or roof cracks? Roof crack
3. Cams or nuts? Cams
4. Hand jam or hand stack? Hand jam
5. Knee lock or chickenwing? Knee lock
6. Tape or no tape? Tape
7. Sandstone cracks or granite cracks? Sandstone
8. Short and hard, or long and pumpy? Long and pumpy
9. Pressure wound or rock rash? Rock rash
10. Colour preference of crack climbing trousers due to unfortunate mistakes, red or brown? Red

MEET THE MASTER
TOM RANDALL

Tom has probably the best crack ticklist in the world. From savage boulder problems to desperate single-pitch nightmares, he has climbed all the hardest cracks from thick to thin. He is perhaps best known for the first ascent of Century Crack (5.14b) in the Canyonlands of Utah.

FAVOURITE CRACK CLIMBING AREA?

It's hard to beat the Orco Valley in Italy because the variety of cracks and the quality of the rock are so high. For sure, you can find more hardcore venues or places that have a higher number of splitters, but Orco is a real paradise for those crack climbers who want a bit extra. It's got slabs, vert tech seams, overhangs, big roofs, and even loads of new routing! The routes can be anything from single pitches to 200 metres long, and the rock eats gear. Big Friend 6s all the way down to bomber RPs. The camping and food in the area are pretty amazing too!

FAVOURITE CRACK CLIMB?

My favourite crack climb is still *London Wall* (E5 6A/5.12b) in the Peak District. It's not the hardest that I've done but is one that I return to time and time again, whatever style I'm climbing it in. I first climbed it when I was at university and E5 was my total limit—I think it was my second one ever—and the runout at the top absolutely terrified me. I was so psyched to have already climbed 75 percent of the route without falling that I committed to the final section knowing I couldn't wimp out. I left all my remaining gear hanging on my last piece and went big.

MEMORABLE CRACK EXPERIENCE?

A significant crack experience that stands out from the last few years is from one of my attempts to climb *Crown of Thorns* (5.14-) with Pete [Whittaker]. This little beauty is down on the White Rim in Canyonlands and is a very similar route to *Century Crack,* except that it's a bit more cruxy but has a couple of decent rests on it to gather your thoughts or shake off an insane level of pump. On the second half of the route—wide and mega-awkward hand/fist stacks and chimney roof—I went total "red line" on the last crux and after giving what felt like my true "last 1 percent," I fell off. As soon as I went tight on the rope I immediately felt really sick and became aware that my whole body was full of lactic acid. I shouted at Pete to lower me very quickly and then spent the next 10 minutes on the ground shaking in pain. Not ideal! I suspect that Pete was quietly laughing at my predicament . . .

THE KNOWLEDGE

My advice for climbing cracks in my favourite area (Orco Valley) would be to choose the correct boots for the route you're going to try. Just because you love your loose Velcro shoes for vertical hand cracks, doesn't mean they're going to work well on a vertical technical finger crack. Think about the demands of the route, how you're going to use your feet, and what's going to give you that edge. Be flexible and plan ahead!

Opposite: *Tom making a rare solo of the iconic gritstone finger crack* London Wall *(E5 6a) at Millstone Edge, the UK's answer to Indian Creek, in the Peak District UK (© Mike Hutton)*

CLIMBING FEET FIRST

It is sometimes easier to climb whole sections of roof crack with your feet leading and your hands following, especially in hand- and fist-width cracks. This style of movement can feel easier on the arms as your feet are out in front of you (acting like arms). When you climb hands first, it is the arms which must lock off to make forwards progression (the strenuous part) with the feet following along. By switching it round, with the feet responsible for the forwards progression and your hands just matching in and following along, you are essentially putting the more strenuous part of the climbing on the feet. The downside to climbing feet first is that you can't make big moves (with your feet) and the whole movement process is slightly slower. On long sections of roof crack it can be nice to mix things up, alternating between climbing both hands-first and feet-first style.

Spin throughs with the hands

Spin throughs with the hands only really occur on wider sections of crack as you have to be able to hang off good foot jams so that you can let go with your hands. If you get to a wider or flared section of crack—one which is tricky for stacking—it can be easier to bypass it with your hands by just using your feet instead.

1. Spin through with your feet (as described above) and place them in the wider section of crack. You can use any kind of leg or foot jam: frogged foot, banana foot, leg bar, and so on.

2. Now, hold firm with your feet/legs and let go with your hands—so you'll be swinging upside down like a bat. Sit up and reach past the wider section into better jams for your hands beyond your feet.

LIP TURNS

A lip turn is where horizontal climbing meets vertical terrain once again. These sections at and after the lip of the roof can often be the cruxes of roof climbs as getting your body back into an upright position can involve tricky sequences. I don't think that any two lip turns that I've done have ever been the same: they always seem to have their own little nuances and sequences—extra holds outside the crack, flares, sidewalls, strange crack angles, and so on—which make it difficult to give specific rules for how to climb them. So, you have to adapt and evolve your climbing to what is available and find the "rule" that works for the specific lip that you are attempting to turn.

In this section we'll take a look at some very basic techniques that you can apply—but, remember, these are by no means rules, just simple concepts.

FINGER, HAND, AND FIST SIZE

The most difficult parts about getting around the lip of a roof on these sizes of crack is first getting your chest around, and then your hips and legs.

WORKING YOUR CHEST AROUND THE LIP OF A ROOF:

The key to getting your chest around the lip of a roof is to remember you have feet! Climbers often completely forget this and start to desperately grind and pull their chest around the lip, leaving their feet uselessly behind. (This is usually because they've reached better holds or jams with their hands and have therefore forgotten about their feet.)

Push your body outwards with your feet, thereby leaving it free from the friction of the lip, *before* you pull upwards with your arms. As you push out with your feet—and not before—move your hands up. If you can get your chest around the lip of a roof without it making contact with the rock, give yourself a pat on the back.

WORKING YOUR HIPS AND LEGS AROUND THE LIP OF A ROOF:

You will get to a point where pushing out with your feet will affect your upwards movement (usually when the lip is around waist or thigh level). When you get to this stage, you need to work your hips and legs around the roof. If you are flexible, you can keep one foot in the roof (using it as a platform to push off) and make a high step with the other foot around the lip of the roof. It will feel bunched up, but once one leg is around you'll be able to stand up easily. If you aren't that flexible, another option is to cut loose onto your jams and throw a toe, heel, or foot jam around the lip from a hanging position. Whichever way you do it, athletic and gymnastic movement will be needed to execute this movement successfully.

HAND / HAND SIZE

This is one of the hardest sizes when it comes to lip turns. If you have skinny knees, your first option would be to use a knee lock technique (see "Hand/Fist Size," later in this chapter). However, this won't be possible for a lot of people, so the best option is to keep leading with a leg.

1. Establish yourself so that you are hand/hand stacking in the roof by the lip. To get your hands into this position, keep moving and jamming your leading leg around the lip of the roof.
2. Take your trailing leg out of the crack. This will allow your body to dangle below the leading leg and not get pulled back underneath by the trailing leg.
3. Place your trailing leg around the lip of the roof, behind your leading leg, and walk both feet up the crack with your hands following behind. You will be completely upside down on less steep terrain, however by going feet first you are creating footholds that wouldn't exist if you let your feet dangle in space below. The movement will feel hard and strenuous, but after a certain distance (about half to full-body length) you will be able to hold firm with your stack and swing your feet below you to the lip of the roof—so you are the "right" way up—and start using standard leg and foot techniques for this size of crack (Chapter 5). Don't

flip back from inverted to the right way up too soon, as if you misjudge it, your legs are likely to slip through the crack and be left dangling in space.

HAND / FIST SIZE

On this size of crack, you can use the inverted technique, as just described, or a "right-way-up," knee lock method.

1. Place your hand/fist stack as far around the lip as possible. To do this, you can either put your leading leg around the lip of the roof, sit up, and stack just behind it, or sit up and do the old "reach around"—reach around and stack past your legs. To reach past your leading leg more easily you can form a pivot manoeuvre (later this chapter).

2. Once your stack is in position, place your leading leg into a knee lock (Chapter 5) at the lip of the roof behind your stacked hands. This might require taking your leg fully out of the crack to get it into this position, or you may be able to just rotate your knee up into the crack from the position it is already in.

3. To help get the knee lock in more easily, drop your trailing foot towards the edge of the crack and place it in an outside foot position on the crack edge (Chapter 5).

4. You will now be in a standard off-widthing position—stacking, knee lock, outside foot—just on very steep terrain, so execute the standard movement process for normal offwidth climbing (Chapter 5).

5. Use your outside foot to initially push your body horizontally away from the lip before pulling upwards, so that your chest doesn't get caught and hinder your movement. The same principles apply here as when moving your body around the lip on finger, hand, and fist cracks.

FIST / FIST SIZE

Lip turns on fist/fist-sized cracks are all about focusing on getting your hips around the lip of the roof. If you can flick those hips around, you'll be singing, swinging, and shuffling on up.

1. At the lip of the roof make sure that your legs are inserted into the crack as far as possible and you are using the appropriate leg techniques (see "Fist/Fist-Sized Offwidth Roof Cracks" earlier this chapter). If your hips are lower than they could potentially be, you'll be making turning the lip much harder for yourself. Keep your hips high.

2. *Hands:* Find the best option for your hands—fist/fist stacking, downwards palming, palming on the lip, under-cutting. You'll often find that on this size of roof crack you will alternate between the techniques; for example, it might be easier to initially undercut the crack, before using downwards palming options when you pull higher. Don't be narrow-minded with your options as different ones will become available as you go through the range of movement.

3. *Legs:* As your hips and upper body get pushed and pulled around the lip, your legs have to compensate for the movement that is occurring or else you will end up in an incredibly uncomfortable—and impossible to move from—position. Imagine your legs are like the hands of a clock: at the start of the movement your leading leg should be at twelve o'clock (inverted straight up above you in the crack) and your trailing leg at about ten o'clock. As you move your hips around the lip, you should rotate your legs back into the crack in a clock motion (clockwise if leading left leg, and vice versa). As your hips get higher and higher, your legs will rotate down until eventually they are at six o'clock and you are in an upright offwidthing position. Standard offwidth techniques can then be performed for this width of crack (Chapter 5).

4. When you are completing this clock-type motion with your legs, don't let them drop out of the bottom of the crack. Keep them securely inside the crack throughout the full movement process and drop them down at the same rate that your hips move up.

5. The "flying pirate" is an offwidth position that can be used on this width of crack when the lip turn is in a corner feature. You will use your legs and feet as described above, however you now have another feature—the corner—which can be beneficial for your hands and arms. The same hand and arm positions can be used in the corner feature of the lip turn as if you were in a standard stemming corner (you don't need to use the crack feature at all for your hands). Hold firm with your feet and legs on the lip of the roof (remember to insert the legs as deep as possible in the crack). Place the palm of one hand on the lip of the roof and the palm of the other hand on the corner wall (fingers pointing away from you). Place your arms slightly behind you and below shoulder level so that you can push your upper body up and into the corner feature. The position should squeeze the shoulder blades together and open the chest. Press your upper body into the corner feature (by pushing on your palms, exactly how you would when stemming), and at the same time start to flick your hips around the lip of the roof. Your bum will either already be on a side wall (if the side wall behind you has extended to make a corner feature at the lip), or it will come into contact as you move your hips around (if the crack wall extends into a corner wall at the lip). Use this to your advantage and get your bum onto and in contact with the corner wall as soon as possible. When your hips are around the lip and your bum is on the side wall things will likely become a lot more relaxing. Keep moving your palmed hands upwards as you make the clock motion (point 3, above) with your legs and feet.

PIVOTING

Pivoting is simply rotating your body around a foot or a leg to help you get back into a more normal upright position from an upside-down position. It's usually done when you go from steep inverted offwidth climbing into less steep terrain, such as on a lip turn.

However, it can be performed when the angle of the crack remains the same steepness throughout and you just want to change from upside-down techniques and positioning back into more standard techniques and positioning. It is simply the act of spinning your upper body past your leading leg/foot. Pivoting can be done on all widths of offwidth crack. Here are a few tricks to help you pivot with perfection.

- *Rotate your body around your leading leg.* The leading leg can initially be placed either in front of or behind your stacks and arms; however, whichever position is chosen it is this leg which your body will rotate around to perform a pivot.
- *Focus on a solid jam with your leading leg.* Your leading leg is your main contact point and what will hold you on (in) to the rock during this movement, so make sure it is good. Your leading leg/foot is the pivot point which your body spins around.
- *Drop your trailing leg further down towards the edge of the crack.* By dropping your trailing leg towards the crack edge you are able to more easily reach past your leading leg with your hands and spin your upper body through. Keeping your trailing leg high will hinder your upper body movement and make the whole procedure feel like a very large and strenuous sit-up. Also, leaving your trailing leg deep in the crack when you spin your upper body past your leading leg can result in it getting stuck while you try to execute the movement. As your trailing leg drops towards the edge of the crack behind you, match this with the movement of your upper body around your leading leg. As one moves down the other moves up, and they balance each other out.
- *Drop your trailing leg out of the crack all together.* This is not something that should be done all the time, but occasionally it can be useful to drop the trailing leg completely out of the crack to achieve the correct body positioning and seat a suitable jam past the leading leg—or to prevent it from getting stuck in the manoeuvre.
- *Use your trailing leg to push your upper body past your leading leg.* After you have brought your trailing leg to the edge of or out of the crack, use it to propel your upper body forwards past your leading leg and seat even higher jams. Using a jammed foot on the edge of the crack, or even a face hold or smear on the rock face, will help with this.
- *Move your leading leg down inside the crack, as your upper body moves past it:* As you move your upper body past your leading leg, don't forget to gradually start dropping the leading leg down so you can eventually start using conventional inside leg offwidth techniques.

Opposite: *Ashley Cracroft placing a massive #12 cam on the first ascent of Tatanka Wing (5.10a) in southern Utah* (© Irene Yee)

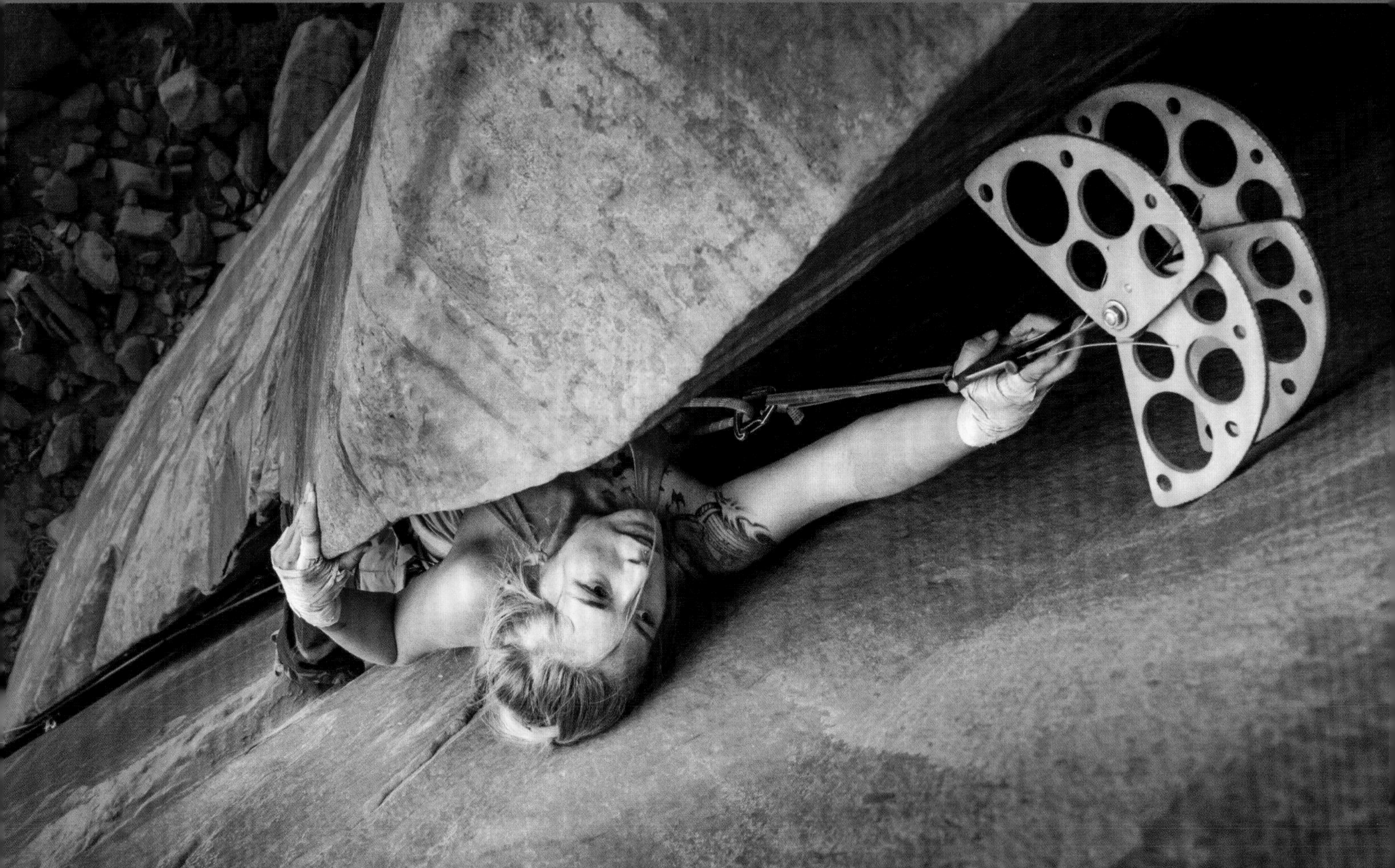

CHAPTER 10

Placing Gear

Cracks lend themselves to being traditionally protected routes and they generally eat gear just like they eat your body, which is great: if you are getting chewed up by the crack, so is the gear which is keeping you safe. In my opinion, the ability to seek out placements, place gear in control, and have the confidence to trust your own gear is as important as the climbing itself. You will never be able to try something at your limit if you don't have a solid awareness and understanding of gear placements.

Placing gear is a skill, and like any skill it takes a huge amount of practice to master all the different aspects involved. A strong climber who has never climbed trad can easily get burnt off by a much weaker, but experienced and trad-savvy climber. So, consider this single chapter to be as important as all the previous chapters combined.

Before getting on to the nitty-gritty of placing gear, there are two questions that you should ask yourself:

Am I aware and knowledgeable? Do you know how the gear works and how to place it? Are you aware of its mechanics and function? You need to make sure you know how to properly use the equipment that you are placing.

Am I confident? Can you confidently judge if a piece of gear is sufficient for the job and your placement is good or bad? This will dictate whether you make the correct climbing decisions once you have placed the gear. Making correct decisions will result in a safe day out. Safety is key: if you neglect it, you won't be around to climb tomorrow.

In this chapter we will look at the three stages to placing gear:
1. Choosing your rack
2. Racking up
3. Placing gear on route

CHOOSING YOUR RACK

The first thing to do before setting off on a climb is select the gear that you think you will need. There is no point in taking huge heavy cams if you are never going to place them, likewise you don't want to leave your tiny micronuts behind and later find yourself in a sticky situation. The process of climbing your chosen route safely starts on the ground.

Look at the route from the ground or from your stance. Stand back, study it from different angles, and gather as much information as you can from just looking at the pitch. If you can't see much of the pitch and know nothing about it, then you will need to take a good range of gear. If you can see the pitch, there is lots of information you can gather.

Take a general overview of what you are climbing. For example, are you climbing a wide crack, a thin crack, or a stem with a seam at the back? These will all take very different gear—if you are climbing a finger crack you won't need a no. 4 cam! Take into consideration the rock type and the types of placements that it offers. There is no point taking lots of nuts on the splitter cracks of Indian Creek; conversely, if you neglect your nuts on a UK sea cliff, you're going to get yourself into a heap of trouble. Once you have made a general judgement you can slim down your rack and remove the extreme pieces, the ones that obviously won't fit the route you are going to climb. As a very general guide:

- splitter cracks often take camming devices
- constricted cracks are good for nuts
- pin scars seat offset cams nicely

If you are confident and can judge the exact gear that you'll need, you can then neglect the remainder of your rack and just select the appropriate pieces. I feel I can only be this precise on completely splitter cracks, and I usually take half a size higher and lower than what I can confidently predict from the ground. If the gear looks complicated or the crack isn't splitter and uniform, then taking one to two sizes higher and lower than your prediction from the ground is a safe option. If you are unsure whether you will need a specific piece of gear, always take it, just in case.

Consider that you might need multiples of certain sizes. On uniform splitter cracks, it's common to take doubles, triples, quadruples, or even more of a single size.

Other factors to be aware of:

- *There might be other gear options:* don't get sucked into just looking at the feature you are climbing—always look out to the side, around arêtes, and in the backs of corners. There might be hidden gems away from the main feature.
- *Small gear is lighter than big gear:* there might be small gear opportunities even if you are climbing wide cracks—such as thin seams and cracks out to the side or in the backs of chimneys. For example, taking ten pieces of small gear could be a lighter and more efficient option than taking five larger pieces. On the other hand, sliding two larger pieces of gear in the crack could be a more efficient and safer option than placing small gear and climbing past it (see "Sliding Cams," later in this chapter). Be the judge and consider your options.

RACKING UP

Once you have chosen your rack, the next thing to do is place it on your harness in a suitable order. You need to know exactly where all the pieces are so that you can select them easily. You don't want to be pumping out on a climb while sifting through all your gear trying to find the appropriate piece. You should know the exact location of it and be able to go directly to it, or at least quickly get to the gear loop it is located on and then only have to select the correct one from a few pieces.

There is no right or wrong way to rack up on your harness; it is subjective and comes down to personal preference. However, there are some tricks which can make things easier—these can be adapted to suit your preferences and current situation.

Group similar pieces of gear together. Simply clipping cams, nuts, and quickdraws into groups will achieve this.

Group similar sizes together. After grouping similar items together, you might want to subdivide these items so that you have similar sizes grouped together. Small, medium, and large pieces, for example. Grouping similar sizes together means that if you are unsure of the exact piece you need, you can judge the size of the placement in the rock as "small," "medium," or "large" and then go directly to the relevant cluster of sizes on your harness.

Balance pieces equally around your harness. If you were to simply group all your pieces together and clip them to different areas of your harness—for example,

all your cams on one side and all your nuts on the other side—you might find that your harness is unbalanced and this makes climbing more difficult. Try to spread your clusters of gear around your harness so that there is an even distribution of weight. You don't want to have the waistband of your harness slipping off one hip because you've placed all your cams and hexes (heavier items) on one side and all your quickdraws (lighter items) on the other side.

Split the same size. If you have doubles of the same piece, you can split them so that you have one on each side of your harness. This not only helps to balance the gear weight and volume on your harness (the previous point), you can also easily locate the first piece of the size you need with either hand and from either side of your harness.

Save space on your harness. If you have a huge rack, your harness can get very full and the gear loops stacked. This can make it difficult to actually unclip pieces from your harness and everything can get tangled together. To help with this:

- *Clip pieces to other pieces.* For example, clip half of your quickdraws into the gear loop on your harness, then the other half through the top karabiner of each quickdraw rather than through the gear loop itself. This prevents lots of karabiners from being clipped directly to the gear loop. You can use this technique with cams as well: clipping the same size to each other; is the simplest way. If you are cunning, you can clip different sizes to each other; however, you have to be confident that the piece clipped directly to the harness is the piece that you are going to use second, not first!

- *Use a master Krab.* Another option is to put two or three smaller cams on to one "master" karabiner (like you would do with nuts, see below), place the cam you want, take it off the master karabiner, and then clip a quickdraw to it. This only works with small cams as they are lighter and easier to hold.
- *Put extendable slings over your shoulder rather than onto your harness.* Alternating the slings over each shoulder as you stack them helps to keep you balanced.
- *Use a bandolier over your shoulder and clip pieces to it.* Bandoliers are also very useful in offwidth climbing as you can easily push the gear to the side of the body that is outside of the crack so that it doesn't disrupt the climbing. If you were to then switch sides while climbing, the gear could be moved around without having to do any unclipping and reclipping to the harness.

Rack protection towards the front of the harness and quickdraws towards the back. Having protection at the front of the harness means you can actually see what you are selecting from your harness—important, as you want to get the correct piece the first time. Selecting the correct quickdraw is less important—apart from length, they are practically all the same—so if you put these at the back you can reach back behind you to grab one without straining to look over your shoulder to select the correct item.

Colour-code karabiners. Match the colours of your karabiners to the pieces of protection they are clipped to. When you have a big, crowded rack, it can be difficult to see which karabiner is connected to which piece of gear, especially in stressful situations. By using colour-coded karabiners you can quickly glance at your gear loop and select the correct-coloured karabiner straight away. This works well with camming devices and hexes, but it can also be used for nuts. You could have a "master karabiner" colour which represents to you, "small," "medium," or "large" nuts.

Racking your nuts. When you rack your nuts, you will have one master karabiner and then a selection of nuts clipped into it. You will place your chosen nut (with all the other nuts still on the master karabiner), unclip the karabiner from the nut, and then clip a quickdraw into the nut. A few tricks can make racking your nuts easier:

- **Don't rack too many nuts on one karabiner.** If you have lots of nuts on one karabiner, they will end up in a massive cluster and the loops of the nuts will thread themselves through one another. Nuts also seem to miraculously unclip themselves from the master karabiner when you have lots on there and you are trying to select the correct one. So, have more master karabiners and fewer nuts on each one.
- **Use an oval-shaped karabiner as your master karabiner.** Because there is more space at the bottom of an oval karabiner, the nuts will sit better and

this stops them from clustering together and sitting on top of one another. Oval karabiners are also exactly the same shape whichever way up you have them, which means that when you decide to place a nut, the remaining nuts won't end up in a tangle at the opposite end of the karabiner.

- *Use karabiners that don't have a wire gate.* Wire-gate karabiners have a "nose" where the wire of the gate shuts down onto the karabiner. This nose can get annoyingly caught in the nut when you are trying to unclip the nut from the master karabiner, a real frustration if you are really pumped. Make sure that there is no "nose" where the gate closes on to the karabiner.

Select the appropriate side of your harness for offwidths and corners. When climbing a corner system or off-width, one side of your body is likely to be in contact with the rock. If your body is in contact and you have racked up as normal, you are likely to have difficulty finding and selecting the piece of gear that you need (your gear will also hinder your movement, especially when offwidth climbing, as it's likely to get caught on things). So, consider putting the pieces that are needed for the climb on the "outside" of the harness; the side which is free from the rock. For example, if you are climbing an offwidth right side in, you should rack your protection on the left side of your harness.

Racking up for redpoints. If you are redpointing a route then you should know everything about the gear that you are going to place. The three things to think about are:

- *Rack the gear in the correct order on your harness.* Place everything on your harness in the same sequence as you will place it on the route—starting pieces at the front, finishing pieces at the back. As you take the first piece of gear off your harness (and place it), your second piece slides forward and becomes your "first" piece. This system means you only ever have to reach for the first piece of gear on your harness—you never have to take the time to look and select.
- *Rack the gear according to which hand you will place it with.* If you are placing a particular piece of gear with your left hand, rack it on the left side of your harness, and vice versa. You should also use the rack ordering system described above for the left and right sides of the harness.
- *Pre-rack quickdraws on the pieces of gear.* If you know a piece of gear will need a quickdraw, pre-rack it to the piece and remove any extra karabiners from camming devices. If you were really being tactical, you could use tape to fix karabiners into position on extendable slings so that they always sit the correct way around and don't spin.

Racking up for onsights. The most important thing when climbing onsight is to continually assess what you've just done and what is coming up next. This changes constantly as you cover new ground and get closer to new sections of climbing, and it means the order of your rack can often change.

When you assess new sections of rock above you, try to plan for what gear you think you might place and either take note of where it is located on your harness, or even move it into a position where it can be more easily accessed. You might even move it to the opposite side of your harness if you think you know which hand you will place it with. This procedure should be done from restful places on the route, where you can look at what is coming up next.

When you have placed a piece of gear, make a mental note that it is gone from your harness, so you don't try to reach for something which is no longer there. If you have doubles of some pieces and you place one of them, remember which side of the harness the other one is on, so you can go straight to it when you need it.

In easy sections of climbing (ones which have lots of different gear options), don't place pieces of gear that you think you might need later on the route. Save these pieces, and place something else instead.

Light is right. If you have a big rack, then using modern, lightweight climbing equipment will make your life much easier. The weight difference between one old piece of equipment and one new piece of equipment isn't all that much. However, over an entire rack, lots of small weight differences soon start to add up. You will notice a huge difference between a rack with 30 pieces of new climbing equipment and a rack with 30 pieces of old climbing equipment.

PLACING PRO ON ROUTE

Now that you have chosen your gear and racked up, it's time to start climbing! There are lots of different factors which need to be thought about when placing gear while climbing. Your gear is what keeps you safe, so it should be carefully considered. In this section we'll take a look at the things that you should be thinking about.

WHEN ARE YOU GOING TO PLACE YOUR PRO?

When is the best time to stop climbing and place pro? Are you safe and can you run it out past the hard section? Are you desperately run-out and pumped, and needing to place a piece to keep yourself safe? It's important to find the best spots to place your gear from, as it's a total heartbreaker to be finger jamming for dear life, fiddling in small cams, only to make a few moves past them to find a massive jug which you could have used instead. I know, as I've done it myself numerous times! Here are a few ideas to help you place your gear in the most comfortable way.

Find the most comfortable positions to place pro from. Always look and feel for the best holds and best positions to place pro from—if you have time to place pro, you have time to check that you are on the best possible handholds and footholds. Remember that the best holds could be hidden.

If the gear placement is time-consuming, you might want to try out different body positions or alternative holds to spread out the increasing fatigue to different parts of your body.

Remember you can always place pro below you—placements can't always be seen from below and you might spot a placement as you climb past it to reach a better hold.

Try to place pro before difficult sections, then blast through the hardest climbing and place more gear when things ease up. This is obviously dependent on your judgement of the route and the risk, and of course if things are becoming dangerous you should consider placing gear even when the climbing is difficult.

Use the climb-up-and-then-down tactic. If there is a difficult section of climbing ahead, sometimes you can climb into reasonably difficult terrain, place some pro as high as possible, then down-climb to a resting stance to shake out and recover. When you are ready to go, your pro is already placed above you, so you can blast through the climbing without having to think about placing any more. This is a tactic I often use all the way up a route when doing a difficult onsight.

Have an idea from the start of what you think or know the route will be like. Is it cruxy and well protected? cruxy and poorly protected? sustained and well protected? sustained and poorly protected?

If you decide in advance what you think it will be like, you'll have a better idea of when to place pro. In general:

- *Cruxy routes:* Cluster your gear below crux sections and then blast through these harder sections of climbing. If the crux section is long and spicy, have the next available piece(s)—possibly in your mouth—ready to place.

- *Sustained routes:* Space the pro more evenly. Place pieces slightly closer together when closer to the ground to keep yourself safe, but space them out more as you get higher.

- *Well-protected routes:* If the route is well protected, then placing one or two pieces at each "gear station" will most likely be adequate.

- *Poorly protected routes:* If you think the pro is dubious, don't hesitate to place more than one or two pieces. I once placed nine pieces of protection all around the same place because I had a very large run-out coming up and I wasn't happy with the quality of the placements. Remember, each piece of gear that rips in a fall reduces the force put on the lower pieces, making the lower poor pieces more likely to hold.

Sometimes you can't place gear as the rock has no placements. In this situation, you have to use your judgement as to whether you have the ability to complete the section of climbing.

WHERE ARE YOU GOING TO PLACE YOUR PRO?

What is the best possible place to put the piece of pro? Are you combining what you have on your rack and what the rock is offering you in the best possible way? You should ensure that where you are placing your protection is the most suitable place for what you have on your rack. There is no point placing a load of gear in totally the wrong place. Here are some ideas to help you place your gear in the most suitable locations.

ROCK QUALITY

The first thing you need to do is judge the quality of the rock—depending on the type of terrain you are covering, this can take anywhere from one second to a few minutes. Remember to use more senses than just sight:

- *Sight:* Look at the rock—does it appear to be sandy/crispy/flakey/solid/smooth/rough/etc.? Look at the bigger picture around the placement—is it a solid crack but part of another system (such as a big flake system) that could peel away? Start to form an idea of what the placement is like.
- *Feel:* Touch the placement with your hands. Does it feel like what you have just looked at? Hit the rock around the placement—does it move or is it stationary? Do bits crumble or fall off around or inside the placement?
- *Sound:* Listen to the placement. Hit the rock around the placement. If it sounds like you're hitting a brick wall, then it will be more solid. If it echoes, vibrates, sounds hollow, or sounds like you're hitting a partition wall, then you might need to reconsider.

POSITIONING OF THE PRO IN RELATION TO THE CLIMBING

When you are placing pro, make sure it isn't going to disrupt the climbing that is ahead of you.

Avoid placing pro in your holds. Sometimes this is not possible; and if this is the only option try to keep the "sweet spot" free for your hands and feet—don't place the piece of pro in the middle of where you will put your hands or feet. Placing nuts at the bottom and cams at the top of handholds or footholds is usually a good tactic.

Avoid placing pro way above your head (if you can). Firstly, you will have to pull up extra rope to clip the piece, thus if you fall while clipping in you will fall much further. Also, if you're climbing a crack and the rope is clipped in, it will run straight down the crack and get in the way of all the jams which are coming up. Instead, place gear at chest to waist height—it's a comfortable height for pulling down on and "seating" or testing the piece, it's easy and safe to clip, and the rope will only get in the way of your feet instead of both your hands and your feet. It is sometimes necessary to place gear above your head, so this point is a guide and by no means a rule.

WHAT PRO ARE YOU GOING TO PLACE?

Have you selected the correct piece of gear for the placement? You should be sure that the piece you are putting in to the placement is the most suitable. There is no point in finding a great location only to then select the incorrect piece and watch it fall out as you climb past it. Here are some ideas to help you select the correct piece of gear for the available placement.

Look at the type of rock:

- *Smoother rock:* Passive protection works well; you'd be surprised how much active protection can slip on very smooth rock surfaces. Active protection needs some friction to help it engage.

- *Crumbly rock:* Active protection works well because when bits crumble off, the protection will keep expanding out into the "new" space.
- *Expanding rock:* Passive protection works well because as it is weighted it will not force the rock to expand as much as when using active protection. It can be useful to use slightly oversized placements to prevent the piece slipping through if the rock does expand.

Look at the shape of the placement:

- *Is the placement parallel-sided or constricted?* This will determine the type of protection you might place. If it's parallel-sided, you might consider active protection; if it's constricted, you might consider passive protection.
- *Is the placement rounded or square-cut on the edge?* This will determine the style of piece you might place. For example, on rounded or flared placements you might select offset pieces (making sure the taper or offset is orientated correctly), whereas on square-cut placements you might select uniform pieces.
- *Does the placement open out in the back or open out at the front?* This will determine how deep or shallow you place your gear to prevent it from pulling straight through the placement.

Look at the size of the placement:

- *Larger placements (hand size and above):* Look to place cams, hexes, or Big Bros (both active and passive protection).

- *Smaller placements (hand size or below):* Look to place nuts, hexes, or cams (both passive and active protection).

Try to learn the size (and colour) of the gear to use in relation to whichever body parts you have inside the crack. For example, if you are hand jamming, you might know that you need to use a gold-coloured camming device. Remember that everybody is a different shape and size, so there's a good chance your gear–body relationship will be different than someone else's—you should learn your own.

HOW ARE YOU GOING TO PLACE YOUR PRO?

How will you properly place the piece of gear you have selected? There is no point in taking into consideration the previous steps, only to then place the piece of gear incorrectly or not in the best possible way. Here are some ideas to help you place your gear correctly. We'll look at the two main pieces of gear used: cams (active) and nuts (passive).

CAMS

Good placements: These are obviously the number-one placements you are looking for—not so overcammed (see below) that they are impossible to retrieve and not too tipped (see below) so that the cams walk. You should aim to place the camming device so that there is still some movement left in the trigger mechanism, but not so much movement that the cam could walk and umbrella (figure 157).

Figure 157. Good cams placement

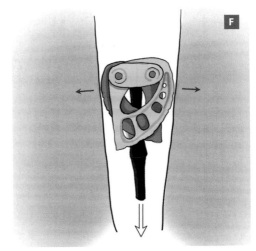

Figure 158. Overcammed cam placement

Overcammed placements: This is the second option you should look for—the cam placed very tightly in the crack (figure 158). These are good solid placements, however it can be really difficult to retrieve the cam. So, think about your second when you're squeezing the lobes shut and pushing the cam right to the back of the crack—it will be bomber, but you might never see it again!

Tipped-out placements: When the crack becomes almost too wide for the camming unit that you have, you will find that just the tips of the cams make contact with the rock (figure 159). These are the last choice of placements you should look for—smaller pieces have the tendency to rip out, and larger pieces like to "walk" into cracks. There is nothing worse than looking down and seeing that your last piece has walked, lost contact with the

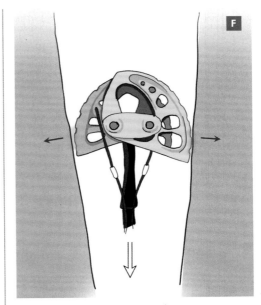

Figure 159. Tipped-out cam placement

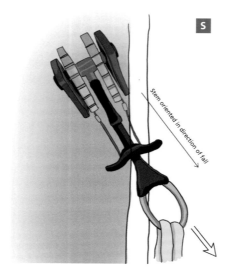

Figure 160. Cam stem orientation

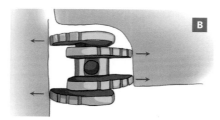

Figure 161. Good shallow cam placement

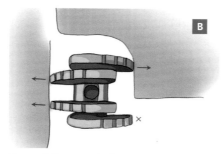

Figure 162. Poor shallow cam placement

rock, slid down the rope, and is now sitting ineffectively on top of a lower piece! To help prevent this, a longer quickdraw can stop the weight and drag of the rope from moving the cam.

Orientation of the stem: You should try to place the cam so that the stem is in line with the force from the direction of the potential fall—pointing downwards, that is not outwards (figure 160). This means that the cam lobes won't rotate and move inside the crack if you fall on to the cam. Sometimes it can be impossible to place cams with the stems pointing in the direction of a fall because the placement may be shallow. Cams with flexible stems can help with this; however, try to make sure that the top two cam lobes are good, as these are the lobes which are likely to rip out first and cause the placement to fail.

Material touching the rock: Make sure all cam lobes are in contact with the rock (figures 161 and 162). This might involve orientating the cam correctly so that the wide and narrow lobes are placed on the correct crack walls.

Horizontal placements: In horizontal cracks, put the wide lobes at the bottom of the placement (if the placement allows) as this will give the cam more stability.

NUTS

Good placements: These are obviously the first placements you are looking for. Both sides of the nut should be making full contact with the rock, and the shape (the curve) of the nut should match the shapes within the rock (figure 163).

Oversized placements: These are the second type of placements you should look for (figure 164). Oversized placements are still excellent placements, as it is impossible for the piece to pull through the crack and fall out of the bottom of the placement. However, because there is limited contact with the rock pieces set this way can easily lift out of the top of your chosen placement when you climb past. Try to prevent this from happening by extending the piece on a long quickdraw—this will stop the weight/ drag of the rope from moving the piece.

Tipped-out placements: These placements are the most risky (figure 165). A nut that is just a little bit too small for the placement will have a tendency to pull straight through the bottom of the placement when your full weight goes through it. It is impossible to

know whether these placements will hold, so, if you are unsure, you should place more than one piece. Or, if you have the ability, you can stack nuts together to help fill the space. You will need two hands in order to stack nuts effectively, so a good resting stance is important for this technique.

Orientation of the nut: Place the nut in the direction you would fall on to it—so pointing downwards, not outwards. If you were to fall on to a nut, it's important that your weight pulls it further into the placement and doesn't rotate it.

Orientation of the placement: Nuts can be oriented in three different ways—so make sure you think of them as three-dimensional shapes:

- *Longways:* This is the normal way to place a nut, with the two largest faces of

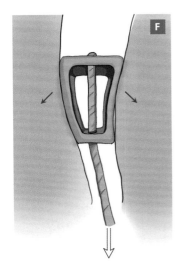

Figure 163. Good nut placement

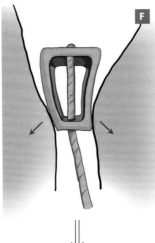

Figure 164. Oversized nut placement

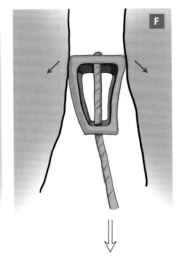

Figure 165. Tipped-out nut placement

the nut in contact with the crack walls. (See figure 163). When you have the correct size of nut and the placement is deep enough, these are the most secure placements.

- *Sideways:* This placement has two sides (often those with a hole in them) of the nut touching the crack walls, and the large face pointing out of the crack and the smaller face pointing into the crack

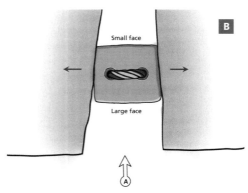

Figure 166. Sideways nut placement: large face forwards

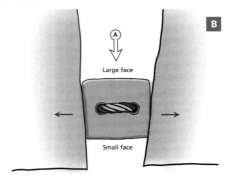

Figure 167. Sideways nut placement: small face forwards

(figure 166). It can be useful to place nuts sideways if you need a wider placement (nuts span a greater width in this orientation), the crack is shallow (nuts have less depth in this orientation), or if the crack is flared (most nuts have a taper to them when sideways which means better rock/gear contact for flared placements (figure 167).

- *Backwards:* This placement is a sideways placement but with the smaller face of the nut facing out of the crack rather than into the crack (so the smaller face is pointing towards you). It is rarely of use, but rock can form strange shapes and placements, so bear this in mind. Remember when placing these pieces to slide the piece from the back of the placement in to the front.

Horizontal placements: In horizontal cracks you are looking for a placement

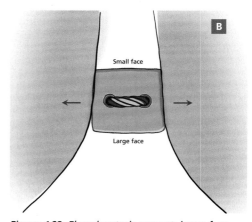

Figure 168. Flared nut placement: large face forwards

where the crack widens at the back and narrows at the front. Slide your nut in from a larger opening to the side of your placement. In my opinion, a good horizontal nut or hex placement can be better than any cam or nut placement in a vertical crack.

KEEPING YOUR PRO EFFECTIVE

Once you have placed your piece of protection, it's important that it stays effective once your rope has been clipped in to it. The way to do this is to use the correct length of quickdraw. Essentially you want to keep the rope in a straight line from your harness to your belayer, as this will result in the least amount of rope drag. Everything should be in line with the crack—including the rope! Here are some general scenarios and things to consider when clipping your gear:

- *Low down on the route:* If the climbing straight off the ground is very difficult, you might just clip the rope straight into the piece or use a single karabiner rather than a quickdraw. If the climbing is easy at the beginning and you are confident, you might extend the quickdraws to help reduce rope drag higher up on the route. Make an informed judgement about the route and your ability.

- *High up on the route:* Unless your pieces are completely bomber (so they can't move or walk), and your pro is in line with the climbing (in which case you could use the shortest quickdraw or clip directly into the piece), you will want to use quickdraws to make sure your pieces don't rotate, move, or lift out when the rope drag starts to build higher up the route.

- *Pro placed to the side of the climbing:* Use longer quickdraws or extendable quickdraws on pro to the side to help guide the rope back towards the centre point—i.e., the line you are climbing. This will prevent the rope from zigzagging and help reduce rope drag.

- *Marginal pieces of pro:* If you think a piece is marginal, could lift out, walk back, or umbrella out, use a long quickdraw to stop the tension in the rope from moving the piece.

PLACING PRO IN CORNER CRACKS

It can often be tricky or strenuous to place pro in corner cracks. There is a corner wall in your way, and you might be climbing in layback style—both of which can obscure your vision. Here are some tips for placing pro in corner cracks:

If you're climbing in a layback position, pull into a straight-on position to place pro. If this is not possible, try to look into the corner to locate the placement, then make the placement blindly from the more comfortable layback position. Then have another look into the corner to check the placement. Look, make placement, check.

If the climbing is too tenuous and you can't pull into the corner to see the placement, you will have to do everything by feel. In this situation I prefer to place cams rather than nuts. There are a few tricks which can help you make a better blind placement:

- Feel for the deeper and parallel spots.
- Judge the width of the crack in relation to the size of your fingers or hands and then use this to select the correct-sized piece.

When you have placed the piece, judge it by both feel and sight. Ask yourself a number of questions to help judge how good it is:

- *How well pulled back is the trigger bar?* It is better to overcam than undercam a blind placement.
- *Is the trigger bar even?* An even trigger bar means both sides of the piece are equally cammed.
- *How far into the crack did the cam go?* Is there a lot or only a little of the stem inside the crack? Generally speaking, a deeper placement is better than a shallow placement, so insert deep!

PLACING PRO IN OFFWIDTH CRACKS

There are certainly a few tips and tricks for placing pro while offwidth climbing. Being half-inserted into the feature that you are climbing can be a nuisance, as gear, rope, and body can get in the way of one another. It's common to knock and disrupt pieces of protection you have already placed, or get the rope trapped between your body and the rock. Both feel like desperate situations where you suddenly feel either completely unprotected or physically unable to move. The wider gear you need is also heavy—and expensive!—so carrying lots of it can be a pain. Here are some options to help overcome these offwidthing gear conundrums:

Lay the rope over your inside knee. Running the rope down the inside of the crack, over the top of your inside thigh, and then over the centre of your kneecap, rather than letting it hang straight down from the attachment point on your harness, works well. This prevents it from getting trapped between your body and the rock and, importantly, keeps it out of the way of the outside foot. When using this method it is important to be as careful as possible with rope management. Focus on keeping the rope running directly down your leg; if it rolls off, it can easily pinch between the rock and your thigh. Keeping the rope on the inside of the crack also means its readily available to clip straight into pieces easily.

Tie in with a long knot. On very tight squeeze chimneys a knot at the front of your harness can mean you are too wide to slide easily through the crack. A solution is to tie in long, so the knot can hang lower than your harness and sit between your legs. If you do this, be very careful to clip the correct piece of rope, the leading end, in to your gear!

Slide a cam. A great method for reducing the amount of gear that you take is to slide a camming device along the rope and inside the crack with you while you climb. This way you are effectively on a "mini top rope" and always protected. Keep the cam towards the edge of the crack so you can easily reach it.

- If you are feeling really luxurious, you can slide two camming devices with you while you climb. This way, when you slide one unit upwards, you are still protected by the other one. This is a great way to climb safely.
- Keeping yourself on a mini top rope does mean that sometimes it can be difficult to slide the cams due to "rope trapping"—when the rope coming up from

your belayer becomes caught between the rock and a body part, usually your leg. One method to prevent this is to clip directly into the piece with a sling (but without weighting it) and leave the rope unclipped from the piece, and then slide the cam with you on this short tether. This does give a degree of protection—but you should be aware that if you do slip you may take a small static fall directly on to the sling, so ensure this tether is no longer than it needs to be.

Use both hands to place your pieces. Placing gear in offwidth cracks can be awkward, so using both hands is a good idea. Remove the gear from your harness with your outside hand and place it above your head on the edge of the crack. Now use your inside hand to move it deeper into the crack to its final position.

Place the piece deeper into the crack to give yourself more room. Leaving a piece of gear and climbing past it without knocking and disrupting it can often be a difficult task. Place the piece deeper into the crack to give yourself more room and avoid accidents.

PLACING PRO IN ROOF CRACKS

The climbing in roof cracks might be well within your ability, but if you set up your gear incorrectly you could end up in a whole world of trouble, with rope drag or pinched ropes leaving you unable to move on easier ground. There are a few points to be noted when placing pro in roof cracks. Think of it as three stages: approaching the roof, climbing the roof, turning the lip of the roof.

APPROACHING THE ROOF

Minimise rope drag by:
- placing extendable quickdraws on protection right at the back of roofs
- reaching out and placing gear as far into the roof as possible

Both these options reduce the sharp-angled turn the rope has to make when moving from vertical to horizontal terrain.

CLIMBING IN THE ROOF

Direction of pull: If you fall off, the direction of pull on your gear is still downwards. This means you want to make sure the cam stem or nut isn't running along the length of the crack (like it would on a vertical crack climb) but is instead pointing towards the ground.

Where to place: Unless you were right at the start of a roof and the less steep terrain was close by, the only thing that you could hit if you fell off a roof would be air—and that doesn't hurt. So, although roof climbing can feel airy, it's actually very safe. Because of this, there is little point in placing pieces in front of you and letting the rope run across the crack, covering your hand holds. Instead, place pieces at around waist level so that you can give them a good tug/test in the correct direction (downwards) and leave your next jams free from gear and rope clutter. The only time you should consider straying from this is if you are at some resting jams and the only available placement is ahead of you, and it's important to place a piece there.

RON FAWCETT

A legend of British climbing who loves climbing just as much now as he did back in the 1970s, Ron put up brilliant first ascents all over the UK. Many of his routes were groundbreaking for the time and are still considered prized ticks for today's top climbers. Ron is famous for his sausage-like fingers, and his first ascent of Strawberries (E7 6b/5.13a) at Tremadog, North Wales, in 1980 heralded a new era of difficulty in British climbing.

FAVOURITE CRACK CLIMBING AREA?

Despite not being a trad climber for some time, it has to be Yosemite: going there as a kid, dossing in the dirt, and climbing with some great mates. Of course, this was in pre-cam days, with hexes in parallel cracks and running it out. Happy days.

FAVOURITE CRACK CLIMB?

It's been a while, but it has to be *Milky Way* (E6 6b/5.12c) at Ilkley's Cow and Calf rocks. It was just up the road from where I was living, and it had consumed a great deal of effort from a number of good climbers. Hard finger locks into a fierce hand crack. At the time the Derbyshire cracks at Millstone were getting all the magazine coverage, but as we know, Yorkshire had flat caps, whippets, and harder—nay, much harder—routes.

MEMORABLE CRACK EXPERIENCE?

It's hard for me to remember crack stuff from decades ago as my memory is crap! Many, many years ago I used to go soloing at Millstone quarry, a truly silly thing to do. I had a circuit that involved lots of E numbers, scary arêtes and, of course, copious quantities of cracks. There was a particularly hard finger crack with a high crux that was rather tricksome for my ample digits. *Coventry Street* (E4 6b/5.12b) was the name, and I would regularly solo up to the hard bit and scuttle back down, but this one occasion I committed, and went for the move. Of course, I had it wired, but without the comfort of a rope and perfect pro, I knew down to the minutest detail

Opposite: Ron on the first ascent of Milky Way *(E6) at Ilkley in North Yorkshire, UK*
(© Fawcett Collection)

where my tips and toes went but slapping the flat jug was so sweet . . . and rather stupid. Never again!

THE KNOWLEDGE

Just do it: you won't learn at the wall, so get out and practise. Sorry if this sounds rather flippant, but once you know the basics, get out there and practise.

Pop Quiz

1. Finger cracks or offwidths? It has to be fingers for me.
2. Stemming or roof cracks? Stemming, I am too weak for roof cracks.
3. Hand jam or hand stack? Hand jams—my hands are big enough without stacking them.
4. Knee lock or chicken wing? Chickenwings? I'm a veggie myself. My knees are shot, too much jumping off pre-mats.
5. Tape or no tape? Never had tape back in the day.
6. Cams or nuts? Nuts. The first time I set off up a route with a set of cams I threw them back down cos they were so heavy.
7. Sandstone cracks or granite cracks? Gritstone is nearly sand so it has to be that.
8. Short and hard, or long and pumpy? Long and pumpy. I have never been too strong but I could hang on for a while before I dropped.
9. Pressure wound or rock rash? These sound like problems I have had after my copious amounts of surgery. Pass!
10. Colour preference of crack climbing trousers due to unfortunate mistakes: red or brown? I am more of a shorts person, usually ill-fitting and grubby, colour immaterial as long as they are cheap.

PLACING PRO AT LIP TURNS

The main problem to be aware of when turning the lip of a roof is your rope getting pinched between the rock and your last cam. To prevent this pinching effect, you have to try to reduce the amount of friction between the moving rope and the cam lobes—or stop them from touching at all. If you don't reduce this friction, you can create some very interesting problems for yourself . . . On more than one occasion my rope has been so stuck I've been unable to move upwards, after climbing past terrain too difficult or dangerous to reverse or jump off to solve the problem. My only option has been to untie and keep shuffling upwards! Don't let this happen to you.

Some solutions:

- Ropes get easily pinched between cam lobes, but not as easily behind other types of gear. On wider cracks try placing a Big Bro as your last piece of pro, and on narrower cracks place nuts. The rope will run much more smoothly around these pieces. I've stuffed lots of other esoteric items at the lip of a roof to stop my rope getting pinched—wooden chocks and climbing shoes, for example!

- If you can only place a cam at the lip of a roof, as you climb past it try to feed the rope between the cam lobes (i.e., down the centre of the cam), rather than letting it sit between cam lobe and rock. When you have it in this position, it's important that your belayer keeps the rope reasonably snug to ensure it stays and runs in this position—communication with your partner is key.

- Once you have turned the lip of the roof, try to find pro that is to the side of the main crack line. This will help stop the rope getting sucked up into the crack and prevent it from running against your last piece in the roof. If there is no pro, you might be able to find small rock features to guide the rope around away from the main crack line. Small crystals or even the friction of the rope on the lip of the roof can work effectively—you'll be surprised!

- If the only place the rope will run is inside the crack, try not to place pro too close to the lip; instead place it further back underneath the roof. This will lessen the sharpness of the angle that the rope has to turn around your last cam. In this situation asking your belayer to give you plenty of slack rope also prevents the rope from getting vigorously sucked up into the crack. Both these options will reduce the amount of friction on your last piece of protection in the roof.

Opposite: Mari Augusta Salvesen giving it everything during the first female ascent of the classic gritstone offwidth Ray's Roof (E7 6c) at Baldstones in the Peak District, UK (© Mike Hutton)

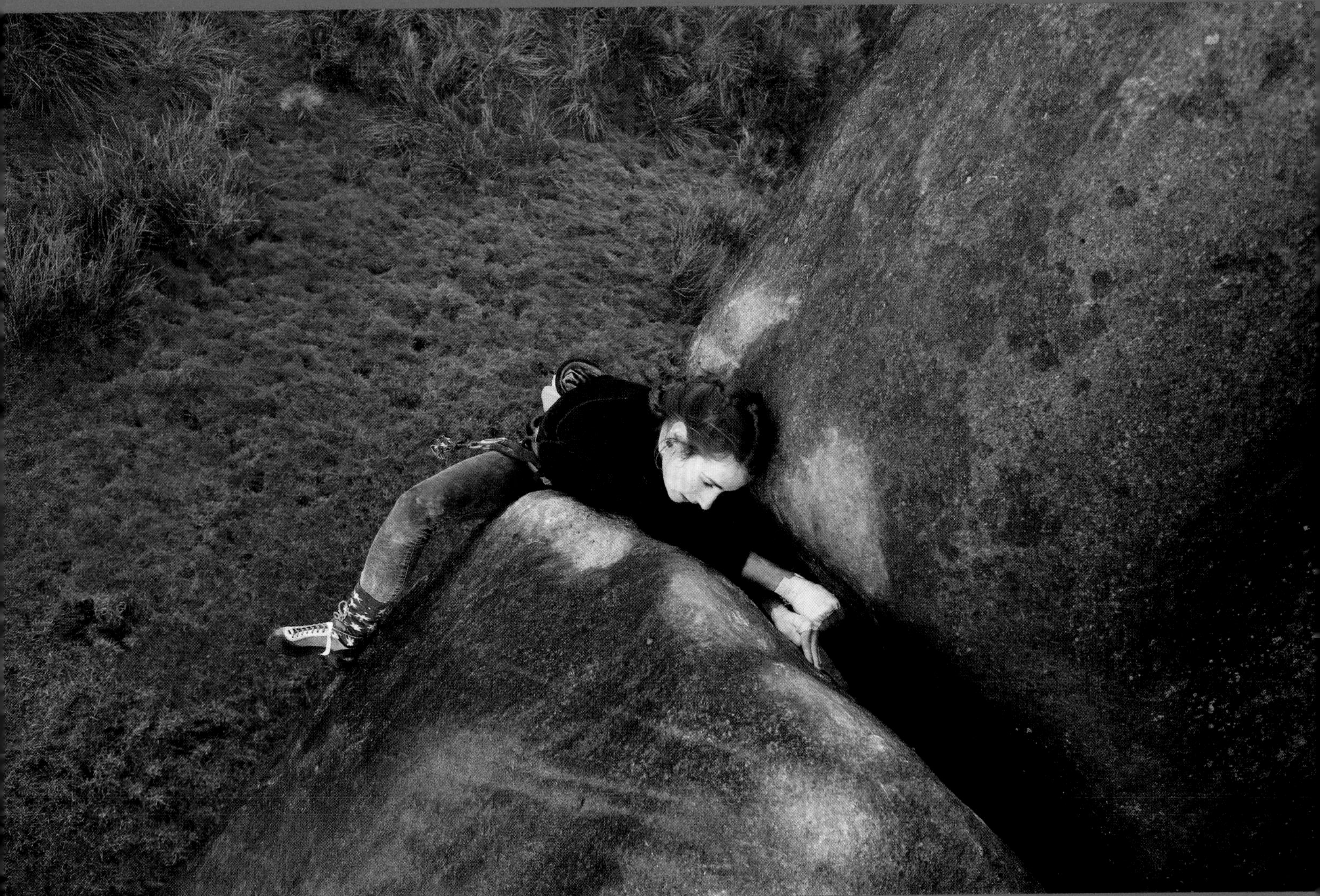

CHAPTER 11

Equipment

This chapter covers the essential equipment you need to enable you to succeed on each size of crack. It's great to know all the techniques, positioning, and movement skills, but if you don't select the right equipment for the task at hand, you will only make life hard and painful for yourself. Selecting the correct equipment can make or break your crack climbing grade. For example, different rock shoes fit different scenarios and crack types, and if you pick the wrong shoes, you'll find that a climb which could have been straightforward is now an impossible battle because your feet don't fit into the crack properly.

Crack climbing can be brutal on the skin, as delicate and sensitive areas are getting rubbed and abraded against the rock. By selecting the correct skin protection, you can increase the amount of time before abrasions, pressure wounds, and, most important, pain kicks in. When you are in pain, you'll find that concentrating on the climbing is almost impossible: your technique will go out the window and your attention will focus on the pain rather than the route.

There are three rules to remember with skin protection:

1. Wrap up, tape up, and/or button up *before* you start crack climbing and not afterwards. Don't tape up when you've had half a battle and are already bleeding.

2. Only wrap up, tape up, button up exactly what you need to, and no more. It's unnecessary to protect parts that don't need to be protected.

3. Repair or replace equipment and protection when it's damaged, don't nonchalantly "push on." When your shirt or tape gloves develop holes, fix them.

By following these three rules you'll protect the body parts that need to be protected, while keeping everything else light and airy.

Gear was covered in the previous chapter; tape and how to tape up is covered in detail in Chapter 12.

FINGER CRACKS

TAPE

As a lot of weight is hanging from what are small body parts, your fingers can become painful very quickly. Tape can be used as protection on the fingers to prevent abrasion and flappers.

If you are really serious and redpointing something that is at or near your limit, you might want to tape only the specific knuckles that will enter the crack. This will keep the other parts of your fingers free from tape so that you still have plenty of skin–rock friction for moves that aren't crack related.

GLUE

There is a lot of pressure and twisting from the fingers in thin cracks, so it is easy for your tape to warp or come loose. You'll find that even the smallest amount of movement in the tape can really affect the quality of a jam.

A solution to this is something your mother would never tell you to do: apply superglue directly to your fingers and then stick the tape on top. If you've not done it before it sounds completely ridiculous—but it works, and it holds the tape in place for much longer. I've never had a problem with the tape becoming so stuck that it's impossible to take off again. The twisting of the fingers and sweat from your hands while climbing tends to loosen the tape so that it comes off easily after a while.

Be incredibly careful when you are applying the superglue not to get your fingers stuck to any other exposed skin, as when you pull it apart you might end up ripping your flesh. Do one finger at a time and spread your fingers apart as you do it. Also make sure that there isn't a chemical reaction between the adhesive of the tape and the superglue when they come together, or everything may just come unstuck and the whole process will be a waste of time!

CLOTHING

As only your toes and fingers will be inside the crack, aim to wear the lightest possible clothing that you can, since skin friction from other body parts won't be needed. Imagine you were climbing a hard sport route; you'd go as light as possible. The same applies here.

SHOES

Selecting the correct shoes for finger cracks comes down to the route you are climbing. You need to ask yourself: are my feet going to be mainly in the crack, or are my feet going to be using footholds outside the crack?

Feet inside the crack: If you think the hard climbing lends itself to putting your feet inside the crack, then use a flat, low-profiled, and soft shoe.

- *Flat:* A flat shoe, with no downturn, has a lower profile and is easier to get into the crack.
- *Low-profiled:* Make sure your toes aren't scrunched up at the end of your shoe. If you can see all the knuckles of your toes protruding through the toe

box this will increase the shoe's profile and prevent your toes from going into the crack. Aim to have the tip of your big toe just tickling the end of your climbing shoe. Again, no aggressive downturns!

■ *Soft:* Having a reasonably soft shoe helps you to wiggle and mould the rubber into the crack. However, if they are too soft you might end up twisting the rubber out of the crack altogether. A happy balance is needed.

Feet outside of the crack: If you are using your feet outside the crack, you should assess the terrain that you are climbing and select a shoe to suit. This means maybe a stiffer shoe if there is edging to be done or a softer shoe if you think you'll be smearing. The same principles apply here as with traditional face climbing.

One more thing to consider is that you don't have to wear the same model of shoe on each foot. Maybe the climb lends itself to using the crack with one foot and edging on face holds around the crack with the other. In this situation you might wear two different shoes at opposite ends of the spectrum; a soft flat shoe for toe jamming and a stiff downturn for edging.

HAND CRACKS

TAPE

I'll split taping for hand cracks into four sections as there are subtle differences for each size.

Thin hands: Your hand should be as narrow as possible with this size so aim to get the tape as thin as possible on the back of the hand and try to not go any thicker than a double layer. I tend not to use a thumb loop in order to keep the area around the thumb— the important part on thin hand jams—slim.

Standard hand jams: A standard tape glove which protects the back of the hand and the area around the thumb is the most beneficial for this size. Try to keep the palm as free from tape as possible so that you can benefit from good skin–rock friction and still use handholds outside the crack effectively.

Cupped hand jams: Lots of pressure goes through the knuckles on this width of crack, so it can be nice to have a few extra layers of tape across the very tops of your knuckles for extra comfort and to prevent pressure bruising from building up as quickly. If you insert your hand further into the crack to gain extra friction from the wrist or base of the forearm, you might consider protecting this area of skin from abrasion with some light wraps of tape.

Ankles: If you are doing long sections of hand crack climbing, your ankles can get internally sore from repeatedly twisting your feet into the crack. You can strap your ankles up with tape (very much like a bandage), or even wear sports ankle supports. This will help support and prevent overstraining of the ligaments down the side of your ankle. It will also reduce the number of cuts and scrapes that you tend to start getting around the ankle bone when the crack gets into cupped hand size.

GLUE

Glue can be used with hand jamming gloves. Apply a spray adhesive, superglue, or a combination of the two.

Spray adhesive: This is a great basic layer of glue to spray over the backs of your hands before applying the tape. There are spray adhesives available which are specifically designed for spraying onto your body before sticking tape over the top. Spray adhesive is particularly useful in hot climbing areas since when your hands are sweating lots you'll find the tape doesn't adhere to your hand as well.

Seam supergluing: You will find that eventually the edges of your tape glove (mostly on thin hand-crack tape gloves) will start to peel back and roll up. This can cause an annoying "cigar" roll of tape down the side of your tape glove which gets caught, eventually preventing your hand from entering the jam as efficiently. This roll also exposes skin. You can slow the process of this rolling by supergluing down the edges of your tape glove at the point where the tape meets skin. A bead of superglue which overlaps both skin and tape works well, or apply superglue to the underside of the tape before sticking it to your hand. You can also use the direction that you lay the tape on to your hand to help prevent the tape from rolling (Chapter 12).

CLOTHING

With thinner and standard hand jamming cracks you'll only be inserting your hands and feet into the crack, so your tape and climbing shoes will provide adequate protection. As a result, wearing light clothing on the rest of your body is a good option. When the crack becomes a little wider (for cupped hand jams) you may want to insert your arm further into the crack. In this situation it can be nice to have some protection at the base of your forearm. There are a few tricks which can help protect the skin on your forearms:

- Wear a long-sleeved T-shirt and tape the sleeves to the wrist straps of your tape gloves, or wear a skintight long-sleeved layer. Either will stop the sleeves of your top from rolling up your arm.
- Extend the wrist strap of your tape glove down your forearm to gain extra protection from the tape. However, be aware that if you have hairy arms, you will get a good waxing when you remove the tape!
- Wearing thin sports elbow supports on your forearms along with a T-shirt is a good warm-weather option.

SHOES

Similar principles apply to shoes for hand cracks as to finger cracks (above). However, there are two other shoe considerations when climbing hand cracks.

- High-top shoes which protect the ankle can be great for internal ligament ankle support if you are doing a lot of foot jamming.
- Shoes with rubber across the tops of the toes can massively improve the "stickiness" of the foot jam. The more rubber to rock contact, the better!

Pop Quiz

1. **Finger cracks or offwidths?** Finger cracks, of course! What a dumb question! Haha!
2. **Stemming or roof cracks?** Roof cracks— best core workout ever!
3. **Hand jam or hand stack?** Hand stack because it is essentially two hand jams on top of one other. And I guess two hands jams are better than one.
4. **Knee lock or chickenwing?** Knee lock: essentially the best rest position of all climbing techniques
5. **Tape or no tape?** Tape. Sometimes it's better without, but it usually means I'll only have one go before my fingers are all gobied
6. **Cams or nuts?** Cams. Only Brits still use nuts.
7. **Sandstone cracks or granite cracks?** Granite: best rock to climb on
8. **Short and hard, or long and pumpy?** Long and pumpy. Ideally with some thank God hand jams here and there . . .
9. **Pressure wound or rock rash?** Rock rash. Pressure wounds take way longer to heal.
10. **Colour preference of crack climbing trousers due to unfortunate mistakes, red or brown?** Red—from wiping the blood from my cuticles

JEAN-PIERRE "PEEWEE" OUELLET

Peewee was one of the first climbers who really started to push 5.13 crack climbing into 5.14, and now has a number of 5.14 crack first ascents to his name. He's a real master when it comes to thin hand jamming. Check out his first ascent of Necronomicon (5.14a) in Canyonlands, Utah—a stunning 30-metre horizontal roof crack.

FAVOURITE CRACK CLIMBING AREA?
Indian Creek/Moab region has to be my favourite. I've spent so much time there. I wouldn't say it's my favorite rock or that my favorite route is there, *but* it is the mecca for crack climbing. The weather is perfect, there's literally a crack every two metres in every direction and as far as you can see. Thousands of cracks everywhere and potential for thousands more. The White Rim area [Canyonlands, Utah] is also a special place for me because of all the roof cracks. Unique underground roof cracks.

FAVOURITE CRACK CLIMB?
Le Toit de Ben (5.13a) in Val-David, Quebec, Canada. It's a super-cool 10-metre roof crack. It was my first hard crack climb. I first climbed it in early 2004 and I've climbed it every year since then. I've used it as a training tool: doing laps on it for pre-paring for *Necronomicon*. It is the best roof crack in Canada. Such a fun route.

MEMORABLE CRACK EXPERIENCE?
While working on *La Zébrée* (5.14a), I had to battle with really poor/wet conditions. I had to come up with ideas to dry the route. I tried everything! Towels, chalk, paper towels, blow torch, stuffing sponges, and tampons in the crack— everything! I even wedged a 6-foot metal gutter in the widest part of crack to try to divert the water away from the crux section (I said *everything*). I came back the next morning, and the gutter was diverting the water into a small waterfall at the top of the route. The crack just stayed wet.

THE KNOWLEDGE
There's a bunch of things to know before going to Indian Creek.
- On your first trip, focus on just a few crack sizes. Don't try to master all the crack sizes at once. It takes time.
- Don't looks for footholds; you can't cheat here!
- Don't be pissed if you fail on a 5.10, you might be able to send the 5.11 two metres to the right (the Creek is very hand-size dependent).
- Don't be shy to put tape gloves on if you want to climb a bunch of days in a row, and don't leave your old tape on the ground— pick up your trash!
- Don't climb right after the rain (in any sandstone areas for that matter). Leave some time for the rock to dry.

PeeWee on his route Necronomicon (5.14a) at Matt's World in Canyonlands National Park, Utah (© Andrew Burr)

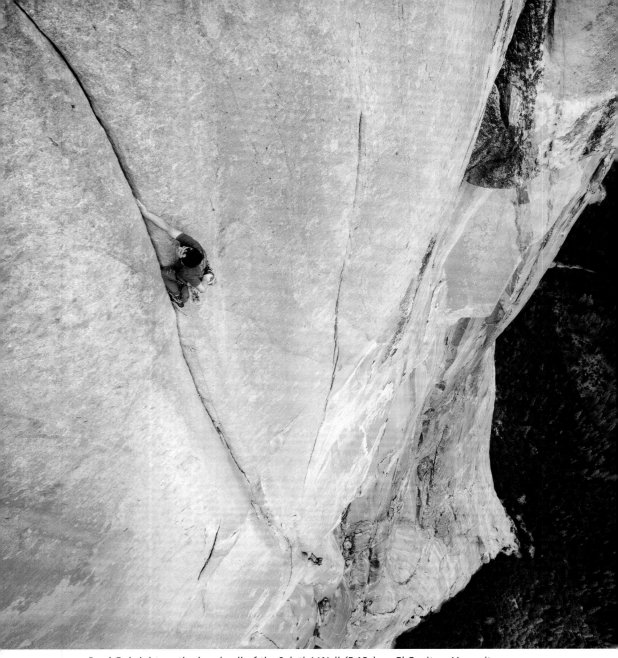

Brad Gobright on the headwall of the Salathé Wall *(5.13c) on El Capitan, Yosemite National Park, California* (© Drew Smith)

FIST CRACKS

TAPE

When taping for fist cracks, it's really important to protect the knuckle below the base of the thumb as this gets a lot of contact with the rock. Start by making thumb loops for your tape gloves (Chapter 12) and adjust how much tape you use around your thumb according to the fist jams you will be using. For example, if it's standard fist jamming, you might choose to tape just the thumb knuckle; but if you are doing a lot of teacupping, then it will be important to also tape the thumb joint. If you do tape the thumb joint, ensure you do it so that you can still bend your thumb afterwards. Movement of the thumb is important in teacup jamming, so you don't want to restrict it by making a tape plaster-cast.

Usually, by making a thumb loop the tape glove will hold itself together well. You will get less "cigar rolling" and so supergluing the edges of the glove isn't as important as on thinner crack gloves. However, if you are going for a hard redpoint or it's important for the tape glove to keep its quality longer, then you might want to use seam supergluing (earlier this chapter).

CLOTHING

Fist cracks seem to be the type of cracks where you're either cruising along, swimming nicely up the edge of the crack with grace, or suddenly you're very involved, jamming in the back of the crack and in deep up to your elbows or armpits. It's important to at least try to judge this from the ground. My approach is this: if things are looking slightly wider I wear a long-sleeved T-shirt and make sure the sleeves will stay down (by either taping them down or by wearing a tight-fitting top); if things are looking narrower, then a T-shirt will be satisfactory, but maybe with some extra tape wraps around my wrists.

If you are going for an all-out, one-go, hard redpoint, then climbing in a T-shirt can still be a good option even if the jams are deep. Your skin might take a bit of a beating, but the friction of your bare forearms against the rock can be beneficial. If you are being really clever, you could lather your forearms in liquid chalk and/or powdered chalk before setting off. You'll look absolutely ridiculous, but it might just give you the extra couple of percent needed to succeed.

SHOES

The important attributes of a fist crack shoe are that it is flat and stiff. These two factors will enable you to stand on your foot like a platform and will stop the shoe from deforming too much when you push it into the crack—it will give you support and rigidity. When you use heel-down technique, it will also stop the shoe from bending excessively or even bending itself out of the crack all together.

When you get into the realms of fist cracks you need to think about protecting your ankle bones from cuts and abrasions. A high-top shoe will instantly solve this problem, and high-top shoes in general tend to be stiffer, so you will be killing two birds with one stone.

The author on Udolni *(VIIIb, approx. E2 5c) at Hlaska, Teplice, Czech Republic* (© Andrew Burr)

OFFWIDTH CRACKS: STACKED TECHNIQUES

TAPE

When taping for stacked cracks, you need to produce a tape glove that can survive a beating. A thicker glove with a few more layers of tape can prevent holes appearing as easily, give more padding and pain relief, and also provide extra width for very wide jams. As a minimum, you should tape for offwidths as you would tape for fist cracks. You can then move into the realms of producing gloves which cover the entirety of your hand—back of the hand, palm, bases of the thumb, index, and pinkie fingers, and even parts of your lower forearm. This gives excellent protection everywhere, even to abrasion on the palm.

Because your palms sweat a lot, it's important to use adhesive spray when taping up or else you'll find the tape will become baggy, like a big soggy nappy. Imagine trying to climb with one of those on your hand—it would slide about all over the place. And also smell like shit.

CLOTHING

When offwidthing, it's easy to think, "I need to get wrapped up because this is going to be full contact." However, when you are using purely stacking techniques, there can be less contact than you might think, especially when hand/hand stacking.

LEGWEAR

With all stacking-width cracks you are going to be putting your legs into the crack at least up to knee depth and then twisting them, so trousers are a must. To stop them from rolling up you can tape the ends to your ankles or go for the "stylish" approach and tuck them in to your socks. It's personal preference, as some people don't like wearing socks with climbing shoes.

If your knee is being inserted in the crack (hand/fist stack upwards), then knee-pads can make things more comfortable. Neoprene sports-support kneepads are great and can be worn either over the top or underneath your trousers, depending on whether you want friction from your trousers or friction from the kneepad (they are likely to be made from different materials and give different results on the rock).

UPPER BODY

If you are purely stacking, your arms might actually be further out from the crack than if you were deep fist jamming, so, surprisingly, a T-shirt can be satisfactory. However, take care: if you misjudge the route and end up having to put your arms into the crack to use different techniques, you might be in trouble! I once made a terrible misjudgement and came away with a tricep so mauled and burnt that it looked like a lawnmower with a blow torch attached had slowly churned its way across my arm. You have been warned! Use your own judgement.

SHOES

The same shoe characteristics are important here as with fist cracks: flat and stiff (earlier this chapter). A stiffer shoe can also help prevent the big toe of your outside foot from taking a massive beating. After a lot of heel-toe action, it can feel like your big toenail is being inserted back into your foot—a stiff shoe delays this feeling. Happy days.

Another factor that should be taken into consideration on this width of crack is the style of shoe fastening you should use. Because you are twisting, turning, and pulling on your feet in many strange ways, the best option is to use lace-up shoes. Slippers are likely to fall off when heel-toe camming, and Velcro straps are likely to unpeel. Laces give the best foot security and won't come undone. If you want to get really technical, then lacing your climbing shoes with flat laces is even better. They are flush to the shoe, meaning the laces won't roll as easily and affect the quality of the jam, and they also don't abrade as quickly. Abrasion and snapping of laces will eventually occur if you climb a lot of cracks—it will even occur from standard foot jamming—so carrying spare laces is always a good idea.

It's very important to keep in mind that when you are offwidth climbing you are using the whole shoe in many different ways, so a shoe with lots of rubber around the heel and across the top of the toe is really useful for extra friction.

One last thing to consider: when you are climbing these widths of cracks in steeper terrain or roofs, you will be hanging a lot from your feet. Even with lace-up shoes, you could still find that the heel of your shoe starts to slip off the back of your foot. The obvious solution is a high-top shoe, however there is another little trick if you don't have a pair of these. Tighten your climbing shoe in a single knot (rather than a bow), then thread the spare lace ends around the back of your ankle and through the pull tabs of your climbing shoe and retie the lace at the front. You can even do an extra wrap underneath the shoe for added support. If the laces aren't long enough, you can thread some tape through the pull tabs and strap it around your ankle to hold the heel of your shoe in place.

CHALK BAG

There are two important chalk bag factors to take in to consideration when climbing all sizes of crack from offwidth up.

- Make sure the chalk bag has a wide opening. You might have heavily taped hands and it is frustrating if you can't get your hand into your chalk bag quickly.
- Make sure your chalk bag is on cord and you can move it around your body on this cord. You don't want the chalk bag clipped or tied in a static position around your back. A lot of the time when off-widthing, chimneying, or stemming, it is useful to be able to move your chalk bag around the side or front of your body so that you can access it more easily when you are in awkward positions.

OFFWIDTH CRACKS: ARM BAR, CHICKENWING, AND SQUEEZE CHIMNEY TECHNIQUES

TAPE

If you are climbing pure arm bar and chickenwing-style cracks then you don't necessarily need to tape up at all, as your hands won't be doing any jamming. If you think the crack may lend itself to holding

crucial face holds or slopers outside of the crack, keeping your hands free from tape to make sure you have full movement, sensitivity, and skin–rock friction is really important.

On the other hand, it is worth considering taping up in case you need to start using stacking techniques or you have to do excessive amounts of powerful palming. You will find that if there is a lot of chickenwinging on a route then you will end up with a red-raw palm as there is so much pressure going through that hand. To tape the palm, you'll obviously have to tape the whole hand. If you really want to be tactical, then using rubber paint on the palms of your tape glove can help give extra palming friction. This takes time and effort, and as you have to prepaint the correct lengths of tape the night before you go climbing, you'll need to have your taping-up method dialled.

Remember, you don't necessarily need to tape both hands, you can use the "Michael Jackson glove" technique: tape only the hand that is doing the extensive palming and leave the other hand free for holding face holds. Shamone!

You need to assess the route and make a judgement about what you think is best. If you're not sure, the better option is always to tape.

CLOTHING

It's important to wrap up well with this size of offwidth because you will be inserting your arms and legs, and even your whole body into the crack. Long sleeves and trousers are a must. Make sure they don't roll up your arms and legs: tape them down, wear close-fitting clothing, or tuck them into other items of clothing, such as your socks. You can also tuck your shirt into your trousers to ensure it doesn't creep up your back.

Another important consideration is the material your clothing is made of since your clothing against the rock provides you with the friction you need to stay on. There is no point pulling on your slippery alpine synthetics; cotton-based products provide the best friction. Wear one thick layer or build up a barrier with multiple thinner layers.

Both elbow pads and kneepads are thoroughly welcome, and again these can be worn either over or under your clothing. It's normal to be fully wrapped up for this style of offwidth.

Partners and peers may get bored with your excessive dressing or preparations, but preparation is key: remember you'll be the victorious one when you're able to climb multiple days in a row and aren't wiping weeping wounds after one redpoint attempt!

SHOES
Follow the same principles as for stacked technique offwidths (earlier this chapter).

CHIMNEYS

TAPE
Tape is not really necessary for chimney climbing. The only time you might consider taping up is if the chimney features other kinds of crack climbing. For example, you might be using chimney techniques with your body and legs, but using jams with your hands at the back of the chimney.

CLOTHING
You are back to the other end of the scale where lighter clothing will feel much more appropriate as you don't need to protect your arms and legs in the same way as on narrower cracks because they're not in direct contact with the rock. Be aware that if the chimney suddenly becomes thinner and you have to start using squeeze chimney techniques, you might enter a whole world of skin abrasion terror—so don't misjudge the route!

The one thing you should consider doing is tucking your top into your bottoms; this will stop your shirt from moving around and exposing skin when you are shuffling your back up the wall.

SHOES
A standard approach to selecting the correct shoes should be applied with chimneys. If it looks like you might be smearing with your feet, then softer shoes will be appropriate. If you are specifically edging, then wear stiffer shoes.

STEMS

TAPE
No tape should be used when stemming. It is really important to have the friction of your bare palms against the rock, and to maintain flexibility and movement in your

hands so you can execute conventional climbing techniques.

One very esoteric option is to wear rubber hand-jamming gloves, but back to front. So, the rubber would be over your palms rather than the backs of your hands.

CLOTHING

Go light! The lighter you are the easier it will be to bend your arms and legs in all the weird and wonderful ways you need to contort them while stemming. Even if you are using chickenwing palming techniques (Chapter 8), I still think you will be better off wearing a short-sleeved top, as it's a marginal technique and so it's beneficial to have skin/rock friction.

SHOES

The same principles apply as with normal climbing: softer shoes for smearing, stiffer shoes for edging.

Opposite: *Finger loop anchoring* (© Pete Whittaker)

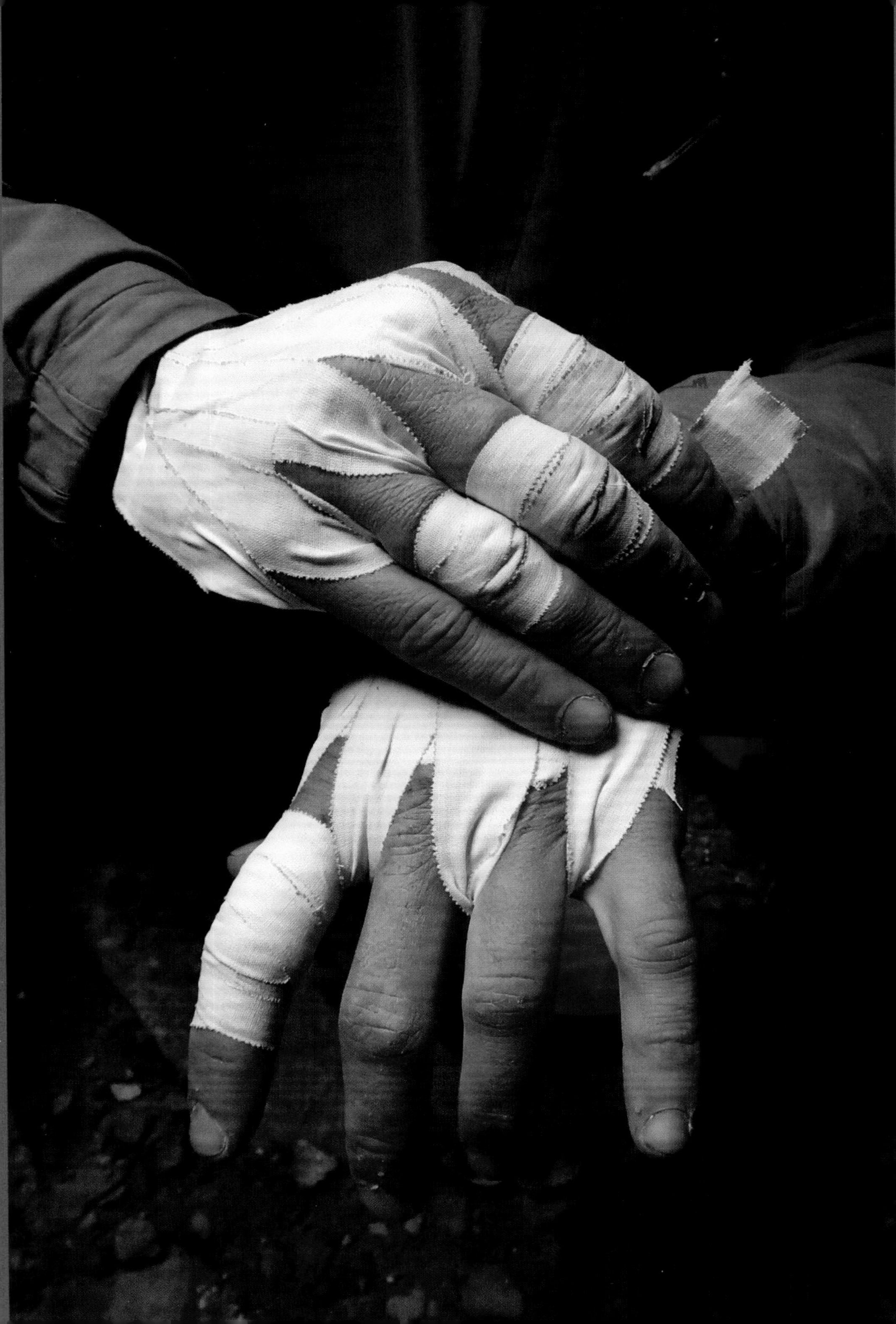

CHAPTER 12

Taping

Taping up gives you a bit of extra protection which allows you to climb cracks for longer and with more enjoyment. It might seem like a tedious or expensive task, but taping up properly can make or break a day out—or even a trip! If you fail to tape up properly on the first day of a week-long trip and proceed to cut your hands to shreds, I guarantee that your remaining days—tape or no tape—will be unpleasant. Rubbing fresh wounds against rock is not fun! Taping up offers the following benefits:

Prevents open wounds. As soon as you abrade or break the skin on your hands and fingers it becomes incredibly sensitive, and the thought of then placing your hand in a crack, putting pressure through it, and pulling up on it is a grim prospect. By using tape, you create a layer (or two or three) of false skin which delays this process of abrasion. Given enough abuse, the tape will abrade and cut just like your skin, however you're creating a barrier to slow this process down.

Prevents pressure wounds. The backs of your hands and fingers are relatively bony and sensitive, so continuous pressure through them will bruise the bone. Imagine someone stepping on and off your hand 50 times—but in a big soft slipper: it wouldn't break the skin, but your hand would be incredibly sore. Taping up gives an extra bit of padding which increases the time before this type of soreness sets in.

Provides extra friction. If you are climbing in a hot climate, you are trying hard, or you are scared, then your hands could become very sweaty, and bare sweaty hands usually equal poor friction on the rock. You'll also notice that while you're climbing it's pretty hard to chalk your whole hand (especially the backs of your hands), making it impossible to absorb all the moisture your hands are producing. Tape prevents sweaty hands from making direct contact with the rock; instead you can use the friction from the tape.

TAPING UP HANDS: THE BASICS

There are a couple of basic yet very crucial things to get right with any kind of taping.

Tape up before you start climbing: Very obvious, but often neglected. It's common for climbers to have one go at a route, realise they are hurting themselves, then make the decision to tape up. Tape up over fresh skin *before* you start climbing, not over cut and bruised skin when you realise that things are going pear-shaped.

Create a second skin: After taping your hands, the finished product is referred to as a "tape glove," however a more appropriate name would be "tape skin." Your tape should be like a second layer of skin on your hand. As you move your hand and the skin wrinkles and creases, your tape should be stuck down yet be flexible enough to move in the same manner. If the tape on your hand is like a baggy washing-up glove, it will slide, crease, and generally be more of a hindrance than a help. If the tape on your hand is too tight, like an undersized mitt, it will restrict your hand movements and you won't be able to execute the correct hand positions for performing the jams effectively. When you think of your tape glove, think "tape skin."

TAPING UP HANDS: PREPARING TO TAPE

Before you even put the tape on to your hand, it's important to correctly prepare both the hand and the tape to ensure you build the best possible tape glove.

PREPARING THE TAPE

The hot and cold treatment: Before you rip strips of tape off the roll, you can prepare the roll so that the tape is stickier and will adhere to your hand more easily. The way to do this is the heating and cooling process: leave the tape to bake in the sun for a full day then let it cool down in the night. The heating and cooling process creates a stickier bond. Make sure it has fully cooled down when you come to rip the tape off the roll and apply it to your hand. Also, don't think you're being clever by putting the tape in the fridge—it will just end up collecting moisture and you'll end up with a cold damp roll of tape. Use a hot then cool and, most important, dry climate.

Different tapes do different jobs: There are lots of different types of tape on the market—some are stickier, some are more flexible and stretchier, some have better friction, and so on. They all have their uses and one tape might be better at one job than another. Using a combination of tapes with different characteristics can help create the best tape glove, as you are unlikely to find a tape which is the best of everything. Here are some common tape characteristics and their benefits:

- *Friction:* You should use tape with the greatest rock–tape friction on the areas of the hand which are in contact with the rock.
- *Hard-wearing:* Hard-wearing tape should be used for covering strips, finger looping, and wrapping. These bits of tape get the most hammer, so

it's important that they can take that beating.

- *Sticky:* Any tape that is in direct contact with the skin—such as the covering strips—should be as sticky as possible. If your first layer of tape against the skin doesn't stick properly, then the whole glove will become baggy and not be the "second skin" that you need.
- *Stretchy:* Stretchy tape is good for pure finger taping and finger anchoring (both later this chapter), as the stretch enables you to still bend and move your fingers as you would normally (which finger taping can often restrict).
- *Tear-resistant:* Tear-resistant tape is a good choice around the wrist as the wrist anchor is often the place where the tape can start to split and tear first.

PREPARING THE HAND

Make sure your hand is hair free: Tape sticks much more easily to hair-free skin, so if you have hairy gorilla hands or wrists, get the razor out and shave it all off before applying any tape. You will also be thankful that you did do this when you come to remove the tape at the end of your session, as it limits the "waxing" effect, making the ordeal less painful.

Make sure your hand is free from chalk and dirt: As when sticking any two things together, the bond is much stronger if the surfaces are clean. The same applies with your hand and the sticky side of the tape.

Make sure your hand is free from sweat and moisture: Again, when sticking any two things together you will have much greater success if the surfaces are dry. Dry your hand of any moisture before applying tape.

TAPE WIDTHS

Throughout this section I'll refer to the following three widths of tape:

- Small: approx. 1–1.5cm
- Medium: approx. 2–2.5cm
- Large: approx. 4–5cm

Don't worry if your tape isn't exactly these sizes. Tape comes in a variety of widths and most brands have sizes which roughly correlate with small, medium, and large widths. Simply choose the closest match. You might also find that with experience you prefer to use thinner or wider tape for different taping methods or to suit the size of your own hands and fingers.

TAPING UP HANDS: THE PROCESS

COVERING METHODS

Covering is the first part of any tape glove. It's the base layer of tape that the rest of the glove is built upon. You should only cover the areas of your hand that will be getting abuse from the crack; keep the remaining areas tape-free for movement and sensitivity. Here we'll look at the different parts of the hand which can be covered, followed by the different methods for covering them—i.e., how to lay the tape on to your hand.

THE AREAS TO COVER

In this order, there are three main areas to look at covering:

1. *The back of the hand and tops of the knuckles:* This is the most sensitive part of the hand, where the bones are closest to the surface and the skin is at its thinnest. Taping here forms the basis of any tape glove whether the crack is narrow or wide.

2. *The base of the thumb and the thumb knuckle:* This can be just as sensitive as the back of the hand but is only really used if cracks become wider and you have to cup and twist or use any form of fist jam.

3. *The palm:* This area of the hand can withstand the biggest beating. The flesh is tougher and thicker and you have to do a lot of (brutal) crack climbing to make it sore. Palm taping is often reserved for offwidth climbing, as chickenwinging and stacking can be harsh on the palm. It's not as common with thinner crack sizes as they generally aren't as brutal. Taping the palm also makes the whole hand much thicker, which can hinder fully inserting your hand into thinner cracks.

APPLICATION METHODS FOR COVERING

Rip the tape off the roll before placing it on to your hand. You will be able to place it exactly how you want it and create a better finish. As you become more experienced, your judgement on tape length will improve.

Pre-rip all your covering strips before applying any of them to your hand. Ripping tape off the roll halfway through the covering process can disrupt the tape you have already applied to that hand.

Don't apply the tape over creased skin. Stretch the skin, apply the tape, then let the natural creases of your hand reform when you relax it. Applying tape in this manner creates the "tape skin" feeling, where the tape moves with the creases in your hand, rather than forming separate tape-only creases. To stretch the skin, flex your fingers, thumb, and wrist into different positions until the skin in the area where you are applying the tape is uncreased and tight.

Overlap the covering strips according to how thick you want the tape glove to be. If you want a thick tape glove, overlap the tape a lot. If you want a thin tape glove, overlap only the edges of the tape. Always have a slight overlap to avoid gaps with skin appearing between the tape.

THE METHODS FOR COVERING

There are three main covering methods:

Vertical strips (tape size: large. See figures 169 A–F): These run from the base of the fingers and on to the wrist. They can be placed on the back, sides, or palm of the hand, and around the thumb. The end of the tape closest to the knuckles should lie just over the top of the knuckle and not extend up the finger (unless using "strap anchoring"), or else you will end up with useless flaps of tape protruding from the end of your tape glove once it is finished.

Horizontal strips (tape size: large. See figures 170 A–C): These run across the width of your hand. So, if placing tape on your finger knuckles, one piece would cover all

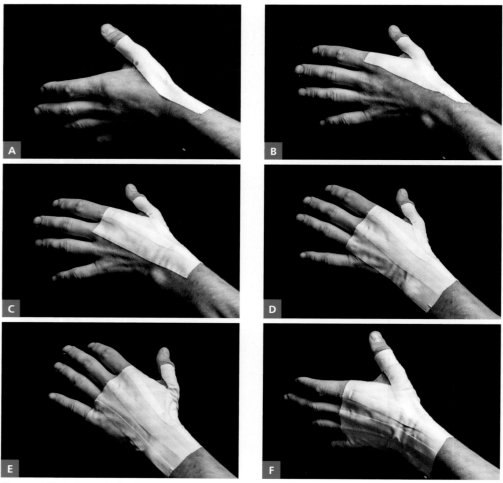

Figures 169 A–F. Vertical strips

four knuckles. They can be placed on the back and palm of the hand. The top edge of the tape that lies across the knuckles shouldn't sit past the webbing of your fingers or it will prevent you from being able to spread your fingers apart.

Diagonal strips (tape size: large. See figures 171 A –E): These run diagonally across your hand. They work well on the palm as they sit into the shape of the palm nicely and the angle helps to prevent "cigar rolling" from occurring during lots of palming

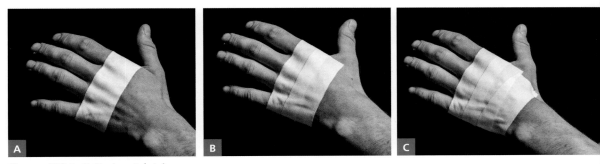

Figures 170 A–C. Horizontal strips

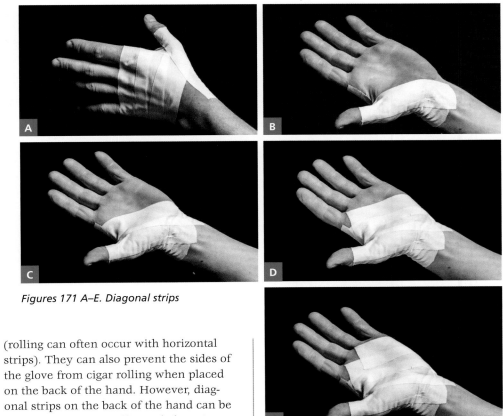

Figures 171 A–E. Diagonal strips

(rolling can often occur with horizontal strips). They can also prevent the sides of the glove from cigar rolling when placed on the back of the hand. However, diagonal strips on the back of the hand can be accomplished more effectively by using

275

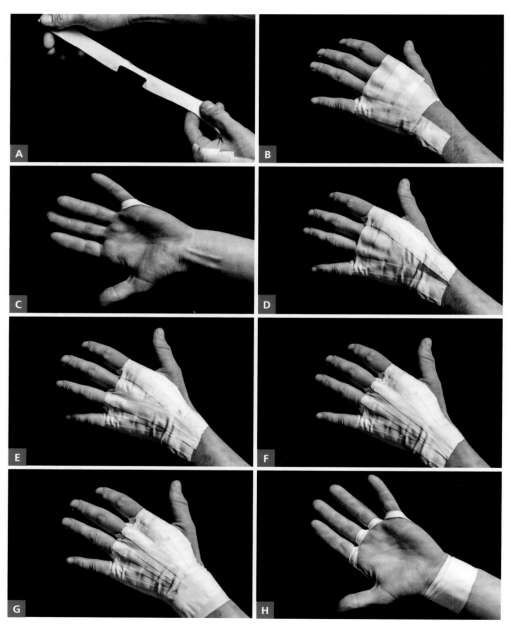

Figures 172 A–H. Finger loop anchoring

either the "finger loop anchoring" or "wrapping" (both below) processes. The corner of the tape shouldn't extend any further than the top of the palm or the knuckles, or else you will again get unnecessary flaps of tape poking out from the top of your glove.

ANCHORING METHODS

Depending on the glove, anchoring is the second or final part to a tape glove. It prevents the tape glove from moving around on your hand as much, and stops the top, bottom, and side edges from rolling up as easily. Remember you're trying to create a "tape skin," and any movement, rolling, or disruption of the tape will negatively affect the quality of your jams.

THE AREAS TO ANCHOR

There are three main areas to anchor your tape glove to—your fingers, your thumb, and your wrist.

FINGERS

Finger loop anchoring (tape size: medium. See figures 172 A–H):

As finger loop anchoring has the tape lying over the tops of (and completely covering) all of the knuckles and looping around the base of each individual finger, it is a great method if you think the tops of your knuckles will take a beating or if you are worried that the top of your tape glove will peel back (which can happen if using the basic wrap—outlined below). The downside to finger loop anchoring is that it is incredibly difficult to get the tape to lie on the back of your hand without any creases or deformities. Horizontal covering strips

on the back of the hand give the best base for loop anchoring. Lay these strips before beginning your loop anchoring.

1. Start with an end of the tape at the wrist. Lay the tape up the back of the hand vertically towards the knuckle of your finger, wrap it around the base of the finger (and in between the finger next to it), then vertically lay it down the back of the hand (slightly overlapping the "upward" strip) to the wrist, so it finishes next to where it started. Do this for all four fingers.

2. The loops around your index and pinkie fingers can also be adjusted so that the strips which form the outer edges of the tape glove can be placed in a diagonal position across the back of the hand; this helps prevent the side of the tape glove from "cigar rolling" as quickly. Be sure to run the diagonal strip over the top of the vertical strip. Tape the pinkie and index fingers first, followed by the ring and middle fingers (the ring and middle finger loops should cover and overlap your diagonal pieces).

3. The small section of tape that is looped around the finger can be folded in half to create a neater finish.

Finger strap anchoring (tape size: large. See figures 173 A–C):

With strap anchoring, the strips of tape can be used as both the (vertical) covering strips and the anchoring strips. Strap anchoring can be done on all four fingers, however it is most commonly used on only the index and pinkie fingers. If it is only done on these two fingers, then you can get a very small amount of peel back over

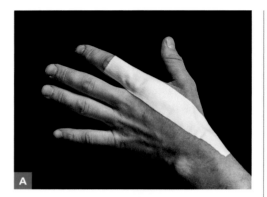

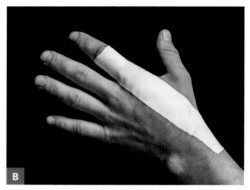

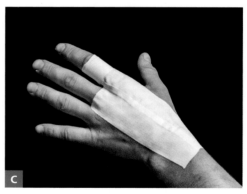

Figures 173 A–C. Finger strap anchoring

the tops of the knuckles. If you do strap all four fingers, you won't get peel back but you will probably find that there is too much tape around the fingers, and that this starts to restrict movement and the flexibility of the hand when trying to hold any kind of face hold.

1. Start with the end of the tape at the second joint of the index finger. Lay a strip down the back of the finger, over the top of the knuckle, down the back of the hand, and to the wrist.

2. Use a thinner piece of tape (tape size: medium) to wrap the base of the finger entirely (between the second joint and the knuckle), anchoring the original vertical strips of tape in place.

Repeat steps 1 and 2 on the pinkie finger. Unlike loop anchoring, strap anchoring should be used in combination with a wrapping method as this helps to hold the whole glove together more effectively.

THUMB

Both loop and strap anchoring, as described above, can be used around the thumb. Loop anchoring gives you basic protection around the base of the thumb, but on anything wider or more gnarly you might still get cut. Strap anchoring protects further up the thumb and can be useful if you are doing difficult teacup jams. However, you might find that strap anchoring can become baggy and might not protect the base of the thumb properly. If you are really concerned about the area around the thumb, then you can use strap and loop anchoring in combination. (See figures 174 A–C).

1. First make the strap anchor (tape size: large). The tape will run from the thumb joint, over the thumb knuckle, and finish on the wrist. Then use a thinner piece of tape (tape size: medium) to wrap the base of the thumb entirely (between the joint and the knuckle), anchoring the strip of tape in place.

2. Now do loop anchoring around the thumb (tape size: large). Start with the end of the tape below the index finger, run it horizontally below the thumb (across the thumb knuckle), then bring it round the base of the thumb (on the palm side of the hand), and up between the thumb and index finger. Finish the end of the tape on the back of the hand, below the index finger again (figure 174 C). The loop that you create should cover any open ends on the strap anchor.

3. If you are being very clever, you can use thumb loop anchoring as part of the horizontal covering strips. This is a good technique for keeping the taped area around the thumb attached to the main glove (with harsh fist jamming you might find that this starts to peel away). Just start with the end of the tape below the pinkie finger rather than below the index finger.

WRIST

The wrist of your tape glove must always be anchored. This piece holds in place all the strips of tape that you have brought down and finished at the wrist. Simple wraps of

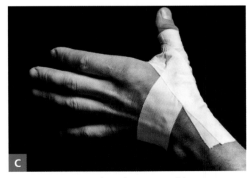

Figures 174 A–C. Thumb strap and loop anchoring

tape work perfectly, and you can extend the tape down the wrist or forearm if you need extra protection. Remember that blood needs to be able to flow to and from your fingers, so don't wrap too tightly: lay the tape on to your wrist; don't pull the roll of tape around the wrist. (Tape size: medium or large.)

As you get pumped while jamming, the flesh and muscle around the wrist will expand, and so the wrist loop can be a common place for tape to split and tear. If this happens and the whole wrist loop splits, your tape glove will very quickly become useless. Some brands of tape tear and split more easily than others. If you find you are having problems with tape splitting around the wrist a good method to prevent that from happening is to do a very small undertuck (sticky side to sticky side) of the tape edge around the wrist loop on the palm side of the hand. This undertuck only needs to be a few millimetres deep, but it creates a double layer of tape and removes this weak spot on the edge where the tape could start to split.

WRAPPING METHODS

Wrapping holds the covering strips together and stops all the tape immediately falling off your hand. However, if you have used finger loop anchoring, then the tape glove will hold itself together already and a wrap isn't always necessary. You can use wrapping methods for very thin tape gloves and also beefy hard-wearing offwidth gloves. It should be noted that if you use a wrap you will end up with tape on the palm of

your hand, so if it's important to keep your palm free from tape—maybe there are some moves on slopers outside the crack where you need the friction of your skin against the rock—then stick to finger loop anchoring.

APPLICATION METHODS FOR WRAPPING

Before looking at the specific wrapping methods, there are a couple of things it's important to note.

- Don't wrap the tape too tight. When you wrap the tape, you'll use methods which circle around your hand, meaning it can be easy to squeeze the knuckles together and restrict your movement (especially the clenching of a fist). To ensure this doesn't happen, semi-clench your fist as you wrap, so that the sides of your hand expand yet you are still able to wrap tape around. Don't stick the tape on to your hand as you are pulling it off the roll as this will make the tape tight. Instead pull out a length of tape (before you start the wrap) then gently lay the tape onto your hand as you do the wrap. Or, even better, pull out the correct length of tape needed for the entire wrap, rip it off the roll, then proceed with the wrapping method. However, be warned, you'll need to be a master taper to get the correct length and avoid tangling it all up.
- During the wrapping process only rip the tape at the end of a complete sequence, not partway through, or you will just create more covering strips rather than a wrap, defeating the point of doing the wrap in the first place.

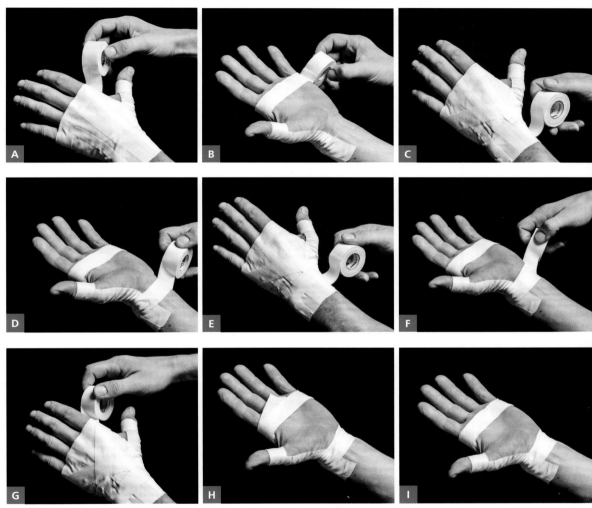

Figures 175 A–J. Wrap 1: the basic wrap

WRAP 1: THE BASIC WRAP

This is one of the most basic wrapping methods, and it can be used to great effect with everything from thin hand jamming tape gloves, to fist crack and offwidth gloves. If you want to make a thinner tape glove the wrap should be done with a thinner tape (medium recommended) and obviously a lighter load of covering strips. For a beefier glove, create a thicker layer of covering strips and use a thicker tape width (large recommended). See figures 175 A–J, J being the finished glove.

1. Turn your hand palm down. Start with the end of the tape just past the pinkie finger and lay it horizontally across the back of your hand, over the tops of your knuckles. Make sure the top edge of the tape doesn't go past the webbing of your fingers or else you won't be able to spread them apart. (A)

2. Turn your hand palm up. Lay the tape horizontally across the top of your palm to meet the point where you started. (B)

3. Turn your hand palm down. Lay the tape diagonally across the back of the hand to a position below the thumb, but on the wrist. (C)

4. Wrap the tape around your wrist once, so that it meets the wrist starting point, below the thumb. (D and E)

5. Wrap it around the wrist again, but only by half, until the tape is below the pinkie finger (but still on the wrist). (F)

6. Using a diagonal motion run the tape back across the back of your hand and in between your index finger and thumb (aiming slightly towards the index). You should have created a tape X on the back of your hand. (G)

7. Turn your hand palm up. Bring the tape to the top centre of your palm. The tape will now meet the horizontal strip you did across your palm earlier. (H) In this position, cut the tape and fold a corner underneath the first horizontal strip (sticky side to sticky side) to help prevent the end from unpeeling. (I)

WRAP 2: THE STACK WRAP

This wrap is only useful if you have used covering strips around your whole hand— back, sides, thumb, palm. It follows a similar principle to the basic wrap however it is done in two parts and you get a diagonal X of tape on both the palm and back of the hand: this is useful for downwards palming and to stop the tape from cigar rolling around the sides of the glove.

PART 1 (TAPE SIZE: LARGE)

See figures 176 A–G; F and G are the finished glove.

1. Turn your hand palm down. Start with the end of the tape on the side of the hand below the base of the pinkie. Lay the tape horizontally across the tops of your knuckles on the back of your hand until you reach the base of your index finger. (A)

2. Turn your hand palm up. Lay the tape diagonally across the palm of your hand to below the pinkie finger, but on the wrist. (B)

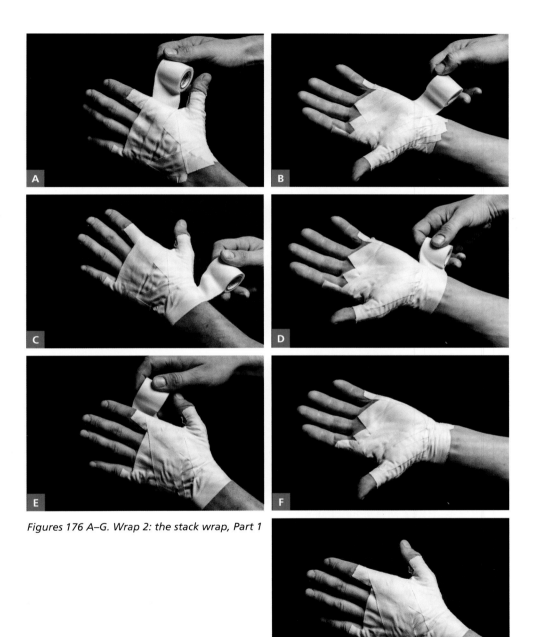

Figures 176 A–G. Wrap 2: the stack wrap, Part 1

3. Do one complete wrap around the wrist, until you meet the wrist starting point again. (C and D)

4. Turn your hand palm down. Lay the tape diagonally across the back of the hand towards the base of the index finger and finish the wrap here. (E)

5. If you don't want any free tape ends on your glove, you can link the end of this tape wrap into an anchoring strap on the index finger; this way no end will be free.

PART 2 (TAPE SIZE: LARGE)

See figures 177 A–H.

1. Turn your hand palm down. Start with the end of the tape where you finished the last wrap. If you don't want any free ends showing, peel back a small section of part 1 and place the start of part 2 underneath it. (A)

2. Turn your hand palm up. Lay the tape horizontally across the top of the palm, until you reach the side of your hand below your pinkie finger. (B)

3. Turn your hand palm down. Lay the tape diagonally across the back of the hand, to the base of the thumb but *not* on to the wrist. (C)

4. Turn your hand palm up and lay the tape diagonally across the pulp of the thumb, through the centre of the palm and finish the wrap below the base of the pinkie finger. (D)

5. If you don't want any free tape ends on your glove, you can link the end of this tape wrap into an anchoring strap on the pinkie finger. (E and F)

6. Finish with anchoring straps around the index, pinkie, thumb, and wrist. (G and H)

TAPING UP HANDS: BUILDING YOUR TAPE GLOVES

Each tape glove you build follows a simple process from start to finish:

1. *Pick a covering method:* Decide if you want to cover just the back of your hand, the back and the thumb, or the entire palm as well.

2. *Pick an anchoring method:* Decide if you want to loop or strap your fingers.

3. *Pick a wrapping method (if necessary):* Pick a wrapping method if you want tape across the palm or you want to try to prevent cigar rolling on the edges of the tape gloves.

SUGGESTED TAPE GLOVE COMBINATIONS

There are so many combinations of methods, strips, rips, and widths of tape to use. Take all the information in this section, tweak it, and adapt it to create a method that fits your hands. Everyone has different hands and different projects— you should tape according to your own. You might even consider taping specifically for a crux jam on the route you are trying.

Here are a few simple suggestions for how you could build your tape glove for the size or style of crack you are climbing.

Thin hands, option 1: Horizontal covering strips only just overlapping, on the back of

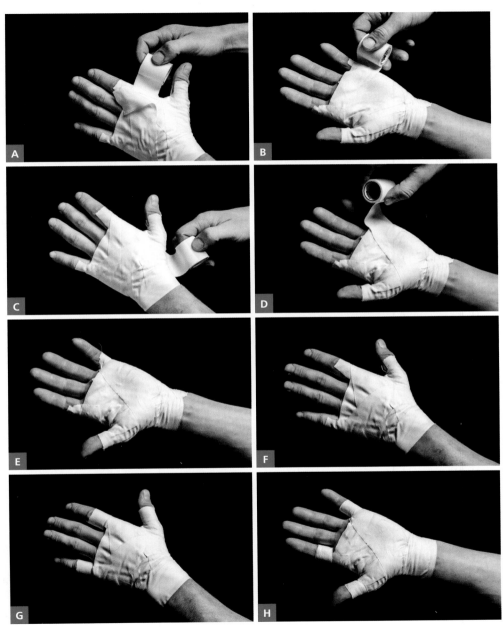

Figures 177 A–H. Wrap 2: the stack wrap, Part 2

the hand only; finger loop anchoring; wrist anchor.

Thin hands, option 2: Vertical covering strips only just overlapping (finger strap anchoring optional), on the back of the hand only; basic wrap (medium-width tape); wrist anchor.

Hands: The same methods as for thin hands, however overlap your covering strips by half and consider adding thumb loop anchoring.

Cupped hands, option 1: Horizontal covering strips overlapping by half with extra layers across the tops of the knuckles, on the back of the hand only; thumb loop anchoring; finger loop anchoring; wrist anchor.

Cupped hands, option 2: Vertical covering strips overlapping by half (finger strap anchoring optional) with extra horizontal layers across the tops of the knuckles, on the back of the hand only; thumb loop anchoring; basic wrap (large-width tape); wrist anchor.

Fists: Horizontal strips (optional) followed by vertical strips (overlapped by half) with finger strap anchoring on the index and pinkie fingers, on the back and sides of the hand only; thumb loop and strap anchoring; basic wrap (large-width tape); wrist anchor.

Offwidth: Horizontal strips (optional) followed by vertical strips (overlapped by half) with finger strap anchoring on the index and pinkie fingers, on the back and sides of the hand only; vertical thumb covering strips with loop and strap anchoring; diagonal covering strips on the palm; stack wrap (large-width tape); wrist anchor.

REUSING YOUR TAPE GLOVES

Freshly taping your hands every single time you go crack climbing can waste tape and can get expensive, so consider reusing your tape gloves multiple times.

There is no definitive answer to the question "How many times can I reuse them?"—it will depend on how careful and precise you are when making, removing, and storing the gloves, plus the amount of damage they suffer during the actual climbing. If you are cruising around in your comfort zone and your gloves stay slick and smooth, there is no reason why you couldn't use them for five to ten sessions—or more. However, if you're thrashing about and your gloves look like they've been mauled by a pack of hyenas, then you might be lucky to get three sessions out of them.

PATCHING YOUR TAPE GLOVES

No matter how smooth your climbing, you will get rips in your tape gloves. You can increase their lifespan by using tape patches. Follow these guidelines when patching:

Clean any irregularities off the tape glove before patching it. When your tape glove rips it might roll into small bobbles of tape—make sure you clean or cut these bits off the glove before adding any tape over the top. Remember you want the tape glove to be as flat to the back of the hand and have as few irregularities as possible.

Patch up the glove while it is on your hand. When you add tape patches to your glove, do it while it is on your hand—this ensures that the tape you are adding matches the shape of your hand.

Cover loose ends. When you add patches, it can be common to have ends of tape showing—these can immediately start to peel when you start jamming again. To prevent this from happening, try to cover up the ends within extra anchoring processes or small wraps.

Be aware that adding patches will make your tape gloves thicker. If you keep ripping your gloves and adding fresh tape, they will inevitably become bigger and thicker. Be aware that after a few sessions a pair of thin hand tape gloves might be useless for that size of crack, however they could now be useful for fist or offwidth cracks. It can be nice to have a small cycle of tape gloves on the go like this.

REMOVING YOUR TAPE GLOVES

Removing tape gloves from your hands without completely destroying them is a small art in itself and needs to be done with the same precision and care that went into making them in the first place. When making the cuts, use scissors to get a clean cut rather than trying to rip the tape with your hands.

Removing gloves with finger or thumb loops and basic wraps: If your glove was made using these methods, then making one simple cut down the wrist loop on the palm side of the hand will be enough to allow you to remove it in one piece (figures 178 and 179). Peel it off the back of the hand (from the first strip of tape that was placed on the hand) from the wrist upwards, making sure all the strips of tape stay stuck together. The glove will usually end up

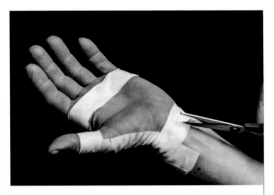

Figure 178. Remove basic wrap

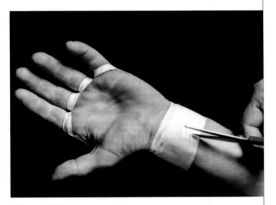

Figure 179. Remove straps

turning inside out; turn it the correct way around again when it's off your hand. When you want to reuse the glove, pop it back on your hand and just do a couple of new wraps of tape around the wrist to secure it in place.

Removing gloves with finger or thumb straps: If you have used a strapping method on your fingers or thumb to anchor the glove then it will be difficult to peel it off your hand. The best method is to first make a cut in the wrist loop, then carefully unwind the straps around the fingers, being careful not to rip the covering strips which go past the knuckle and up to the second finger joint. Take the glove off your hand in the same way as described above. When you want to reuse the glove, pop it back on and do a new wrist strap and new finger and thumb straps.

Removing gloves which cover the palm: If you have used taping methods which cover the palm of your hand, you will struggle to take the glove off and reuse it effectively. If you do want to reuse it, then the cut you make needs to be as small as possible. First remove any finger straps (as described above), then cut the glove from the side of the wrist up the underside of the thumb; use scissors to get a clean cut (figure 180). At this point, you might be able to slide the glove off your hand without any further cutting damage; if you are struggling, then you may have to cut the tape glove the

Figure 180. Remove stack wrap

whole way up the side of your hand. If you want to reuse the glove, the only parts you have to re-tape and repair are around the thumb and the wrist loop—plus any finger straps you might have removed.

Removing your gloves pain free: As mentioned earlier, shaving the hair off your hand and wrist will help to eliminate the waxing effect when you remove the glove. Peeling back and unsticking the glove bit by bit is usually the most painless way of removing it, rather than just quickly tearing it off your hand. Removing the glove slowly also helps you to keep it in one piece, whereas doing it quickly and carefree will end up creasing, folding, and damaging it, thus shortening its lifespan.

STORING YOUR TAPE GLOVES

This part will probably read like the "storage" section in the manual of a new product you might have bought: *store in a clean and dry environment.* When you use your tape gloves over and over, they will inevitably lose some of their stickiness. You can increase the longevity of "the stick" by doing simple things such as not stuffing them at the bottom of your climbing bag where they will end up mingling with chalk dust and your sweaty climbing shoes. Keeping them in a ziplock bag (or even a small plastic box with a tight-fitting lid to stop them from creasing) in the top of your pack will preserve their life.

Also, don't crumple your gloves up in a mess before putting them away. Fold any finger loops, finger straps, or wrist loops into the centre of the glove, then fold the

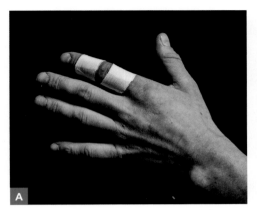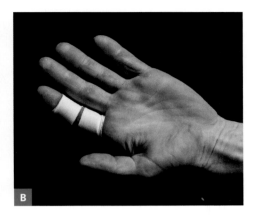

Figure 181 A and B. Finger taping, no joint

glove in half so that none of the sticky part is exposed—thus preventing dirt, grit, and chalk from sticking to it—and make sure to keep it flat. As with any items of equipment, if you want your gloves to last, take good care of them.

TAPING UP FINGERS

Taping the fingers for thinner cracks can be tricky, as the widest part—your joint—is the section of your finger which suffers the most abrasion. However, taping the joints also restricts movement (although a slightly stretchy tape can help with this problem). So, it comes down to your needs: do you need movement, or do you need protection?

A thinner tape—something around 1cm in width—works best for all finger taping. Here are three options for taping the fingers:

No joint coverage. This method just covers the fleshy parts in between the finger joints and knuckle. Simply wrap thin strips of tape around your finger between the joints (figures 181 A and B).

Semi-joint coverage. This method covers the same fleshy parts of the finger as above, however it also creates an X pattern across the side of the joint; this provides some protection but keeps the top of the joint free, allowing for some movement. The process for taping the index finger is illustrated in figures 182 A–M. This process shows a full wrap and can be reasonably bulky on the finger.

However, if you want it to be thinner and provide a greater range of movement through the knuckle, then a thinner version can be done. Use a tape width of 2cm (instead of the original 1cm) and instead of creating an X across the side of the joint, only lay one diagonal strip across it. With the thicker width of tape, the flesh on the side of the joint will still be protected from abrasion but the layers of tape will be thinner and therefore more flexible. The downside is that thinner tape (i.e., not a

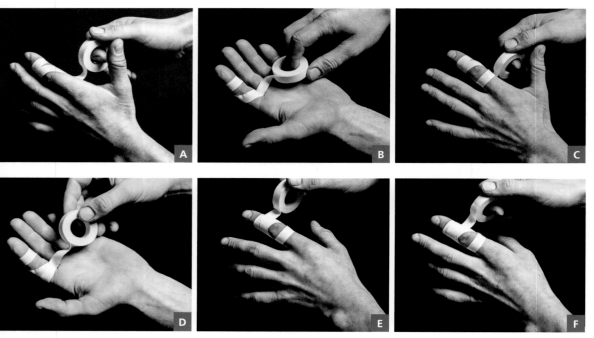

Figures 182 A–M. A Semi-joint coverage

double layer) has a tendency to split and rip more easily, and if you are doing multiple aggressive finger jams in a row it's not uncommon for you to finish a sequence and find that you've split the tape and also ripped through the skin—so be careful. To create this taping method, follow figure 182, steps A through E.

Full joint coverage. This method covers the entire finger. While it offers great protection, it can also make your finger feel like it is in a mini plaster-cast. Start at the top of the area you want to cover and work down your finger using a cross-hatching method. See figures 183 A–H

1. With your hand in a palm-down position, first lay a horizontal strip across the top of the finger and then around the back of it.
2. The second time you come across the top of the finger, half-overlap your first strip, but in a diagonal motion—and then go around the back again.
3. Follow this process of one horizontal strip, followed by a half-overlapping diagonal strip, all the way down the section of finger that needs to be covered.

The tape will end up double thickness, as you will have half-overlapped everything, in a cross-hatched pattern.

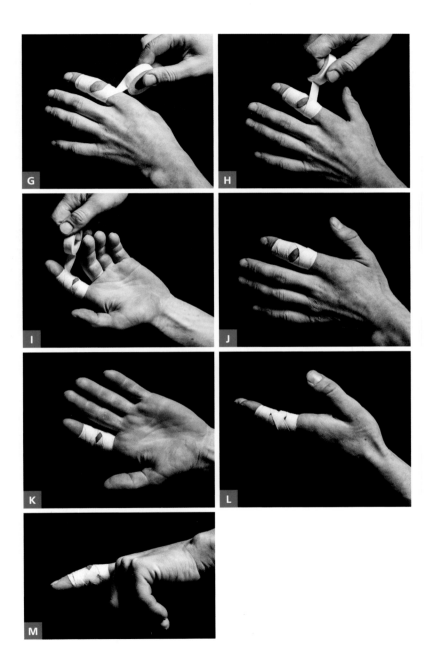

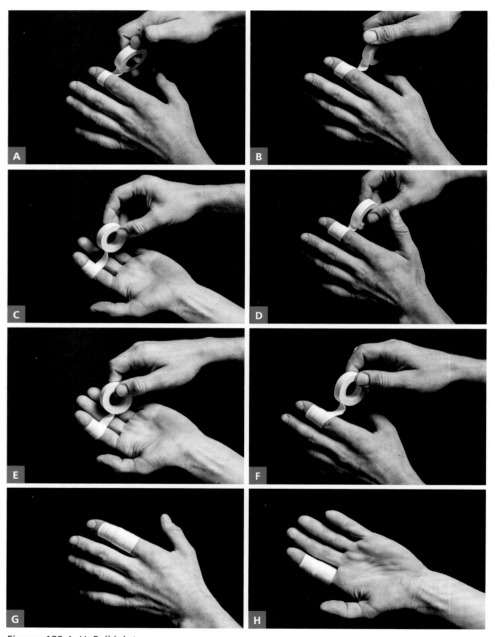

Figures 183 A–H. Full joint coverage.

CRACK GLOVES

There are a variety of different makes and models of crack gloves available and there are reasons for and against using them instead of tape gloves. Here we'll go through the pros and cons and you can decide whether it's tape or crack gloves that best fit your needs.

Pros:

- *Rubber backed:* Crack gloves are rubber backed so the friction can often feel better than the friction from tape. The rubber can also provide better protection against pressure wounds, slowing the bruising of the bones in the back of the hand.

- *Ripping:* Crack gloves can withstand much more of a beating before they develop holes. This means the longevity of the glove is better, and also you won't pull your hand out of a brutal jam to find that you've ripped through the glove and damaged the skin, which can often occur with tape.

- *Ease of use:* They are quick to put on and take off—much faster than the time it would take to tape up. This is obviously great if you're in a hurry, but also fantastic for multi-pitch climbing where you might have some crack pitches and some face pitches. You can free up your hands for the face pitches (and clip the gloves to the back of your harness out the way), and still have the freedom to quickly put them back on before the crack pitches, if necessary.

- *Price:* Crack gloves are much more economical than tape. You would spend much more money on tape in the time that it would take for a pair of crack gloves to wear out.

Cons:

- *Thickness:* You can't alter the basic bulk of crack gloves. So, if a jam is very thin, you might not be able to get as much of your hand in the crack as you would like, making the jam feel worse than it should.

- *Specificity:* You can't alter the style of the glove to suit the route you are climbing. When you use tape, you can zone in on specific areas and really make the tape fit the route or a specific jam. Crack gloves offer only a single solution for hand protection.

- *Rolling and movement:* Unlike tape, crack gloves aren't sticky on the inside so they do feel like a glove rather than a "second skin." This means they can move around on the back of your hand—especially if you're sweating a lot—massively affecting the quality of the jam. Because the crack glove isn't stuck to your hand, the edges can easily get caught, flap up, and become obstructive on thinner jams.

- *Wrist loop:* The wrist loops on crack gloves are often quite thick, which can prevent you getting your hand into the crack past the wrist on slightly thinner jams—this is certainly an annoyance.

In conclusion, crack gloves are good for easier, basic, and convenient jamming; but if you are climbing cracks that involve technical jamming, then tape is the way forwards.

Pop Quiz

1. Finger cracks or offwidths? Finger cracks
2. Stemming or roof cracks? Roof cracks
3. Hand jam or hand stack? Hand jam
4. Knee lock or chickenwing? Knee lock
5. Tape or no tape? No tape
6. Cams or nuts? Cams
7. Sandstone cracks or granite cracks? Granite cracks
8. Short and hard, or long and pumpy? Long and pumpy
9. Pressure wound or rock rash? Rock rash
10. Colour preference of crack climbing trousers due to unfortunate mistakes, red or brown? Brown

WILL STANHOPE

Having soloed up to 5.13 on cracks, repeated some of the hardest testpieces and then put up his own, Will has established himself as one of the most technically able crack climbers that there is. In 2015, he made the first free ascent of the Tom Egan Memorial Route (5.14) on the east face of Snowpatch Spire in the Bugaboos, British Columbia.

FAVOURITE CRACK CLIMBING AREA?

I know it's a bit of a cliché, but I'd have to say Indian Creek, Utah. The sheer variety of splitters is mind-boggling. If you have a weakness that you'd like to work on, say, offwidths, for example, there is an endless number of cracks to choose from. It's also incredibly expansive, so it's really easy to escape the crowds if you'd prefer to be alone. And the place is an easy, hassle-free hang, and oh-so gorgeous.

FAVOURITE CRACK CLIMB?

This route called *Crime of the Century* (5.11c) at the Smoke Bluffs in Squamish might be my favourite. I first tried it when I was in my early teens and was mystified how to climb it. It's a thin crack, slightly flaring in spots, and has a handful of funky off finger-jams as well. More than any other, that pitch really taught me how to climb thin cracks. The approach is mega short, so it's really convenient to throw a few laps if I have some free time.

MEMORABLE CRACK EXPERIENCE?

In 2012 I freed a route on the right side of El Cap called *The Prophet* (5.13d). *The Prophet*'s crux pitch is dubbed The A1 Beauty and is this beautiful, very thin, curving splitter a few pitches from the rim. The pitch culminates in this desperate lurch for a finger jam, pretty run-out, with your rope running around an arête. Anyways, the sun had set, my gas tank was pretty much empty, and I barely managed to stick the jam. It was an electrifying moment that I'll never forget.

THE KNOWLEDGE

Work your weaknesses! Although it can seem dis-heartening at first, you'll be surprised how quickly these specific techniques come if you're willing to lose a bit of skin and put your ego aside. If, say, finger stacks are giving you trouble, force yourself to climb on them. They'll feel like second nature in no time!

Opposite: *Hardest pure pitch of crack climbing in the world? Will Stanhope frees the "Blood on the Crack" pitch (5.14) of the* Tom Egan Memorial Route *in the Bugaboos, British Columbia, Canada. The pitch's name is reference to the sage wisdom of Bob Dylan and the human sacrifices given to this piece of rock—both of which were in ample supply during the three years it took Will and partner Matt Segal to free-climb the route. Their story is told in the short REEL ROCK 11 film* Boys in the Bugs. *(© Kyle Berkompas/REEL ROCK Film Tour)*

Acknowledgments

Writing a book . . . I wonder if my English teacher would have ever expected me to do that?!

Well here it is, after an uncountable number of hours of work. What a monumental task it was trying to condense a lifetime's worth of practice and dedication into 90,000 or so understandable words.

So many people have helped me along the way, either with their time, skills, or knowledge. I'll start right from the beginning and thank chronologically.

This book would have never been produced if I hadn't started climbing! Thanks, family Whittaker, for the climbing adventures—scrambling up gullies, walking round the mountains, training support at the climbing wall, and countless belays on routes— all from the age of six. Also, thanks Mum and Dad for being supportive in helping me to pursue the totally bizarre concept that is climbing.

There would be nothing to write if I hadn't gained all this crack knowledge from practice. There is only one person to thank here and it's Tom. All the adventures and training we have done together has combined our knowledge, developed it, and given me a far greater understanding of the subject. I can't put a price on what I have learnt from climbing with him over the last 11 years. Tom, you legend!

A book can't start without an idea. Nice one, Dad, for planting the seed—you put the idea in my head.

Where do you then go with a wealth of knowledge and an idea? A publisher. Thanks Vertebrate and Mountaineers Books, especially Jon and Kate, for accepting my idea and trusting my ability to produce content that you would be proud to publish.

To help make my words make any sense at all, I knew there had to be illustrations. Visuals. This was going to be an integral part of the book. Alex, your work is incredible. It's a total pleasure to have your work alongside with my words. It's your work that brings the book to life. Brilliant, mate! Also, sorry for being such a perfectionist, and making you have to put up with my messages of . . . "Here's more photos for you," and "Can you just . . . ?"

Thanks Mum and Mari for putting in the hours to either be model or photographer for the content that Alex needed to base his illustrations on. An impossible task if I'd tried to do it alone.

Thanks a bunch to the other crack addicts that I interviewed. Some of you I know in person, others I don't, but I appreciate you giving your time to provide me with funny and insightful answers which I hope the readers will enjoy. When our paths cross, remind me to buy you a beer. Lynn, I left one in your haul bag above the Great Roof last October; I hope you found it and it wasn't too warm.

Photographers! Thanks for providing the inspiration amongst the pages. Photographs make people psyched and want to get out there and do it. It's amazing you've managed to capture some of the obscure techniques that I describe.

Thanks to those people who I double-checked knowledge with, when their understanding of the subject area was better than my own.

And, finally, a massive thanks has to go to Mary and Peggy (the editor and designer of the Mountaineers Books edition), John (the editor of the Vertebrate Publishing edition), and Jane (the designer of the Vertebrate Publishing edition) who I worked closely with to get the book just how I wanted. I can't thank them enough for their patience in putting up with me being a perfectionist—this arrow here and that word there. When I came back with an excessive amount of rewrites and corrections after draft one, it was like I'd given them a whole new book: sorry! I'm forever in debt of cake and doughnuts to you to show my appreciation and say thanks!

Index

About the Author

Drawn to climbing by the challenge and adventure, **Pete Whittaker** seeks out pioneering first ascents and revels in pushing his personal limits. Having grown up in the UK's Peak District surrounded by the area's world-famous gritstone crags, he has been climbing since the age of six and has gone on to rack up an impressive mix of climbing achievements on a variety of rock types and styles across the globe. As one half of the Wide Boyz duo with Tom Randall, Pete has become synonymous with hard crack climbing. He has taken techniques learnt on his local crags and applied them with great effect all over the world, most notably on the huge roof cracks in the desert areas of Utah and on the big walls of Yosemite.

In 2014 Pete flashed the classic *Freerider* (5.12d) on El Capitan, Yosemite, and in 2016 he became the first person to make a free-solo ascent of El Capitan in under 24 hours. He followed this up in 2018 with a single-day solo link-up of both El Capitan and Half Dome.

On his local gritstone, Pete's major first ascents include *Dynamics of Change* (E9 7a), *Bigger Baron* (E10 7a), and *Sleepy Hollow* (E10 7a). Further afield, he has made the first ascents of *Century Crack* (5.14b), the world's hardest offwidth crack, *The Millenium Arch* (5.14a), and *Lamb of God* (5.14b)—his hardest crack to date, all in Canyonlands National Park, Utah.

Pete's hard crack credentials also include the first ascents of *Black Mamba* (5.14b), *Crown of Thorns* (5.14a), and *Cruzifix* (5.14a), and repeats of *Recovery Drink* (5.14c) in Jøssingfjord, 0Norway and *Cobra Crack* (5.14a) in Squamish, Canada—considered two of the hardest crack climbs in the world. And he has climbed one of the world's most famous roof cracks, *Greenspit* (F8b, trad) in Vall dell'Orco, Italy, as well as dozens more crack routes graded in the 5.13 bracket. Pete was the the first person to flash a 5.13 offwidth with his first-go ascent of *Belly Full of Bad Berries* (5.13a/b) in Indian Creek, Utah, in 2011. Pete believes he has only scratched the surface of what is possible with hard crack climbing.

MOUNTAINEERS BOOKS is a leading publisher of mountaineering literature and guides—including our flagship title, *Mountaineering: The Freedom of the Hills*—as well as adventure narratives, natural history, and general outdoor recreation. Through our two imprints, Skipstone and Braided River, we also publish titles on sustainability and conservation. We are committed to supporting the environmental and educational goals of our organization by providing expert information on human-powered adventure, sustainable practices at home and on the trail, and preservation of wilderness.

The Mountaineers, founded in 1906, is a 501(c)(3) nonprofit outdoor recreation and conservation organization whose mission is to enrich lives and communities by helping people "explore, conserve, learn about, and enjoy the lands and waters of the Pacific Northwest and beyond." One of the largest such organizations in the United States, it sponsors classes and year-round outdoor activities throughout the Pacific Northwest, including climbing, hiking, backcountry skiing, snowshoeing, camping, kayaking, sailing, and more. The Mountaineers also supports its mission through its publishing division, Mountaineers Books, and promotes environmental education and citizen engagement. For more information, visit The Mountaineers Program Center, 7700 Sand Point Way NE, Seattle, WA 98115-3996; phone 206-521-6001; www.mountaineers.org; or email info@mountaineers.org.

Our publications are made possible through the generosity of donors and through sales of more than 700 titles on outdoor recreation, sustainable lifestyle, and conservation. To donate, purchase books, or learn more, visit us online:

MOUNTAINEERS BOOKS
1001 SW Klickitat Way, Suite 201 • Seattle, WA 98134
800-553-4453 • mbooks@mountaineersbooks.org • www.mountaineersbooks.org

An independent nonprofit publisher since 1960

OTHER TITLES YOU MIGHT ENJOY FROM MOUNTAINEERS BOOKS

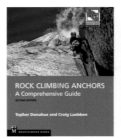

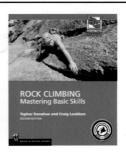